NEPAL

Praise for the Book

'Nepal, one of the leading democracies in Asia, has unfortunately got engulfed by several sociopolitical issues during [the] last [few] decades, thereby impeding its healthy growth of both economy and politics. Contributed by esteemed Nepalese academics and practitioners, this publication dwells upon the various problems confronted by this mountainous country and provides some perspectives as well to get rid of them. Thus, an extremely important volume on Nepal has lately become available.'

Akira Nakamura, Professor Emeritus, Meiji University, Tokyo;
Fellow, National Academy of Public Administration (USA)

'Building a new polity based on democratic and context-appropriate principles is a long and hard journey. This book, written by engaged Nepalese scholars and practitioners, illuminates the challenges along the way. Those of us who are similarly engaged in our country's peace-building and constitutional reform processes will find meaningful lessons from these authors' analysis and insights that are relevant to our own cases.'

Miriam Coronel Ferrer, Philippines Government
negotiator for peace talks with the Moro Islamic Liberation Front;
Professor of Political Science, University of the Philippines

'Nepalese people are very patient. They are continuously bearing political leaders who are pursuing their clientelistic and personal interests rather than representing Nepali people in the nation-building process. As a result, Nepalese are facing upheavals in all fronts and yearning for stability in politics and development. Contributors have dwelt upon these matters in this volume. Although one could have difference of opinion with regard to the issues and perspectives discussed and provided by the contributors to address current upheavals, I consider it as an authentic reference document for all who are interested on contemporary Nepal—a document giving a voice to the many people/citizens of Nepal.'

Ulrike Müller-Böker, Professor and Head of Human Geography Unit,
Department of Geography, University of Zurich, Switzerland

'Nepal, for a long time, has been embarking on what social scientists called "the road to modernization", assuming that this process would lead to greater homogenization and integration, not just of national societies but also of the international realm. Sadly, the last twenty-five years have witnessed, in many countries, an upsurge of particularism eclipsing universalism of subnational identities and fissiparous tendencies with destabilizing, immobilizing impact and consequences. Nepal has been one of the most striking and unhappy examples of this counter-trend. The contributors of this volume are seeking to reverse this trend to suggest a meaning and identity of Nepal that is more than a cartographic designation.'

Norman Uphoff, Professor of Government and
International Agriculture, Cornell University, New York

NEPAL

~A Country in Transition~

Edited by

Dwarika Nath Dhungel . Madan Kumar Dahal

RUPA

Published by
Rupa Publications India Pvt. Ltd 2018
7/16, Ansari Road, Daryaganj
New Delhi 110002

Sales centres:
Allahabad Bengaluru Chennai
Hyderabad Jaipur Kathmandu
Kolkata Mumbai

ISBN: 978-93-5304-064-2

First impression 2018

10 9 8 7 6 5 4 2 3 1

Printed at Nutech Print Services, Faridabad

To

the contemporary as well as future generation of Nepal

for ensuring their security and prosperity

Map of Nepal showing its seven provinces and seventy-seven districts

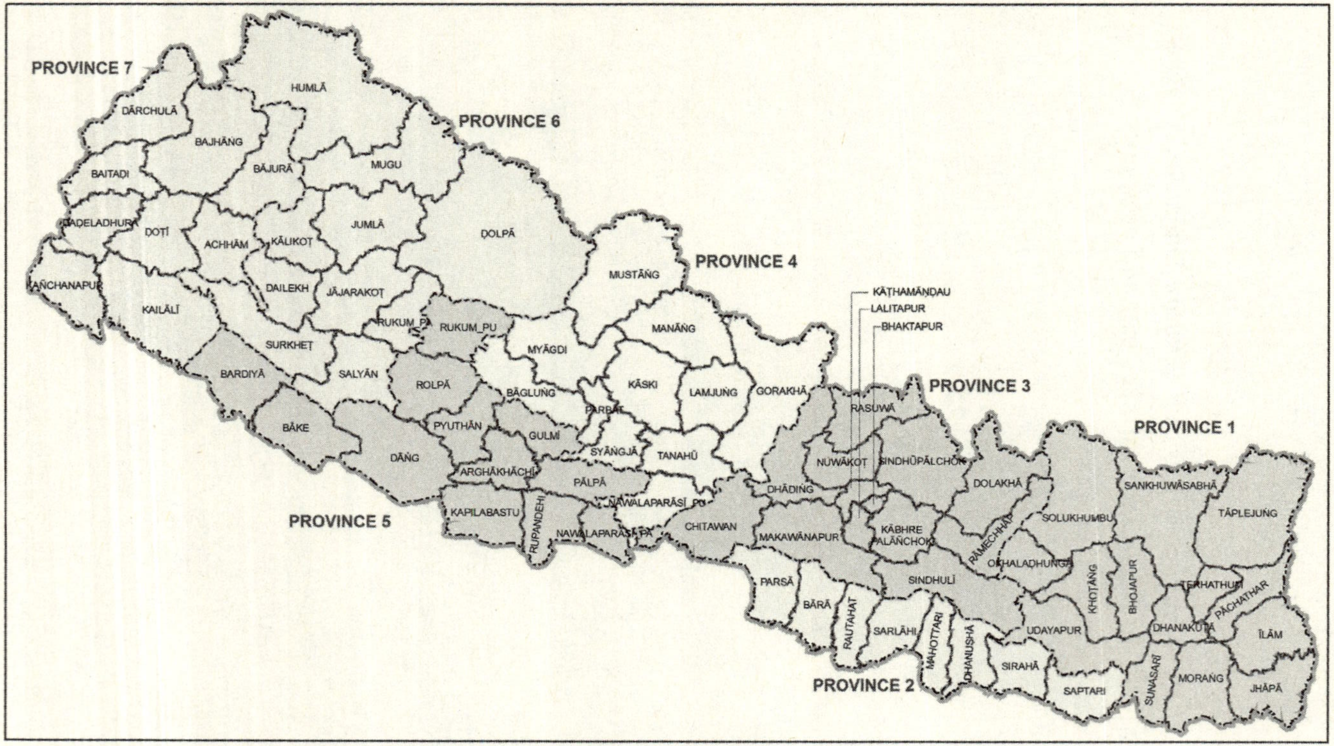

Source: Department of Survey, Government of Nepal

CONTENTS

FOREWORD

Nepal was never physically colonized but it could not help being infected by the colonial discourse. The legacy of colonialism abounds in Nepal as much as it abounds in the rest of South Asia. The naming of Mount Everest, for instance. Although locally called Sagarmatha, the latter never got the recognition beyond Nepal. This is as much a fault of the colonial power as it is of the Nepalese, and I would include the South Asians as well, who had succumbed to the colonial naming of the highest peak of the world even after the demise of the British Empire in South Asia and the rest of the world. There is an interesting story to the naming of the peak, and this would make clear the point that I am trying to flag here.

International practice has always been to name a discovery after either a local designation or the person responsible for the discovery. The naming of the Mount Everest was an exception. The race for discovering the highest peak in the world reached a momentum in the nineteenth century with the introduction of newer methods of calculating geological spheres. The responsibility came to Radhanath Sikdar (1813–70), a brilliant mathematician from Bengal with proficiency in spherical trigonometry. At the insistence of Colonel Andrew Scott Waugh, Director of the Great Trigonometric Survey, Sikdar took up the effort, and after calculating what was then referred to as Peak XV from six different observations, concluded that this was indeed the highest peak in the world. If the international practice were followed, the name of the peak would have either been Mount Sikdar or Mount Sagarmatha. Waugh, however, decided to name the peak after his former boss, George Everest, who after initial objections agreed to the name. Sikdar was soon conveniently forgotten. Sagarmatha, too, was never internationally recognized. The post-colonial record of Nepal's quest for stability and development is no better

'Secularism', 'electoral politics', 'majoritarianism', 'Westminster parliamentary system', 'planned economic development' or what amounted to be a development in the image of the modern Western state, all have an imprint of a colonial discourse that a non-colonized Nepal has come to replicate almost unwittingly. In this context, shocking though it may be, there is some merit in Tri Ratna Manandhar's contention that, 'To satisfy the vast Hindu population, the word "secular" may be deleted from the constitution.' This will probably be viewed as a plea for majoritarianism bordering on communalism but it can also be viewed from the standpoint of what religion, or more precisely, dharma, is all about in Nepal or South Asia.

Etymologically, the two are different, where 'religion', originating from the Latin, 're-ligio', meant 'to bind', 'to unite'; dharma, on the other hand, originating from the Sanskrit 'dhr + ma', meant the way a mother would nourish her child. It is precisely for this reason that Rabindranath Tagore pointed out that the closest word that we have for the Western concept of 'civilization' is dharma. This also helps us to understand Mahatma Gandhi's extraordinary statement that, 'Those who try to divide religion from politics, understand neither religion nor politics.' The civilizational quest of the Nepalese, as it would be the case with the rest of the South Asians, has always been dharmic! Secularism or separating dharma from politics remains less meaningful to the South Asians, including the Nepalese. How do we then bring back this civilizational quest without falling for the West's fragmentary, if not divisive, notion of secularism? Indeed, this is a challenge that requires greater contemplation and imaginative thinking.

'Stability' certainly is an issue of governance, but as the authors of this volume have aptly demonstrated, Nepal is suffering from 'malgovernance'; in fact, at times, lack of governance has made it, to use the words of Dwarika Nath Dhungel and Madan Kumar Dahal, 'gloomy and sluggish.'

The evidence of this is found in Nepal having six constitutions during the last sixty-seven years (the first one in 1948 and the current one promulgated in 2015) that is, on average, one constitution every ten years! I guess it is time for Nepal to start thinking out of the box on the issue of having a 'written' constitution. Since the South Asians, including the Nepalese, are oral people and not textual, why doesn't Nepal start thinking of having an *unwritten* constitution instead of the overly tried written one? There are several countries, including New Zealand, Canada, Israel and, of course, former colonial power, the UK, that have unwritten constitutions and face no 'constitutional' or 'legal' barriers in running their respective governments. I cannot help pointing out here that the Delhi Sultanate (1206–1526) as well as the Mughal dynasty (1526–1857) that 'governed' a large part of the Indian subcontinent for over three hundred years never had any written constitution. The idea is to go bill-by-bill or convention-by-convention and not have everything written down in *one* 'sacred' document.

Moreover, none of the written constitutions in South Asia have fully worked. They had so many 'amendments' that the original content, often the 'spirit,' was displaced or simply erased. And that includes the Indian Constitution as well! Not surprisingly, the state of the current Nepali constitution is no different, as Dwarika Nath Dhungel and Jan Sharma came to the conclusion that, 'The NC, CPN-UML and CPN-M, which should have worked together and owned the constitution, are now politically at loggerheads on...issues.' In this context, an *unwritten* constitution would also help Nepal fend itself from India, which, according to Bipin Adhikari, seems to be in the business of using 'the process of democratization' to 'create instability' in Nepal and 'space for India and Indian interests.' Conspiratorial though it may sound, this is a point that merits attention, particularly in view of the public perception both within and outside Nepal of such politicking by India.

Noteworthy here is the fact that Nepal's current constitution, and even the one promulgated in 1990, did make a qualitative break from the constitutions of several South Asian countries, particularly in having a separate chapter on 'political parties.' This is important because political parties, as Tri Ratna Manandhar rightly points out, are 'the backbone of democracy.' Having their rights and responsibilities incorporated in the constitution (Part 29 of the 2015 Constitution of Nepal), not only makes them accountable but also empowers them. However, despite having certain responsibilities enshrined in the constitution, including holding party elections at all levels and submitting an audit report annually, political parties in Nepal are able to get away without practising them. This is mainly because the constitution did not specify the penalty for the would-be violators. The outcome of this has been to carry out the cause of democracy *without*, indeed, with little or no democracy or transparency *within*! This is bound to invite favouritism, corruption and poor governance. But that is not all.

Electoral politics has transformed the political parties into assemblies of ethnic/caste identities and 'self-seeking' members, both of which are inimical to the cause of democracy. Dilli Ram Dahal captures this well in his chapter, 'Social Structure of the Nepali Society.' In this context, the 'ethnic awakening' that Aditya Man Shrestha, Chiranjibi Bhandari and Rajib Timalsina refer to when reflecting on the 'Maoist conflagration' seems to have backfired! Equally alarming is the picture shown by Dwarika Nath Dhungel, Dipak Gyawali and Mahendra Sapkota in their chapter on the governance of the country and their blunt expression that, 'the interests of most of the ministers...misuse power and amass wealth to the maximum extent possible for personal benefit as well as to finance the next election.' Indeed, 'only long-term political stability in the country,' as Rabi Raj Thapa and Chiran Jung Thapa judiciously remarked, 'can enhance Nepal's prospects.'

But can there be 'political stability' without development? The answer is obviously a 'No,' and this Madan Kumar Dahal has rightly identified. But then, the question that needs to be flagged is: What is 'development' in the age of globalization? Certainly, it cannot be 'self-reliant' in the traditional sense of the meaning. Rather, globalization, with 'production' becoming *international* for the first time in the history of capitalism, provides an opportunity for a win-win situation in the relationship between developed and developing economies. In this context, India's fear of growing Sino–Nepalese economic relationship is counterproductive, if not bordering on infantilism. Rather, Nepal could be an ideal place for a joint Sino–Indian–Nepalese economic collaboration, particularly in the backdrop of India's $100 billion trading relationship with China. In fact, Mohan Prasad Lohani and Nishchal Nath Pandey made an implicit reference to this when they pointed out that Nepal can benefit from its neighbours' economic growth and prosperity. Indeed, such tripartite collaboration could bolster not only Nepal's economic development but also the development of Northeast India, which is in a dire need of economic growth.

The vibrancy of the oral people depends on having dialogues, discussions and debates. If that were throttled then the same group of people would end up demonstrating their vibrancy violently. It would be wise for the party-in-power in Nepal to recognize this and take measures to create space for the public discourse to thrive and flourish so that the people of Nepal can creatively and peacefully come out of the abyss. On a quest of this kind, the essays collected in this book would prove immensely valuable. My heartiest congratulations to all the authors!

Imtiaz Ahmed, Professor, Department of International Relations, University of Dhaka, Bangladesh, and former Executive Director, Regional Centre for Strategic Studies, Colombo, Sri Lanka

PREFACE

Nepal is geostrategically located between two of the fastest-growing economies of the world—China and India. It is endowed with enormous potentiality and inhabited by people from different social, cultural and religious backgrounds who live in the high Himalayan, middle mountain and lush green and fertile Tarai regions. World over, Nepal enjoys the unique image as a country of Mt Everest, Pashupatinath Temple and Lumbini—the birthplace of Lord Buddha. At present, however, it looks sick and tired in every sphere, be it political, economic, social, foreign/diplomatic, security or governance. Such is the country's situation, despite the fact that it has been practising a multiparty democratic form of government and has adopted an open, liberal and market economy.

The high ideals of democracy and good governance enshrined in its sanctified documents are honoured overwhelmingly in breach. The gulf between what is committed in principle and what is actually practised remains one of the widest to be found anywhere in the world. A state of stalemate pervades the nation in all fields. Thus, questions arise: (i) Why does a country having vast potential in many fields looks so gloomy and sluggish? and (ii) What could be done to make Nepal a happy and peaceful country once again?

Through this compendium, the native scholars have tried to seek answers to these questions through their analytical and diagnostic lenses. In other words, this book is an attempt to examine the current state of affairs, including an analysis of recent trends in the areas of history, society, constitution, economy, politics, foreign policy, security, corruption, governance and conflict.

Although we do not stake a claim to pioneering the effort through this book, this is an attempt to sincerely analyse the crux of the ongoing upheavals on multiple fronts, as well as developing a comprehensive understanding of the problems facing Nepal with a commitment to contribute in the acceleration of economic prosperity, preserving democracy, strengthening national unity, maintaining territorial integrity and upholding the sovereignty of the country. This is also a very modest attempt on our part to contribute to the enrichment of literature on Nepal.

A galaxy of scholars has contributed to this endeavour. To name a few: Babu Ram Acharya, Dilli Raman Regmi, Keshar Bahadur KC, Surya Bikram Gyawali, Naya Raj Panta, Imansing Chemjong, Harka Gurung, Sylvian Levi, Percival Landon, Giuseppe Tucci, Leo E. Rose, Christopher von Fürer-Haimendorf, Erika Leuchtag, Han Suyin, Toni Hagen, Wang Hongwei, Hu Shisheng and Assad Hussain.

We are grateful to our contributors, namely Tri Ratna Manandhar, Dilli Ram Dahal, Bipin Adhikari, Jan Sharma, Mohan Prasad Lohani, Nishchal Nath Pandey, Rabi Raj Thapa, Chiran Jung Thapa, Aditya Man Shrestha, Chiranjibi Bhandari, Rajib Timilsina, Dipak Gyawali and Mahendra Raj Sapkota, for taking pains to accomplish the assignment within the stipulated time frame.

In the preparation of the chapters, our contributors have received inputs, support and motivation from many other people. They are: Ananta Ram Bhattarai, former Additional Inspector General of Nepal Police; Asish Thapa, Executive Director, Transparency International-Nepal (TI-Nepal); Batsa Gopal Baidya, senior artist; Bharat Thapa, former Chairperson, TI-Nepal; Devi Ram Sharma, former Chief, Nepal Investigation Department; Dina Nath, Programme Officer, TI-Nepal; Govinda Nepal, Professor of Economics, former Economic Advisor, Ministry of Finance (MoF), and former National Planning Commission; Jaya Raj Acharya, Professor of English and former Nepalese Ambassador to United Nations; Krishna Acharya, a retired civil servant; Prakash Chandra Lohani, former Finance and Foreign Minister; Dr Prajwal Dhungel; Rajesh Jha 'Ahirraj', Editor, Madheshvani; Raman Misra, Senior Social Demographer; Sudhindra Sharma, Executive Director, Inter Disciplinary Analysts; Ganesh Mandal, Medeshi Civil Society Activist; Hari Bahadur Thapa, News Editor, Kantipur News; Kedar

Khadka, Executive Chairperson, Go Go Foundation; Keshab Paudel, Editor, New Spotlight; Krishna Nepal, retired civil servant; Kuber Rana, former Inspector General of Nepal Police; Laxman Ghimire, former State Minister for Water Resources; Madhukar Shumshere JB Rana, former Finance Minister; Milan Shrestha, Advocate and Lecturer of Political Science, Tribhuvan University; Naveen Adhikari, Lecturer, Economics Department, Tribhuvan University; Dr. Prachanda Pradhan, Senior Researcher, Social Sciences; Ratan Bhandari, Water Resources Activist; Santa Bahadur Pun, former Officer on Special Duty, Ministry of Water Resources and former Managing Director, Nepal Electricity Authority; Sunder Nath Bhattarai, former Nepalese Ambassador to Thailand; Chandra Shah, Election Commission, Nepal; and Trilok Singh Thapa Magar, Senior Sociologist. Each of them deserves our sincere appreciation.

Likewise, we are extremely thankful to Imtiaz Ahmed, Professor, Department of International Relations, University of Dhaka, Bangladesh, and former Executive Director, Regional Centre for Strategic Studies (RCSS), Colombo, Sri Lanka, for readily agreeing to our request of writing a foreword to this book.

We are immensely grateful to Shyam Prasad Adhikari, a development anthropologist, for all his support, motivation and encouragement in the completion of this work.

We are also grateful to Kapish G. Mehra, Managing Director, Rupa Publications India, New Delhi, for giving us this opportunity and supporting us. Special thanks to Yamini Chaudhary, Senior Commissioning Editor, and the team at Rupa for their editorial inputs.

Also, our profound thanks to Anil Shrestha in bringing the book to its current shape. Equally thankful to Madhav Lal Maharjan, of Mandala Book Point, Kathmandu, for all his help, support and encouragement.

We are indebted to our respective family members, including Neera Dahal, Niru Dhungel and Sudha Lohani, for their cooperation, support and hospitality throughout the discussions and until the completion of the very challenging and tight schedule.

We envisage that this book will address the demand for a

comprehensive understanding of contemporary Nepal, comprising many facets at national, regional and global levels. Furthermore, we hope that it will contribute to understanding the reasons that have been causing problems in Nepal for the past few decades, as well as the factors that might cure its ills. In this regard, we may recall William Shakespeare's famous lines in his play, *Julius Caesar*,

> The fault, dear Brutus, is not in our stars, but in ourselves.

Kathmandu, Nepal
April 2018

Dwarika Nath Dhungel
Madan Kumar Dahal

INTRODUCTION

Nepal is a country rich in natural resources and known for many things, including its contribution to international peace through the United Nations' (UN's) peacekeeping operations. While it has been a party-less democracy since 1960 and a restored parliamentary system of democracy for more than a quarter century since 1990, the dispensation has remained a paradox all these years. Despite democracy being idealistically defined as a government of the people, for the people and by the people, most of the masses in Nepal—characterized by pervasive poverty and persistent underdevelopment—continue to suffer from extreme deprivations. While trying to heal from the scars of the decade-old (1996–2006) bloody insurgency launched by the Communist Party of Nepal-Maoist (CPN-M), which had caused immense loss of human lives and property, through election to the constituent assembly (CA) for drafting the fundamental law of the land, the country got entangled in a political whirlpool and economic stagnation.

The country has been going through a steady process of deterioration over the decades, and occasional mishaps like the earthquake in April 2015 have further made people's lives miserable. But after the elections to all the three layers of the government structure—753 local government units, seven provincial governments and one federal government, as per the provisions of the Constitution of Nepal 2015—the country, from all indications, is on the path of political stability. But the economy is not in a good shape. There is still suspicion as to whether the country would remain politically stable in the days to come and whether the economy would grow. In other words, the downhill slide has been taking place under a dispensation that is supposedly democratic, under which popular well-being must have been the supreme consideration for all people ensconced in the positions of power. Would it not happen in the days to come? It is fundamental to find the reasons for Nepal remaining unstable and in a poor condition. Is it history or social structure or the economic policies? Or, is it the country's political system, or foreign and diplomatic policy, or national security policy, or insurgency, or agitation, or movement or overall governance situations? These yet-to-be answered questions are covered in this book, which is divided into nine chapters, covering Nepal's history, society, constitution, economy, politics, foreign policy, security, conflict and governance and corruption.

Chapter 1 provides a scenario of Nepal's history, which is full of glory and heroic saga of generations of brave-hearted people who never came under any foreign occupation. As envisioned by Prithvi Narayan Shah, the founding father of the nation, in his *Divya Upadesh* (Divine Dictum), Nepal is 'a yam between two boulders'—a historic but immutable axiom to reflect the country's status in antiquity. This chapter also traces the history of Nepal from the ancient time, to the unification, to the present-day situation and provides some perspectives for the future from history's viewpoint.

Chapter 2 deals with the Nepali society that embodies the great merit and unique example of unity among diversity. The society in general, the author writes, comprises multi-ethnicity, multi-language and multi-culture and religion—an excellent example of social equilibrium, cultural and religious harmony, deep-rooted sense of belonging among families and communities and love and respect for each other in the past. Unfortunately, the whole society is divided and fractured today and, therefore, extremely weak to defend. The author further highlights the essence of the deep cultural roots and heritage of Nepal—one of the very few ancient countries in the world associated with the origin of the Vedas. However, the modern Nepali society, the contributor thinks, is seriously engaged in the quest of peace and tranquillity through social and cultural harmony to ensure a better future for Nepal.

Chapter 3 is devoted to the development of the constitution and its sustainability in Nepal. It is indeed a poignant episode for the Nepalese people. This country has witnessed promulgation of a series of seven constitutions within a period of seven decades. And, the author is of the opinion that none of these constitutions got the opportunity to evolve and develop based on experience and necessities. Each of them came to an abrupt end. Even the Constitution of Nepal 2015, the latest one, is facing tough times. While controversies on the contents are there, no less are the geopolitical impacts. The chapter also provides details as to how the new constitution came into existence after the fall of the monarchy. The new constitution is characterized by the Federal Democratic Republic order—a great manifestation of sovereignty that lies with people and also the strong evidence of power and authority of Nepalese people to independently formulate a constitution in accordance with their aspirations. However, the author mentions that it is extremely challenging to fully implement the new constitution because all of its political innovations—federalism, secularism and mixed system of representation with parliamentary type of government—are being contested, and geopolitical considerations are not clear.

Chapter 4 deals with the economic oscillation facing Nepal for a long time. The economy, the contributor thinks, is passing through a crucial phase of 'low-level equilibrium trap' circumscribed by poverty and stagnation. The macroeconomic indicators and international comparison exhibit that Nepal is trailing behind other South Asian countries and is ranked one of the poorest countries in the world according to the classification of World Atlas. The growth rate squeezed to 0.77 per cent—lowest in the last twenty-five years—in 2015–16, attributable to the earthquake, economic impasse and prolonged agitations. Nepal's economic development is a challenging proposition, for reconstruction and rehabilitation activities are moving at a snail's pace; capital expenditure suffers from 'under-spending' syndrome; status of infrastructure, especially of hydropower is very poor and inadequate; and exportable items are extremely limited, resulting in macroeconomic instability. The prime concern, this chapter explains, is to return the economy to normalcy after accomplishing the task of reconstruction and rehabilitation activities within the next two or three years; move towards a 'self-reliant' economy by mobilizing viable economic potential of the mountains, hills and Tarai/Madhes; upgrade the country from Least Developed Country (LDC) status to that of developing economy by 2022 and thereby achieving the Gross National Income (GNI) per capita at par with middle-income countries by 2030; and, finally, make Nepal the Switzerland of Asia by 2040.

Chapter 5 dwells on contemporary political developments in the country, especially focusing on the developments since 2006. The authors are of the opinion that Nepal's tryst with democracy remains elusive ever since the collapse of the Rana oligarchy in 1951 and the advent of democratic innovations after the promulgation of a written constitution. The Constitution of Nepal 2015 is the country's seventh constitution and is already confronting challenges even after the elections to all the three layers of government and political public positions. The hope that it will institutionalize a Federal Democratic Republic to lay the foundation of a stable political order to catch up with its neighbours—China and India—is yet to happen, thereby causing worry to common people. This chapter explores what went wrong. Also, reasons and consequences of the latest political developments and uncertainties are touched upon, in addition to the strategy to pull the country out of the murky democratic order.

Chapter 6 highlights Nepal's foreign relations. Since the country's exposure to the international arena, especially after 1951, diplomatic relations have been established with 144 countries and Nepal is one of the countries that have been making continuous contributions to world peace through the UN peacekeeping operations and missions. More importantly, the contributors look upon Nepal's strategic location between two economic powers—India in the south and China, the second largest economy in the world, in the north—as a great advantage and opportunity to ensure economic prosperity by mobilizing cooperation from the two economies. In addition, they are of the opinion that Nepal has been receiving bilateral, regional and multilateral cooperation without any disruption and with increasing size, despite a series of political changes. But they feel that over the period, especially after the movement of 2005–06, Nepal's foreign policymakers seem to have failed to understand its geostrategic location and adopt as well as adjust its policy accordingly. Thus, the contributors hold the view that the Nepal's foreign and diplomatic policies seem not to be in line with its location in South Asia and as such its role in the international and regional arenas seems to be gradually eroding.

Chapter 7 is concerned with the national security and related aspects of Nepal. The contributors dwell upon the different security-related institutions—Nepal Army (NA), Armed Police Force (APF) and Nepal Police, and National Investigation Department (NID)—and the problems associated with them. The chapter also deals with the new security challenges that Nepal is facing.

Chapter 8 surveys the successive traumas Nepal encountered from the Maoist insurgency from 1996 to 2006 followed by the Madhes agitation triggered in 2007. It dwells on the Maoist armed revolt resulting in more than 17,000 casualties and untold damage to property, which ended with an agreement between the Maoists and seven political parties. The rebels and the political parties joined hands to end the arbitrary rule of the king but, once at the helm of affairs, abolished the 240-year-old monarchy in 2008. In the political peace process, the Maoists achieved many of their pronounced agenda, like federalization, secularism and republicanism, but Nepal is yet to achieve the avowed pace of development.

This chapter also reviews the prolonged agitation of the Madhes-based parties, which has equally shocked the Nepalese people since 2007. To begin with, Prime Minister Girija Prasad (G.P.) Koirala conceded to their demands for regional autonomy and proportional representation in all branches of the state under a federal system that his successors could not meet. The results gave a death blow to the fruitless first CA and when its second incarnation produced the much-awaited Constitution of Nepal 2015, the dissenting Madhesi parties boycotted it, launched a months-long agitation, resulting in loss of a large number of lives, and, subsequently, India 'unofficially' imposed an economic blockade on Nepal. People in Nepal have been reeling under these unforeseen ordeals for more than two decades with no light yet seen at the end of the tunnel.

And finally, Chapter 9 discusses the state of corruption and poor governance in Nepal in the context of the sayings of King Ram Shah of Gorkha, whose righteous rule was characterized by the popular saying, *Nyaya napaye Gorkha janu* (If you want justice, go to Gorkha) and divine dictums of the founder of today's Nepal, King Prithvi Narayan Shah, (*Niya nisaf bigarnya bhanyako ghus dinya ra ghus khanya. En dui ko ta dhan jib gari liyako pani paap chhaina. Ee rajaka mahasatur hun*—Justice is crippled with bribe-giving and bribe-taking. If the life and property of these two are seized, no sin is incurred. They are the greatest enemies of the king).

This chapter refers to corruption in the country as a pernicious problem. Political corruption has gone beyond the pursuit for personal gain by the political parties, politicians and their henchmen and has, thus, been structurally entrenched. The elected representatives of different political parties and individuals seek plum and lucrative positions, and then use their pelf to assure their re-election and hold onto power. From the executives of big enterprises to even a village schoolteacher, appointments are made more by kickbacks than by normal and established criteria. The same is true with promotions, placements and transfers in most of the public services. This has demoralized, politicized and even criminalized the bureaucracy, disabling it from performing its normal expected functions. The country, as per the contributors, has not improved in the latest Corruption Perception Index of TI. In 2012, Nepal's position was 139th with a score of 27 points; the position was almost same at 122nd with a score of 31 points after six years in 2017. In 2017, among South Asian nations, Nepal was just ahead of Afghanistan (177th with 15 points) and Bangladesh (143rd with 28 points). In addition to dealing with corruption in all sectors, the authors have also suggested measures to check corruption, one of which is to award life imprisonment for serious corruption offences.

1

HISTORICAL PERSPECTIVE

Tri Ratna Manandhar

Nepal—a Himalayan state bounded by China in the north and India in the south, east and west—has remained independent of foreign rule from the very beginning of its history, though it has fought wars with its northern (China) and southern (Britain) neighbours during different periods. After many ups and downs in history, democracy was finally restored in Nepal in 1990, but even after the lapse of more than a quarter of a century, the country could not make satisfactory progress as a nation. Rather, it has been embroiled in a series of crises—political, social and economic—and has now become a fragile state.

United and Divided Nepal

Although the archaeological and chronological history of Nepal can be traced back to millions of years, its epigraphic history starts only from the fifth century AD. The Changu Narayan inscription of AD 464 is very significant as it records the country's history for the first time. The political boundary of the then Nepal was almost of the present shape, covering an area west of Kamarupa (Assam) and east of Kartapuradi (Kumaon). The Licchavi rulers directly ruled from Dumja in the east to Gorkha in the west; beyond these, feudal chiefs ruled the eastern and western areas under the suzerainty of the Licchavis. Whenever the Licchavi rulers became weak, the feudal chiefs rose in revolt and tried to claim their autonomous status, but each time, the central government was successful in suppressing them (Bajracharya, 1973).

Historians claim that Licchavi Nepal was a prosperous state. Land and agriculture were the main bases of the country's economy. The country was the centre for entrepôt trade between India and Tibet. Cottage industry was also well-developed. The period also witnessed minting of a variety of coins, though limited in quantity. While analysing the economic condition of Licchavi Nepal, we must take into account its taxation system. Commonly known as 'trikara', the main taxes were termed as Bhoga, Bhaga and Kara, which were levied on agriculture, trade and commerce, and cattle, respectively. It seems that taxes were the main sources of income for the government, and as such the people had to pay different kinds of taxes (Bajracharya, 1973).

Another significant aspect of the Licchavi Nepal was the existence of religious harmony between Hinduism and Buddhism. One Chinese pilgrim in the seventh century writes that in Nepal, Hindu and Buddhist temples stood side by side and the people worshipped in both temples with equal respect (Bajracharya, 1973).

The Licchavis developed a sound local administrative system by instituting effective local units, clearly defining their obligations and responsibilities, but they did not limit the absolute power of the king. The inscriptions state that the king's command was a law unto the people. The administration was well-organized, but only till the king and the higher authorities allowed them.

The social system of the day was well-defined and effectively implemented, but with many exceptions. Sati system was prevalent, but not compulsory. Divorce was allowed in some specific cases, but it was considered a shameful act. Guthi (trust) lands were established to perform various social and charitable activities, but these guthis were only active in some specific areas and for some specific periods. The permanency of a sound social system was generally lacking.

Coming to foreign relations, Nepal was in good terms with Tibet. Princess Bhrikuti was married to a Tibetan king, with whose help, Narendra Dev, the son of the deposed king of Nepal, could recapture his throne. Nepal had normal relations, at least at people's level, with the states of India to the south because of easy communication.

The Licchavi rulers effectively governed the country up to the eighth century, after which they gradually lost their power and position. Exploiting this opportunity, the federal chiefs of the east and the west proclaimed autonomous states of their own. The situation worsened after a couple of centuries, when the Licchavi kings had to share power with an emerging nobility, the Mallas, who finally got overall control of the state and government by the end of the fourteenth century, ending the very existence of the Licchavis in the history of Nepal (Shaha, 1992).

Along with political turmoil, there were also religious disruptions. The chronicles mention the visit of the Sankaracharya to Nepal and his destruction of Buddhist literature and monasteries and harassment of Buddhist population. But Buddhism continued to flourish because of the active role played by scholars such as Padmasambhava, Santaraksita and Kamalasila from India (Ram, 1977). By the end of the fourteenth century, King Jayasthiti Malla had divided the entire population into Shaiva and Buddhist sects, clearly defining their status, duties and responsibilities. The state now came to be known as Nepal Mandala.

With the gradual decline of the Licchavi rule, one powerful, independent state emerged in the west, comprising Gandaki and Karnali regions, which came to be known as the Khasa kingdom. Occasionally, these rulers even extended their kingdom to certain areas of India. Similarly, a new state was created in the east, mainly situated in the Koshi and Narayani areas, which came to be known as the Doya kingdom, with its capital at Simraungarh. Its founder ruler, who came from the south, was a feudal chief and later proclaimed himself an independent ruler (Shaha, 1992).

Of these three independent states, Nepal Mandala was the most prosperous. One chronicle mentions that its agricultural lands were most productive, and engagement in agricultural activities for three months would give products sufficient for one year. And that is why it became a target of the eastern and western kingdoms, which occasionally attacked it to gain economic benefits. These three kingdoms further disintegrated by the end of the fifteenth century. The

Khasa kingdom was divided into forty-six small kingdoms—twenty-two, known as Baisi, in the Karnali region and twenty-four, known as Chaubisi, in the Gandaki region. Similarly, the Doya kingdom was divided into four or five small principalities—all ruled by the Sen Dynasty. The Nepal Mandala also split into three independent states, viz. Kantipur, Bhaktapur and Lalitpur, all under the Malla rulers belonging to a single family. One peculiar feature of this disintegration was the adoption of monarchy by all these states. No republican state is ever known to exist in the history of Nepal till 2008.

One important phenomenon of the medieval history of Nepal was the entry of Muslims and Christians to the Nepal Mandala in the fifteenth and seventeenth centuries, respectively. The Muslims entered Nepal as businessmen and were permitted to live under certain terms and conditions. They could conduct their business uninterrupted with the support of the government. Only one or two minor incidents against Muslims are recorded in the entire medieval period. The entry of Christians, however, was different. They entered Nepal on their way to Tibet or back from there. Unlike Muslims, Christians were more active in converting Nepali people to Christianity. Thus, they were expelled immediately after the conquest of the Kathmandu valley by King Prithvi Narayan Shah.

During the seventeenth century, the Nepal Mandala extended its trade relations with Tibet through a treaty to establish Nepali trading houses at Lhasa. In addition, the Nepal government got rights to mint coins for Tibet, for which the Tibetan government would pay in gold or silver. Trade relations with India were mostly informal, with most of the border states engaged in one way or the other.

The three states of the Nepal valley frequently fought with each other with limited or unspecified objectives. The adjoining states of east and west were also involved in these political struggles to fulfil their minor interests. It made these states politically weak and dependent on one another, the result of which was their annexation by the king of Gorkha—Prithvi Narayan Shah—and his successors, leading to the unification of Nepal as a nation.

Just like the Licchavis, the Malla rulers, though being Hindus, had equal respect for Buddhism. It was a time when people at large constructed Hindu temples and Buddhist monasteries and offered liberal donations for their upkeep and progress. As regards to social life, the Nepali society was largely governed by Jayasthiti Malla's code, which put the caste system as a permanent feature of Nepali society, fixing different occupations on the basis of one's caste. The duplication in occupation was rare, and everyone was satisfied with his job. But, over the period, distinction was created or emerged between higher and lower circles within the social system, which led to unseen conflicts.

A number of fairs and festivals were observed by people partly as religious practice and partly as means of entertainment. The state patronized several national festivals, and the people donated land (guthis) to perform their own festivals. The guthis were extended at state and private level, and the system became a regular feature of the Nepali social life. The medieval period also witnessed the development of art and architecture. The government sent a team of artists under Araniko to Tibet and China, who earned fame there and eventually settled in China permanently (Petech, 1984).

Unification of Nepal and After

As already mentioned, Nepal was divided into more than fifty small states during the medieval period. Out of them, only three kingdoms of the Kathmandu valley (mentioned as Nepal valley) termed themselves as Nepal. None of the Baisi, Chaubisi or Sena kingdoms of the east used the word for their state; rather, they mentioned with pride that they had made attacks on Nepal, viz. Kantipur or Lalitpur or Bhaktapur. In fact, the three kingdoms of the Kathmandu valley, along with the adjoining ones, were known as Nepal Mandala during the early medieval period. After its division into three major states, they continued to use the term 'Nepal' for themselves.

Prithvi Narayan Shah was an ambitious king, but it was not possible for him to move towards the west of the Gorkha. There were powerful states such as Kaski, Lamjung, Tanahu and Palpa, with whom the Gorkhali king could not think of waging a war. So, he tried to move towards the east, and the sole aim of his military campaign was to conquer the states of the Kathmandu valley for economic benefits. By 1769, he was able to conquer the valley kingdoms and also successfully repulse the attacks of the Bengal and British armies. By this time, he seriously realized the necessity to protect the conquered areas as a unified state, and the idea of unification came in his mind in the last phase of his life.

Prithvi Narayan is criticized for some of his acts during his military campaigns. He executed his disloyal commander in the most inhuman manner; cut the noses of the people of Kirtipur who had resisted his invasions for nine years; imposed an economic blockade on the Kathmandu valley, making peoples' life miserable; and burnt hundreds of houses in Bhaktapur in course of his invasion. But the one commendable act he did was the founding of a standing army to defend the nation against foreign invasions, which became an integral part of Nepal's history (Jangi Adda, 2013).

He is also attributed to shifting the capital to Kathmandu, realizing its overall geographic and strategic importance. Historians agree that Prithvi Narayan Shah had become a 'Nepali' from Gorkhali. His strategy was to continue the local traditions of the states he had conquered, primarily to avoid their opposition to the new regime. That is why he completed the final rites of Indra Jatra immediately after the conquest of Kantipur and continued the Kipat land system of the Limbus of the east after his conquest of that area.

Prithvi Narayan Shah adopted a dual policy in administration. He chose some of his loyal servants and their families to control different branches of civil administration, but followed the 'merit' policy in the army. Thus, clashes among courtiers interrupted the progress of the nation after his death, but the military campaign in the west continued successfully.

After his death, Regent Queen Rajendra Laxmi conquered the three powerful Chaubisi states, viz. Kaski, Lamjung and Tanahu, and Bahadur Shah, who became the regent after Rajendra Laxmi's death, conquered the remaining Chaubisi and Baisi states. He instructed his army commanders to recognize the autonomous status of a state which voluntarily surrendered before the NA, with the respective rulers enjoying judicial and financial authority along with the title of 'Raja'. As a result, almost all the petty states were annexed to Nepal within a few months, and without big battles.

After Bahadur Shah, Nepal's mission to expand the territory was halted for almost a decade because of political turmoil. But it resumed in 1804 under the leadership of Bhimsen Thapa. Across the Mahakali River, Kumaon had already been conquered, and now the NA marched forward and annexed Garhwal and a group of small states known as Barha and Atharathakurai. The Nepali territory was extended up to the Sutlej River in the west, but the government could not win the confidence of the people of those areas, whose administration posed a great challenge to the Nepali rulers.

Nepal had to fight wars with the East India Company, which wanted to stop its march towards the west. It lost the war because of the non-cooperative attitude of the conquered areas, and was compelled to sign the Treaty of Sugauli in 1816, by which it lost one-third of its territory and had to abide by the British directions in conducting foreign relations. Whatever may be the negative impact of the war, its positive outcome was the ending of the seventy-five-year-old mission to expand the territory of Nepal. The political boundary fixed in 1816 remains intact till today, except for some changes in 1860 (Stiller, 1973).

Prithvi Narayan Shah's initial objective was the conquest of Nepal Mandala and not that of Baisi and Chaubisi, but he later realized the necessity of preserving his conquered states from British influence. Prithvi Narayan's successors well understood this reality and founded a 'big Nepal' by unifying all petty states that were once part of greater Nepal. Hence, it will be appropriate to conclude that, though Prithvi Narayan Shah's military campaign started as an act of expansion of Gorkha, it ended in the unification of Nepal.

After the Sugauli Treaty, Bhimsen Thapa tried to take revenge against the British with the help of Indian states, but to no avail. On the contrary, he was dismissed from power after King Rajendra attained the age of maturity (18 years). Rajendra was an ambitious ruler, but he could not control his two wives who were equally ambitious and opposed to each other. The queens were backed by two rival groups of courtiers, i.e. Pandeys and Thapas. The nine-year period of political instability (1837–46) resulted in the emergence of a little known nobility, Kunwars, who ruled Nepal as dictator prime ministers for more than a century as 'Ranas'.

The unification period and its aftermath (1742–1846) were marked by a few changes in administration, society and the economy. Earlier, all the petty states had their own administrative systems with different social values and economic policies. After unification, the greatest challenge to the Nepal government was to develop a uniform administrative system, a common social policy and a strong state economy. During the last days of his life, Prithvi Narayan Shah gave instructions to his officials on state policies, which were later compiled into what is now called *Divya Upadesh.*

The implementation of these instructions was very rare because they were known only to a few courtiers and the document itself was first discovered only after the end of the Rana regime in 1951. Still, the *Divya Upadesh* sheds light on the thoughts of a king who wanted to preserve the political identity of his new state and protect it from foreign domination or influence. It had some impact on administrative and social policies; attempts were made to govern the country through a universal code, create a unified social structure and develop a new economic policy. Mention should be made of a special court formed by Bhimsen Thapa in 1827 to look after the cases of misuse of authority by government officials—higher or lower (HMG, 1965/66).

Despite its declared policy of maintaining friendship with China and the British, Nepal witnessed her diplomatic failure when she was involved in wars with both the neighbours during the unification period. The country lost both the wars and her attempts to pit the neighbours against one another also failed. Bhimsen's attempt to challenge the British domination with the help of Indian states also did not materialize.

The Rana Regime

The Kunwars, with Jung Bahadur Kunwar as the leader of the group, came to power in 1846. Through Kot, Bhandarkhal and Alau episodes, he eliminated the opponent courtiers, queen and the king, respectively, and established his family rule by reducing the position of kings to that of a nominal head of the state. In addition, Jung raised the status of his family by calling themselves 'Ranas' through a royal order in 1848, assumed the royal title of Maharaja of Kaski and Lamjung in 1856 and got dictatorial powers of state and government in 1857 as the Prime Minister of Nepal (Manandhar, 1986).

All through the Rana regime (1846–1951), the prime motive of Jung and his successors was to preserve and continue their dictatorial role, and for this they pursued a variety of policies. Jung contracted matrimonial alliance with the royal family—a tradition continued by his successors. The objective behind this was to prevent the royal family from taking back the supreme power of the state from the hands of the Ranas. They also tried to suppress the rival groups, but failed. Several political organizations were founded, chief among them were Praja Parishad and Nepali Congress (NC), whose activities finally sounded the death knell on the Rana rule.

In foreign relations, the Ranas adopted pro-British policies mainly to protect their dynastic rule in Nepal. Jung helped the British to suppress the Indian Mutiny of 1857, and prime ministers Chandra and Juddha rendered valuable services to the British during the first and second world wars, respectively. The result was the signing of the Nepal–Britain Treaty in 1923, through which the British unequivocally recognized the independent status of Nepal. The Gorkha recruitment was an outcome of the Nepal–Britain relations. The enlistment of Nepali people in the British Army had started in 1816, but in the pre-Rana days it went into most difficult phases as the Nepali government was not in favour of sending its men to the British service. But things changed during the Rana regime, and from Bir Shumsher's time, the recruitment went undisturbed, with the active support of the Nepal government (Husain, 1970). Up to the end of their rule, the Ranas considered the British as their guardian and protector.

The Rana rulers tried to maintain cordial relations with China with some ups and downs on different issues. Jung waged a successful war against Tibet in 1855 by keeping China in good humour. In 1883, Tibetan lamas plundered the property of Nepali merchants in Lhasa, and the Nepali government firmly stood behind her merchants to get full compensation for lost property, even by resisting Chinese intervention. Similarly, in 1928, when a Sherpa was arrested by Tibetans from the Nepali Legation at Lhasa, the country threatened to launch a war if the issue was not solved in its favour.

During the last years of the Rana regime, Nepal extended diplomatic relations with America and France. It also established formal diplomatic relations with independent India and signed friendship and commercial treaties in 1950 to gain its tacit support to their regime. But at this juncture, the Ranas failed, and the family autocracy was ended with active intervention of the Indian government in favour of Nepali revolutionaries.

The century-long Rana regime had introduced a number of reforms in socio-economic and administrative fields. Through these, the Rana rulers wanted to go down in history as great reformers, and thereby win the favour of illiterate masses by providing certain facilities in their daily lives. However, most of these reforms were meant for the ruling family and their adherents and the common people could hardly enjoy their benefits. The Rana rulers could deprive any person or group of any privilege without giving any reason whatsoever. That is why, in 1951, when the autocratic regime collapsed, people found that the country had been left far behind in the race of progress (Jain, 1972).

A number of factors led to the demise of the Rana regime, chief among them were the British withdrawal from India and clashes and divisions in the Rana family. Besides, the joint platform of King Tribhuvan and Nepali revolutionaries led by the NC party, whose leader was B.P. Koirala, also played a decisive role in overthrowing autocracy. In this anti-Rana movement, the Indian government, particularly Prime Minister Jawaharlal Nehru, played an intervening role dictating both the Rana government and Nepali revolutionaries to accept a compromise formula. The so-called Delhi Pact provided for the (a) emergence of the king as the real head of the state, (b) formation of an interim government representing Rana oligarchy and Nepali revolutionaries and (c) election of a CA within two years to frame a democratic constitution. The family autocracy thus ended and democratic era began in the history of Nepal.

Democratic Experiments (1951–1960)

The democratic experiment started in Nepal amidst numerous impediments. King Tribhuvan became the head of the state and government, but guarded by Indian diplomats; peoples' representatives had to share power with past dictator Ranas; and even among the peoples' representatives, only the NC got the lion's share, with complete negligence of other political parties. Most serious of all, Pandit Nehru was not in favour of a democratic government in Nepal and he rather wanted a loose combination of the NC and the Ranas through his policy of 'middle way'. The NC accepted the challenge, but left no stone unturned to oust the Ranas from the cabinet.

Tribhuvan fully supported the Congress, and within nine months, the Rana–Congress coalition government collapsed. However, the king, on the advice of Nehru, betrayed the NC and set aside the claim of B.P. Koirala to be the prime minister and a new government was formed under M.P. Koirala—the half-brother of B.P. Koirala. As a result, the NC cabinet also collapsed in another nine months.

Since 1953, Tribhuvan had not been in good health, and in his absence, M.P. Koirala became all-powerful. He sought help from minor parties—Praja Parishad and Nepali National Congress—to run the government, but completely ignored NC, which was now split into four different factions led by B.P. Koirala, M.P. Koirala, Bhadrakali Mishra and Bal Chandra Sharma. In this critical period, the Nepal Communist Party (NCP) emerged as an alternative political force in the country, but it was banned soon. By March 1955, when King Tribhuvan died, the political situation of Nepal was at its worst (Manandhar and Sharma, 1996/97).

Nepali politics underwent a substantial change after Mahendra ascended the throne. The new monarch was determined to govern the country under his direct leadership, and for this to happen, the proposed election to the CA was the main obstacle. Mahendra tried to pollute the political air against the CA through two leaders—Tanka Prashad Acharya and Dr K.I. Singh—who were appointed prime ministers one after another, mainly to disseminate the political objective of the monarch. In this context, the Supreme Court also acted in the king's favour by misinterpreting the provisions of the interim constitution of 1951 (Manandhar and Sharma, 1996/97).

In addition, the major political parties were sharply divided on the election issue, with the minor parties actively engaged in making political bargains by exploiting the controversial election question. The division in the political parties provided an opportunity for the king to act as an arbitrator. After many moves and counter-moves, Mahendra finally ruled out people's right to frame the constitution and declared election to the parliament, under a constitution, to be given by him. The minor parties endorsed the royal verdict without any reservation, and the big political parties, such as the NC, also reluctantly accepted it. In effect, the nation accepted 'King Mahendra's personalized version of democracy rather than King Tribhuvan's vision of a government functioning within the framework of a constitution framed by the people' (Joshi and Rose, 1966).

By 1951, Nepal had established diplomatic relations with Britain, India, America and France, and no other diplomatic relations were contracted during Tribhuvan's four-year rule. It was only after the prime ministers of India and China met in Beijing in 1954 that Nepal contracted diplomatic relations with other countries. According to a former diplomat, Yadu Nath Khanal, India agreed to Nepal's diplomatic extensions only after China accepted to consider Nepal as under the sphere of India's influence.

After ascending the throne, Mahendra's foremost objective was to establish diplomatic relations with China as a counterbalance to India's domination. This, he did within five months. The only obstruction to this move was the question of Tibet, which had been paying an annual tribute of 10,000 Nepali Rupees (NPR) to Nepal since 1856 and where the Nepalese envoy enjoyed extra-territorial jurisdiction. Mahendra sacrificed Nepal's dominant position in Tibet to ensure friendship with China (Ramakant, 1976).

The first general election in the history of Nepal started in February 1959, and the king announced the election date only after getting secret reports from his trusted agents that no party would get absolute majority in the parliament. That is why, in the constitution promulgated only a week before the election, the king was authorized to impose his direct rule for one year if no party got absolute majority in the House. In addition, he was equipped with discretionary powers which were beyond the jurisdiction of the Supreme Court.

However, the election took a surprising turn, with the NC bagging two-thirds majority in the Lower House. After initial hesitation, Mahendra appointed B.P. Koirala as the first elected prime minister of Nepal, but created an obstruction in his working by appointing anti-Congress figures in the Upper House of the parliament. The government got a setback as the major plans and policies were to be approved by both the houses of the parliament. A couple of treaties and acts, such as the Gandak Agreement, signed with India in 1959 on the use of waters of the Gandak River, and the Birta Abolition Bill, nationalizing the lands of big landlords, came under heavy criticism.

During the eighteen-month parliamentary rule, Nepal's relationships with India and China neither improved nor worsened. It signed a new treaty with India, which sought the expansion of trade between the two countries and the encouragement to their collaboration in economic development. Relations with China were mildly disturbed by the Sagarmatha issue, when China made her claim over Mount Everest, and the Mustang incident, in which Chinese troops fired on Nepalese border guards near Kore Pass in Mustang.

All these activities encouraged the king to fulfil his old ambition of becoming a powerful monarch. He finally staged a coup in December 1960 by dismissing the elected cabinet, dissolving the parliament and suspending the constitution (Gupta, 1964).

While analysing Mahendra's intention to stage a coup, two

hypotheses, contrary to one another, have to be examined. First, the elected government's unpopular activities created an uneasy situation in the country, and the king was compelled to dismiss the cabinet and dissolve the parliament to bring peace in the country. Second, the elected government was moving successfully to implement its plans and programmes, which undermined the king's position. And, in order to regain his power and position, the king dismissed the government (Manandhar and Sharma, 1996/97).

Both the hypotheses are true to some extent. The elected government was unpopular in the eyes of the opposition parties, but the king realized that if the cabinet successfully implemented its plans and programmes even at the teeth of opposition, he would be reduced to a nominal head of state, despite his wide powers in the constitution. So, he exploited the opportunity, dismissed the elected government, and eventually ended the parliamentary democracy. The compromise made between the hereditary monarch and the elected cabinet through the 1959 constitution ended in failure.

The Panchayat Rule (1961–1990)

The 1960 coup was aimed not only at the dismissal of the elected government but also at the ending of parliamentary democracy. But the king's motive was not exposed even to trusted officials. In his royal proclamation, Mahendra levelled several charges against the NC government, but did not speak a single word against the parliamentary system. However, his activities during the first few months gave a clear indication that the country would not return to a parliamentary system.

The first blow came when the king imposed a ban on political parties, which are the backbone of a parliamentary democracy. Along with that, he put forth an outline of the Panchayat system, which he was going to introduce as a system of government. Once he assumed full power, he initiated several new experiments to show that it was the crown which could play an effective role in national politics and lead the country to progress and development. He formed the National

Planning Commission under his own chair, appointed royal tour commissions to investigate the grievances of the people and founded a new ministry of National Guidance to supervise the working of class and professional organizations formed under official control.

The king also appointed an official ad hoc committee consisting of his trusted officials to survey political institutions in Yugoslavia, Egypt, Pakistan and Indonesia in order to determine whether the political experiences of those countries might be instructive in the establishment of a new political system in Nepal. The report of this committee, if there is any, was never made public, but it is widely believed that the Panchayat system did embrace some of the features, such as the 'national guidance' system of Egypt and Indonesia, the 'basic democracy' system of Pakistan, the 'class organization' system of Egypt and Yugoslavia and the 'guided democracy' system of Indonesia. The party-less character of the Panchayat system was also largely influenced by the system of one-party dictatorship in these countries (Joshi and Rose, 1966).

In order to provide legal basis to his direct rule, King Mahendra promulgated Nepal Special Arrangement Act 1961, which gave supreme executive and legislative powers to the king. The council of ministers, to be constituted under the king's chair, was powerless as the ministers were only to carry out the directives of the king. In the same process, Mahendra took over the defence portfolio to himself to directly deal with the opposition groups through the NA.

The NC leaders who could escape arrest, gathered in Patna, India, to determine their future plans and programmes. They decided to launch a resistance movement against the royal regime in border districts with the sympathy and cooperation of India. The rebel activities came to a climax when an attempt was made on the life of King Mahendra in Janakpur in January 1962. The government adopted tough measures to deal with the rebel movement and requested the Indian government to check their activities at the Indian borders. When India showed its favour to NC leaders, Nepal turned over to China for support. In quick response, the Chinese defence minister publicly declared to help Nepal in case 'any foreign army makes a foolhardy attempt to attack it' (Devkota, 1983/84). Soon after, the Chinese forces attacked Sino-Indian borders, which compelled the NC to suspend its movement, presumably on the advice of the Indian government.

At home, the government made every attempt to convince the people that the parliamentary system had failed and the country should adopt the Panchayat system, which 'is democratic and known to Nepali people since ancient times'. The government announced a new administrative division of the country consisting of fourteen zones and seventy-five districts. In addition, a four-tier Panchayat structure—Village Panchayat or Town Panchayat, District Panchayat, Zonal Panchayat and National Panchayat—was established as national legislature. For the first time, local panchayats were established in the country.

Laws relating to different tiers of Panchayat were publicized and elections were held for village and town panchayats. To get support from political leaders to his new system, King Mahendra summoned an intellectual conference, attended mostly by the political leaders opposed to the NC. The participants unanimously endorsed the royal verdict, though they vehemently criticized the working of the government. They also adopted resolutions expressing their full faith in the Panchayat system and resolving to support the steps initiated by the king (Joshi and Rose, 1966).

Finally, in December 1962, King Mahendra announced a new constitution which gave the king supreme power in all fields. It mentioned: 'The sovereignty of Nepal is vested in His Majesty and all powers—executive, legislative, and judicial—emanate from him.' He had full control over the council of ministers as he formed it under his own chair, and there was no post of prime minister. The ministers, though members of the National Panchayat, were responsible to the king and the latter could dismiss them at any time. The indirectly elected National Panchayat was more of an advisory council than a legislative body. The king could abrogate any bill passed by the legislature and convert any bill rejected by the National Panchayat into law. He also possessed unlimited emergency power through which he could suspend all the provisions of the constitution for an unlimited period. However, the supremacy of the Supreme Court was accepted, with the exception that the king could direct the apex court to revise its decision. On the whole, the king was all in all, with no authority or institution to check his actions.

Once the Panchayat system was adopted formally, attempts were made to publicize it through several means. The government officials, especially in districts, were instructed to create an atmosphere in favour of the new system. If the officials failed to do so, they were reprimanded or even dismissed in some cases. On the other hand, if they succeeded in creating a public opinion in support of the Panchayat system, they were rewarded with promotion, and the government remained silent even if they indulged in corruption. Political leaders, especially from the NC and NCP, were given high posts if they deserted their party and joined the king's regime. One of the criteria for promotion of government or non-government officials was that he/she should have full faith in the Panchayat system.

The king's regime gave the slogan of one institution (i.e. monarchy), one language (i.e. Nepali) and one religion (i.e. Hinduism). Nepal was declared a Hindu state, although every citizen was free to profess his or her own religion in accordance with tradition and custom. Conversion activities, including voluntary conversion, were strictly prohibited, and the top leaders, including the king, openly declared Buddhism as a branch of Hinduism.

On the king's initiative, the Nepal government introduced some notable administrative, social and economic changes. The elected government (1959–60) had already abolished the state courts (Rajya Adalat), and now King Mahendra abolished the 'Rajyas', which had been functioning as semi-autonomous units since the unification period. For this act, Mahendra was hailed as the 'real' unifier of Nepal. In 1963, the king promulgated a new civil code, abrogating the century-old civil code of the country. Equality before law was declared to be the main motto of the code, and it did not make any discrimination in punishment on the basis of caste, creed or sex. After a year, a new land act was announced, giving some specific privileges to the tenants. The peasants hailed it as a revolutionary step in economic history, but the act greatly affected several guthis, which were dependent on lands cultivated by tenants.

Several class and professional organizations were formed under official control and, among them, the youth, women, labourers, peasants and ex-servicemen were represented in the national legislature. One graduate constituency was also established from where four representatives were elected to the national legislature. But this constituency became a headache to the government when some of its candidates who had condemned the Panchayat system and demanded restoration of parliamentary rule were elected by the voters. The government tried to control students' activities by forming an organization under official control. It is said that the government had plans to represent them in the National Panchayat, but because of vehement opposition from students themselves, the plan was dropped.

After imposing his direct rule in 1960, the king promised to restore the political system in five or seven years, as per the will of the people. To remain true to his words, Mahendra, in 1967, gave some 'liberal' concessions through a constitutional amendment. One sentimental change was, that in the national anthem, the words 'we Nepali brothers' were replaced by the words 'we Nepali people'.

After a few months, Mahendra sent a message to the National Panchayat, seeking their opinion on a suitable system in the country. Before the legislature gave its opinion, several organizations asserted that the Panchayat system was the best system for Nepal. As a result, the National Panchayat passed a unanimous resolution declaring it as a system with no alternative. Soon after, the king gave a new slogan of 'Back to the village national campaign' (BVNC), under which every governmental or non-governmental employee had to work in his or her village for one week in a year to disseminate the principles and objectives of the Panchayat system to the people (Shaha, 1978). It is widely believed that the campaign was a political mobilization in support of the Panchayat system. It did not, however, produce any concrete result.

King Birendra, who succeeded his father following his death in 1972, was educated at different institutions in Britain, America and

Japan, and people expected him to be a progressive ruler. As expected, the new king did not utter a single word on the Panchayat system in his initial speeches. But the situation changed after three weeks when he had to admit Panchayat system as a suitable polity for Nepal. It is said that Birendra made this announcement under pressure from his family members, chiefly his wife, Aishwarya, and brother, Gyanendra.

Apart from the royal family, the palace secretariat was working in its own direction, and the Panchayat leaders were moving with their own interests. In this triangular contest, the bureaucracy lagged far behind, with officials taking the side of one group or another. On the other hand, the people were waiting for innovations from the new king in public interest, but they were highly disappointed when, through a constitutional amendment in 1975, the BVNC, which was only a slogan during Mahendra's time, was made a constitutional and most powerful body with the responsibility to mobilize people politically for the country's overall development. It played a paramount role in the election of National Panchayat and other local elections because the candidature for any level election had to be endorsed by the BVNC. The result was that most of the members of the central- and local-level elections were not elected but declared elected on the recommendation of the BVNC (Shaha, 1978). Along with political leaders, the general population was also greatly annoyed by this procedure as it deprived them of their voting right in local elections. The student community exploited the opportunity and launched a movement with educational demands, with the support of banned political parties.

The situation turned so serious that in May 1979, King Birendra had to make an announcement to hold a referendum to decide whether to continue the Panchayat system or introduce a multiparty system. Although the ban on political parties was not lifted, people were given freedom to express their views on either of the systems. At first, the Panchayat leaders were largely demoralized, but they gradually developed confidence to campaign in favour of the Panchayat system. On the contrary, the leaders of banned political parties were greatly encouraged in the beginning, but the lack of coordination among themselves and their self-centred policies alienated them from the people. More than that, the king's announcement (December 1979) to bring changes along the parliamentary lines, irrespective of referendum results, further weakened the position of the multiparty leaders. The result was the defeat of the multiparty system by a slim margin in the referendum that took place after a year (May 1980).

It would not be out of place to mention Birendra's Zone of Peace (ZoP) proposal, which governed a major part of Nepal's foreign relations for more than a decade. On the occasion of his coronation in February 1975, the king made a proposition that 'Nepal be declared a zone of peace'. This subsequently became a major theme in Nepal's foreign policy statements. Many countries endorsed the proposal within a short period, and after much persuasion, the great powers also accepted it, though with some comments. But the negative response came from India, whose leaders dismissed the proposal by stating that India wanted the whole of South Asia or sometimes Asia or the world to be declared a ZoP. Hence, the proposal remained only a political slogan (Rose and Scholz, 1980).

After referendum, King Birendra introduced some liberal changes in the constitution focusing on the National Panchayat. The changes were: direct election of the National Panchayat members, appointment of prime minister on the recommendation of the National Panchayat and the cabinet being responsible to it. But the ban on political parties made it hardly possible to contest the election and recommend the prime minister on ideological basis. Therefore, the major political parties, including the NC, boycotted the two consecutive general elections of 1981 and 1986. Instead, in 1985, the NC, with the support of a few communist groups, launched a protest campaign against the ban on political parties. But a series of bomb explosions in the capital killing five and injuring dozens changed the political scenario, and the NC called off its non-violent movement.

The year 1989 witnessed the lapse of trade and transit treaties between Nepal and India, and the Nepali people suffered a lot due to disruption in the supply of essential goods from India. The political parties accused the government and the Panchayat system for this setback. Seven communist factions formed a United Left Front (ULF), and the NC held a national conference in Kathmandu in January 1990, also attended by Indian leaders, which declared launching of a peaceful movement from 18 February 1990. The NC-led movement, with the active support of the ULF, started on the scheduled date. Although the fifty-day movement could not get momentum for a few weeks, it succeeded at last when King Birendra declared lifting of the ban on political parties and deleting the word 'party-less' from the constitution at his meeting with the leaders of the NC and ULF (Brown, 1996).

From Constitutional Monarchy to Republican State

Multiparty democracy was restored in Nepal in a most favourable atmosphere. However, there were some ups and downs. The NC Government collapsed within three years, not because of opposition, but because of internal clashes. The second general election, held in November 1994, produced a hung parliament, with Communist Party of Nepal-Unified Marxist-Leninist (CPN-UML) getting more seats than the NC and Man Mohan Adhikari, in his capacity as the leader of the largest party in the House of Representatives (HoR), forming the minority government. But the Adhikari government fell within nine months as a result of the vote of no confidence. A consequence of this was the emergence of a coalition government culture in the country resulting in six different governments within five years and also the beginning of massive corruption at political level just to save the government.[1] The third general election, held in 1999, however, once again, gave mandate to the NC to rule and the CPN-UML to sit in the opposition. The people gave their verdict in favour of political stability. But this time, the political situation was quite different.

One extreme group in the CPN formed the Maoist faction, which adopted violent measures to destabilize the parliamentary government in the name of People's War, and the governments, one after another, failed to check their violent activities. In addition, there was a formal division in each of the three major political parties, NC, CPN-UML and National Democratic Party (NDP)—party of former Panchas.

Although the breakaway parties were not powerful, they could weaken the parent organizations to a large extent.

In 2001, an unimaginable incident took place—the massacre of the members of the royal family—which took the lives of King Birendra, Queen Aishwarya, heir apparent and other royal family members including the crown prince Deependra. The throne passed into the hands of Birendra's only surviving brother, Gyanendra, who was known for his ambitions and conservative nature in the past.

Within two months, Prime Minister G.P. Koirala was forced to resign, as the new king 'did not give him an opportunity to suppress the Maoist insurgency with the help of the army' (Whelpton, 2005). Gyanendra tried to bring the Maoists to the negotiating table partly as an attempt to bring peace to the country, and partly to encounter the major political parties, which were trying to minimize the role of the monarch. But the three rounds of talks between the government and the Maoists ended in failure. Hostilities were resumed and thousands lost their lives. The country was put under a state of Emergency, army was mobilized to suppress the Maoists and the government enacted anti-terrorist laws to suppress the rebel activities (Jha, 2014).

Sher Bahadur Deuba, the leader of the NC, who became prime minister upon the resignation of G.P. Koirala, declared Emergency in November 2001 to quell the CPN-M insurgency. When the question of the extension of Emergency came up after three months, the NC was divided on the issue. Party President G.P. Koirala opposed the extension as it minimized the fundamental rights of the people, but Prime Minister Deuba sided with the king on the issue and recommended dissolution of the HoR to avoid defeat in the Emergency motion. The HoR was finally dissolved and fresh elections were called, leading to a formal split in the ruling NC party, and the king got an opportunity to become the most powerful.

The holding of parliamentary election within six months became a most conflicting issue and King Gyanendra decided to suppress the Maoists and the political parties by a single stroke. On 1 February 2005, the king struck suddenly by taking over the reins of administration in his own hands and imposed his direct rule with a cabinet of his choice under his own chair. Most of the ministers, including two vice-chairpersons were drawn from the politicians and bureaucrats of the Panchayat era (Toffin, 2013). A state of Emergency was declared, fundamental rights were suspended, telephone lines were cut off (for the first time in the history of Nepal) and media became the main target of the government (Sharma, 1998).

Under such situation, the Maoists and the political parties thought it inevitable to come together to fight the king's autocratic rule, and the Indian government played a vital role in bringing them together. In November, under the mediation of the Indian government, the seven agitating political parties and the Maoists signed a 12-point agreement in New Delhi, pledging to end the dictatorial rule of the king and establish 'purna loktantra' (complete democracy), indirectly a republic (Sharma, 1998).

Meanwhile, certain events put the king and his government in an awkward position. People boycotted the municipal elections, limiting the voter turnout to less than 20 per cent in many places; the Supreme Court declared the king-formed anti-corruption court illegal, invalidating all of its decisions; and the Maoists' violent activities intensified in different parts of the country. Even at this stage, King Gyanendra showed no sign of negotiation. The agitating political parties, with the active support of the Maoists, started a mass movement in the first week of April 2006. Within two weeks, the movement took an unexpected turn with the participation of thousands of people on the streets.

At this critical juncture, the Indian government tried to intervene by sending Karan Singh, a senior leader of the Indian National Congress, which was in power then, to meet the king with a message from the Indian government. On his advice, King Gyanendra gave a royal message to the nation on 21 April, asking the agitating political parties to submit a name for appointment as prime minister. Though the king's formula was hailed by India and other countries as a positive step, the political parties and the Maoists rejected it outrightly because the royal message did not mention anything about the restoration of dissolved HoR. In the midst of violent agitation, the king had to surrender before the people and was forced to issue another proclamation after three days, reconvening the dissolved HoR, which finally ended the nineteen-day agitation against the monarch.

Within a few days, the lower house of the parliament met in a completely new situation, and it made a 25-point declaration which divested the king of all powers—nominal or real—and vested supreme power of state and government to the cabinet and parliament. The provisions of the constitution, contradictory to the declaration, were considered to be null and void (Sharma, 1998).

Unconfirmed reports say that when King Gyanendra reconvened the dissolved house on 24 April, the NC and the CPN-UML had assured him that they would not abolish the kingship, rather would continue the constitutional monarchy. But the Maoists, who knew they would be the first victims if the king re-emerged in politics, were strict on the abolition of monarchy as early as possible. Finally, a compromise was made in the interim constitution (promulgated in January 2007), which stripped the king of all powers and the fate of monarchy was to be decided in the first meeting of the elected CA. The Tarai/Madhes-based parties opposed the constitution and demanded their representation in all sectors of the state, as a result of which the constitution was amended within two months, guaranteeing the representation of Madhesis, indigenous groups and backward people in all organs of the state.

A new legislature was constituted with the representation of the Maoists in sufficient number, who, inside as well as outside the house, constantly demanded the abolition of monarchy by the HoR. When Prime Minister G.P. Koirala, who was also the NC president, hinted at the possibility of installing a baby king (the infant grandson of King Gyanendra), he came under such a massive attack that he had to withdraw his words. Once again a compromise was made through which the house of parliament was empowered to declare Nepal a republic if the king in any way tried to obstruct the election of the CA. The Maoists were not satisfied even at this stage. Finally, through another amendment in the interim constitution, Nepal was declared a republic with a provision that it should be ratified in the first meeting of the CA for implementation.

The election of the CA was postponed twice. The first postponement took place because of 'the lack of time for preparation', and it was postponed for the second time over a controversy on proportional representation among the Maoist and other political parties. Finally, the election of the CA took place in April 2008. And, contrary to expectation, the Maoist party captured 120 out of 240 elected seats and emerged as the largest party in the House. At its first meeting (28 May 2008), the country was formally declared a republic with full power to implement it immediately.

The abolition of monarchy was almost an unimaginable event in the history of Nepal. Even the Maoists might not have thought that the establishment of a republic would be so easy. Three factors were largely responsible for it: King Gyanendra's own ambition to become an active ruler and his actions of completely ignoring the political parties and the Maoists; coming together of the Maoists and the political parties against the king's regime; and the decisive role of the Indian government to abolish monarchy from Nepal (Jha, 2012), although it is widely believed that Karan Singh had assured King Gyanendra that, 'India would not allow the king to be disgraced or the institution of the monarchy to be abolished' (Muni, 2012).

Monarchy has been abolished and a republican state founded in Nepal, but political parties, including the Maoists, have not been able to put the state on the right track. Their activities during the last eight years compel us to believe that they can neither govern the country in a republican style nor take the nation to the path of development. The first CA extended its term from two to four years, but it could not even draft a constitution. Under the directive of the Supreme Court, it was dissolved in 2012 and the election to a new CA became a matter of debate. The Maoist party, which was in power at the time of dissolution, wanted to hold the next election under the existing government. But other political parties vehemently opposed it. A compromise formula was accepted by all, through which one non-party government was formed under the leadership of the chief justice of Supreme Court with former bureaucrats as ministers, which successfully conducted the election within a year (November 2013).

Although the newly elected CA pledged to promulgate a democratic constitution by January 2015, time passed even without entering into a formal process. The political parties were sharply divided, especially on the issues of political system (presidential or parliamentary), nature of federalism, including the demarcation of provinces and election system for both central and state legislatures. But the great earthquake in April 2015 compelled the parliamentarians to realize the fact that they should be united at this critical hour of natural calamity. Finally, a new constitution was endorsed by the CA in September 2015.

The Tarai/Madhes-based parties boycotted the proceedings and launched a movement with a demand to abrogate the newly promulgated constitution. Their activities in the border areas led to the blockade of petroleum, gas, medicine and other necessary goods by the Indian government for more than six months. People suffered a lot, and no compromise was forthcoming. However, the decisive stand taken by the government compelled the Tarai/Madhes-based parties to modify the nature of their movement, the indirect result of which was the ending of the Indian blockade.

The story did not end here. The Tarai/Madhes-based parties continued their agitation, and the government failed to satisfy them. As per constitutional provisions, the elections to the local level, state legislatures and federal parliament were successfully completed by January 2018, with the Left front (CPN-UML + CPN-MC) winning nearly two-third seats in the federal parliament, six out of seven state legislatures and most of the seats at the local level. The new government assured political stability at least for the next five years; however, in view of past experiences, the Nepalese people have their reservations on this front.

In Conclusion

History repeats itself when people do not learn lessons from it or ignore its messages. The main objective of the study of history is to evaluate the positive and negative aspects of our deeds in the past, and correct them in the future. On the basis of the above discussion on the development of Nepalese life throughout its different phases of history, the following perspectives can be reached:

- Nepal has been an independent state from the beginning, but its disintegration during the medieval period was a dark aspect of its history. The preservation of independence and its rightful place in the comity of nations should be our ultimate goal. Religious and social harmony has been a unique feature of Nepalese social life in different phases of history. It should be continued, and no provocation should be made for socio-religious conflicts, which may become more serious than the political issues. For this, and to satisfy the vast Hindu population, the word 'secular' may be deleted from the constitution.
- People strongly doubt that the federal system will work properly in Nepal. A large number of people fear that it may herald the disintegration of the country. Thus, the issue needs to be looked into very seriously and sorted out, giving due consideration to the intrinsic interrelationship between the three ecological regions of the country, viz. Himalayan, mountainous and Tarai regions.
- Democracy is the government of the people, for the people and by the people. Nepal has witnessed governments of the people and by the people, but never for the people. If a nation works for its people, the system becomes superb even if it is not a system by the people or of the people. Any system, if it is not for the people, is meaningless.
- As said by Prithvi Narayan Shah, the people are the wealth of a nation. Economic prosperity of the people reflects the sound economy of the state, but economic disparity leads the country to anarchy.
- Political parties are the backbone of democracy, but they should be formed on the basis of ideologies and not on personal or group interest. Any split in political party for personal or group benefit should be discouraged.
- The history of political parties in Nepal is a record of clash

and disintegration, rather than of solidarity and achievement. Irrespective of a party's ideologies, alliances and counter-alliances are made with the sole objective of capturing power or getting a share in the government, which is evidenced by the fact that almost all parties—whether major or minor—got a share in the government within eight years of the proclamation of a republic. To the people, political leaders seem to have become self-seeking rather than their representatives.

- Reservation of seats for indigenous people, Dalits or women[2] should not be a permanent feature of the system, because it minimizes merit. However, every opportunity should be given to weaker sections of the society to make them capable of being competitive in every sphere of life.
- The system of proportional representation in legislature has proved to be disastrous. Political stability is rarely possible under such mode. Family connections and 'financial contributions' play major role in such nominations, which may prove harmful to the nation.
- The Maoists fought a 'People's War' for over a decade. Once they joined the mainstream, their past actions have become a subject of debate and criticism. As such, their actions and contributions to the transformation of Nepalese state and society need to be assessed and at the same time the grievances of the victims of the insurgency should be addressed.
- Court conflicts have been a permanent feature of Nepalese politics since ancient times, which even led to the disintegration of the country into more than fifty petty states during the medieval period. The nine-year court politics (1837–46) led to the formation of a dictatorial system for more than a century, and the ending of the parliamentary system within a short period in 1960 was also the result of inter- and intra-conflicts, which once again established the king's dictatorial rule for three decades. Unfortunately, this phenomenon has continued to the present-day politics of Nepal, indicating that Nepalese politicians have not learnt any lesson from history.

- Because of Nepal's unique geographical position, over-dependency on India is a challenge to it. Economists and planners should develop a long-term plan to minimize Nepal's dependency on India and counter Indian domination. Effective implementation of such a plan by Nepalese government will definitely enhance the country's future.

Tri Ratna Manandhar *is former Vice Chancellor, Lumbini Buddhist University, and former Professor and Head of the Department of History at Tribhuvan University.*

Bibliography

Government and Allied Publications

His Majesty's Government, Nepal/Ministry of Law and Justice (HMGN). 1965–66. *Sri Panch Surendra Bikram Shah Devko Sashan Kalama Baneko Muluki Ain (Civil Code Enacted during the Reign Of His Majesty Surendra Bikram Shah Dev.*

Jangi Adda. 2012–13. *Nepali Senako Itihas (History of Nepali Army).* Kathmandu: Army Headquarters.

Other Publications

Bajracharya, D. 1973. *Licchavi Kalaka Abhilekh (Inscriptions of Licchavi Period).* Kathmandu: Institute of Nepal and Asian Studies.

Brown, L.T. 1996. *The Challenge to Democracy in Nepal.* London: Routledge.

Carr, E.H. 1976. *What is History?* London: Penguin Books.

Devkota, G.B. 1983–84. *Nepalko Rajnitik Darpan, Tesro Bhag (Political Mirror of Nepal, Part III).* Kathmandu: Upendra Bahadur Devkota.

Gupta, A. 1964. *Politics in Nepal.* Bombay: Allied Publishers Pvt. Ltd.

Husain, A. 1970. *British India's Relations with the Kingdom of Nepal.* London: George Allen and Unwin Ltd.

Institute for Integrated Development Studies (IIDS). 2000. 'The Fourth Parliamentary Election: A Study of Evolving Democratic Process in Nepal.'

Jain, M.S. 1972. *The Emergence of a New Aristocracy in Nepal.* Agra: Sri Ram Mehra and Co.

Jha, P. 2012. 'A Nepali Perspective on International Involvement in Nepal.' In: Eissiedel, von S., Malone, D.M. and Pradhan, S. (Eds.) *Nepal in Transition: From People's War to Fragile Peace.* New Delhi: Center on International Cooperation, Cambridge University Press.

Jha, P. 2014. *Battles of the New Republic.* New Delhi: Aleph Book Company.

Joshi, B.L. and Rose, L.E. 1966. *Democratic Innovations in Nepal.* Berkeley: University of California Press.

Manandhar, T.R. and Sharma, N. 1996–97. *Adhunik Nepalko Rajnaitik Ityihas (Political History of Modern Nepal).* Kathmandu: Centre for Nepal and Asian Studies.

Manandhar, T.R. 1986. *Nepal: The Years of Trouble.* Kathmandu: Purna Devi Manandhar.

Muni, S.D. 2012. 'Bringing the Maoists down from the Hills.' In Eissiedel, von S., Malone, D.M. and Pradhan, S. (Eds.) *Nepal in Transition–From People's War to Fragile Peace.* New Delhi: Center for International Cooperation, Cambridge University Press.

Nepali, C. 1965–66. *Bhimsen Thapa ra Tatkalin Nepal (Bhimsen Thapa and Contemporary Nepal).* Kathmandu: Ratna Pustak Bhandar.

Petech, L. 1984. *Mediaeval History of Nepal (Second Edition).* Roma: Istituto Italiano Per II Medio Ed Estremo Oriente.

Ramakant. 1976. *Nepal-China and India.* New Delhi: Abhinav Publications.

Ram, R. 1977. *A History of Buddhism in Nepal.* Patna: Janabharati Prakashan.

Rose, L.E. and Scholz, J.T. 1980. *Nepal: Profile of a Himalayan Kingdom.* New Delhi: Select Book Service.

Shaha, R. 1978. *Nepali Politics: Retrospect and Prospect (Second Edition).* Delhi: Oxford University Press.

Shaha, R. 1992. *Ancient and Medieval Nepal.* Kathmandu: Ratna Pustak Bhandar.

Sharma, J. 1998. *Democracy without Roots.* Delhi: Book Faith India.

Stiller, L.F. 1973. *The Rise of the House of Gorkha.* Ranchi: The Patna Jesuit Society.

Toffin, G. 2013. *From Monarchy to Republic.* Kathmandu: Vajra Books.

Whelpton, J. 2005. *A History of Nepal.* Cambridge: University of Cambridge.

Endnotes

1. Sher Bahadur Deuba-headed government of NC, Rastriya Prajatantra Party (RPP) and Nepal Sadbhavana Party (NSP) lasting for eighteen months; Lokendra Bahadur Chand-led government of RPP, CPN-UML

and NSP lasting for seven months; Surya Bahadur Thapa-led government of RPP, NC and NSP, with a tenure of six months; G.P. Koirala-led NC government with four months; G.P. Koirala-led NC and CPN-UML government with four months; and G.P. Koirala-led government of NC, CPN-UML and NSP with five months' duration. Institute for Integrated Development Studies (IIDS). 2000. *The Fourth Parliamentary Election: A Study of the Evolving Democratic Process in Nepal.*

2. The Constitution of Nepal 2015 reserves one-third seats for women in the federal parliament. In addition, seats are reserved for Dalit, indigenous, Khas Arya, Madhesi, Tharu, Muslim and background regions based on their population. Same applies in the case of state legislature as well. Two members from every ward of Gaun Palika and municipal council should be women. The executive of the committee of the village council should be comprised of four women, one Dalit and one other minority. The executive committee of the municipality should have five women and three people from Dailt and minority communities. In the civil, military and police services, too, 45 per cent of seats allotted for open competition are reserved for women, indigenous people, Madhesi, Dalit, disabled and backward area people.

2

SOCIAL STRUCTURE OF THE NEPALI SOCIETY

Dilli Ram Dahal

In anthropology and sociology, the term 'social structure' is loosely applied to any existing pattern of social behaviour or ordered interrelationships between the different elements of a social system or society. The different facets of kinship, religious, economic, political and other institutions of society may be said to comprise its social structure (Marshall, 1994). According to Radcliffe-Brown (1952), in a given social structure, 'human beings are interconnected by a complex network of actually existing relations.' The components of social structure are persons and a person occupies a position in a given social structure.

Though there is plenty of anthropological literature discussing the basic social structure of various ethnic/caste groups of Nepal, a consolidated account of its social structure was first presented by a Nepali anthropologist, Dor Bahadur Bista. But considering the wide scope and complexity of the subject matter, Bista focused his discussion on the social structure of Nepali society on two sensitive sociological topics—hierarchy and Chakari (sycophancy)—overlooking its basic features and other interrelated issues (Bista, 1989). No doubt, these topics have been affecting the everyday life of Nepalese people over the years. These terms are, however, elastic in nature and many times their forms are more subjective than objective in content.

Bista (1989) stated that it is not good to classify Nepali society into distinct categories of caste or ethnic groups, and a matrix of caste/ethnicity is simply a pigeonhole degrading other social features of the society. In brief, he neglected the more complicated scenarios of existing social structure which affect the intergroup relations, social change and development of Nepal. I, however, feel that the understanding of the basic social structure of each ethnic/caste group is a prerequisite for grasping the changing nature of the Nepali society as a whole. This process not only enhances the knowledge of various groups of people in temporal sequence but also facilitates the process of national integration in the long run.

The biggest burning problem in present-day Nepal is the caste/ethnicity issue with the right of cultural territory, language and religion of people. In other words, the leaders of the various ethnic/caste groups of Nepal, in resisting the power of the state, have clung to a myriad of oppositional identities in the name of Adibasi/Janajati, Madhesi, Kiranti and so on, claiming separate cultural identity for themselves, as if this cultural identity were primordial (Dahal, 2013).

The cultural territorial issue has now spilled over into state politics as various cultural groups within Nepal, have been claiming their traditional habitat as their own territorial state. The claim of Madhesi Morcha, a united political front of Nepal Tarai, that the Tarai or Madhes belongs to Madhesi people is a case in point. Proper understanding of the basic social structure of various ethnic or caste groups would provide a base or foundation for the Nepali social structure in historical and modern contexts and a rational basis for claiming a separate cultural territory as part of federal provinces for the groups in question.

As ethnicity plays the key role in understanding the basic features of Nepali social structure, it is theoretically important to give a broader picture of the multi-ethnic nature of the Nepali society in general. In recent years, the reconstruction of 'self' has become a paramount issue in the everyday life of Nepalese people. In this chapter, we discuss how caste/ethnic, linguistic, religious and other forms of social institutions have inflicted the various processes of the cohesive nature of the Nepali society in recent years. The major question is:

Can we envision a unified Nepali social structure in these competing social institutions of various cultural groups of people? This chapter further argues that the vulnerability of the Madhesi movements or the indigenous movements in the name of creating a homogenous cultural identity or social structure has limited choice considering the multicultural nature of Nepali society throughout history.

An Overview

Culture is a sensitive term and often hard to define. Long ago, the idea of culture was recognized under different terms such as 'customs', 'traditions' or 'social habits' of people. Certainly from Herodotus (a Greek historian and philosopher of the fifth century BC) onwards, it was known that the patterns of human behaviour varied from place to place, and many accounts have been made for these variations. Anthropologists have defined culture from a universal outlook to a conceptual, particularistic framework of a given society. In the Nepalese context, culture can be understood as a historical phenomenon or heritage, as well as living systems emphasizing family structure, kinship, marriage and other economic, political and religious institutions.

Though Nepal has been discussed widely in many Hindu scriptures, such as the Puranas, the Ramayana and the Mahabharata, and it is also considered an abode of thousands of gods and goddesses, very little is known about the people and culture of this country during that period in time. It was only after the conquest of the Kathmandu valley by King Prithvi Narayan Shah in 1768 did Nepal start being known as a land of 'char varna and chhattis jaat' (four distinct colour groups and thirty-six castes), indicating a multicultural nation. Since then, Nepal has remained a cultural mosaic, forming a unique multi-ethnic and multi-caste society.

As Nepal was divided into small kingdoms and principalities before 1768, it is difficult to provide an overview of the Nepali social structure; however, it can be fairly said that it was traditional in nature. Family, kinship, caste and village were the main forms of social institutions and people were highly orthodox in their religious values and divided along geographical, linguistic and cultural lines because of geographical isolation. Overall, people's life was guided by their own supernatural faiths and the concepts of good and bad or heaven and hell.

Nevertheless, efforts to describe the culture of Nepali ethnic/caste groups along with history began nearly two centuries ago. Western fascination with Nepal dates back to the earliest encounters (Buchanan Hamilton, 1819; Hodgson, 1874) and robustly continues to the present day. Since the work of anthropologist Christoph von Fürer-Haimendorf on Sherpas (1964), there has been overwhelming anthropological evidence concerning the diversity of cultures in the Nepali society and its various facets. In brief, today's Nepali culture, in essence, can be described in three distinct elements:

i. A culture or social structure of people, representing various groups such as Hindu groups with caste origin versus ethnic/tribal groups, Muslims and others (Sikh, Bengali, Marwari and Christians);
ii. Racially, there are two distinct groups of people: Indo-Aryan (Caucasoid) and Mongoloid. Certain small groups of people, e.g. Satar and Jhangad, are treated in separate racial categories, Austro-Asiatic (Satar) and Dravidian (Jhangad);
iii. In terms of cultural tradition or civilization, Nepal, as a whole, can be said to present a distinctive interface between the Hindu and Buddhist civilizations. The Nepali cultural tradition is heavily influenced by the Hindu civilization from the south and the Tibetan culture or Buddhist civilization of the north. Furthermore, there are many groups (primarily ethnic groups) who are not influenced by the Hindu or Buddhist religious-cultural traditions. They are partly influenced by both traditions. Their traditions can be popularly labelled as 'animism' or 'folk tradition' or 'local tradition'.

In the larger context of providing an overview of the Nepali social structure, it will be better to provide the data of the Central Bureau of Statistics (CBS), which has been providing data by caste/ethnicity, language and religion since the 1991 Census. The latest census, conducted in 2011, provides a list of 125 distinct ethnic/caste groups, 123 languages and ten religious groups in the country. The ethnic/caste groups can be divided into eight broad categories to discern their distinct pattern of social structure: (i) Caste-origin hill groups, (ii) Hill Adibasi/Janajati groups, (iii) Hill Dalit, (iv) Caste-origin Madhesi groups, (v) Caste-origin low-caste Madhesi groups or Dalits, (vi) Tarai (Madhesi) Adibasi/Janajati, (vii) Musalman or Muslims and (viii) other cultural groups. (see Table 1)

Table 1: Ethnic/caste groups of Nepal, 2011 Census

Cultural groups	Number of ethnic/caste groups	Total population and percentage
Caste-origin hill groups	4	8,278,401 (31.2)
Hill Adibasi/Janajati groups	50	7,228,463 (27.3)
Hill Dalits	5	2,151,526 (8.1)
Caste-origin Madhesi groups	3+31=34	220,382 (0.8) + 3,851,941 (14.5)
Madhesi Dalits	15	1,192,517 (4.5)
Madhesi (Tarai) Adibasi/Janajati groups	13	2,039,407 (7.7)
Musalman (Muslim)	1	1,164,255 (4.4)
Other cultural groups	4*	91,852 (0.3)
Unidentified (but noted within these broad cultural categories)		275,670 (1.0)
Total	126	26,494,504 (100.0)

*'Foreigner' as other cultural category is also included here; otherwise, the total number of ethnic/caste groups is only 125.

Source: Dahal, 2014

Caste-origin groups

The caste origin groups have some distinct social structure and cultural features: (i) hierarchical structure; (ii) hereditary basis of membership; (iii) endogamy (marrying within one's own cultural group); (iv) mostly Hindus in their religious values and (v) purity and pollution, which govern the day-to-day life of people based on Hindu religious principles. There are three distinct caste-origin groups in Nepal: (i) caste-origin hill groups, (ii) caste-origin Tarai (Madhesi) groups and (iii) caste-origin Newar groups.

The caste-origin hill groups can be divided into two broad social categories: i) cultural groups wearing the sacred thread such as Brahmin, Thakuri, Chhetri and Sanyasi and ii) low-caste Hindu groups or Dalits such as Kami, Sarki, Damai, Badi and Gaine.

The social structure of caste-origin hill groups is simple, reflecting only three groups in hierarchy in the Varna model (Brahman, Chhetri and Sudra) and there are no four Varna (colour) such as the Vaisya category within this model. The Sanyasi/Dasnami cultural group, like the hill Brahmin and Chhetri groups, wears the sacred thread but does not perform all Samskaras (rite de passage) like other hill caste Hindus do. These caste-origin hill caste groups are monolingual—only speaking the Nepali language. More than 99 per cent of these groups are Hindus. Most of their houses are scattered. They are one of the most mobile groups in Nepal as they constantly move from one place to another for better livelihood. According to Sharma (2004), the footloose Parbate Hindus went and settled everywhere in Nepal. Normally, the status of women among them is low—they marry at early age compared to Adibasi/Janajati groups and have little decision-making power and control over resources (CEDA, 2001). To sum up, hill caste people have fewer castes in total compared to Newar and Madhesi people and a simple hierarchy in their social structure. Kinship network is not very cohesive and functional as that of Newars.

Nevertheless, considering the numerical strengths, control of resources, i.e. land, possession of political power and socio-religious status, Western education, jobs in administration contributing to prestige and power, high-caste Hindu Brahmin Chhetri groups, including Thakuri (certain clan members of Thakuri were kings of Nepal until a few years ago), can be considered the 'dominant castes' in Nepal as a whole.

Regarding the low-caste hill Dalit groups, Rastriya Dalit Ayog (National Commission on Dalits) has given a separate caste name to the following hill Dalit groups:

- Viswakarma for Kami, Lohar, Sunar, Ode, Chunara, Parki, Tamata
- Sarki for Mijar, Charmakar, Bhul
- Pariyar for Damai, Darji, Suchikar, Nagarchi, Dholi and Hudke
- Gandharva for Gaine
- Badi

Dalits are treated as 'untouchable' in Nepal even today, though the caste system was abolished with the promulgation of Muluki Ain 1963 (National Code). The members of higher castes (all high-caste Hindus, including Adibasi/Janajati groups) do not accept cooked food and water from them, keeping intact the exclusion model in their day-to-day life (Bhattachan, et al., 2002). On the other hand, Dalits themselves practise the Hindu model of untouchability and instead of seeking inclusion within them, exclusion is very much alive in their social structure. They marry within their own cultural groups and refrain from eating cooked food and water from other groups. They are the most backward groups in social, economic and political platforms of Nepal (Dahal et al., 2002). Many of them have to work in the traditional model of patron–client relationship for their survival even today.

Each hill Dalit group has its own traditional occupation beyond farming. Kami make and repair iron tools, Damai sew clothes, Sarki are leather workers, Gaine sing songs and Badi make earthen pots. Many of them also work under the Balighare system or patron–client relationship; their wages are fixed on annual basis in grains, depending upon the size of the landlord's land and number of members in the family.

Adibasi/Janajati (Ethnic groups/Nationalities)

The National Committee of Nationalities has noted fifty-nine distinct cultural groups as Adibasi/Janajati (*Nepal Rajpatra*, 2 February 2002). The Adibasi/Janajati Utthan Rastriya Prathisthan defines Adibasi/Janajati as: 'Nationality (Janajati) is that community which has its own mother tongue and traditional culture and yet do not fall under the conventional fourfold Varna of Hindu or Hindu hierarchical caste structure.'

This definition seems extremely elusive and arbitrary in the context of Nepal as many of these are adherent Hindus. For example, the Newar group, whose population is labelled under the Janajati category, has 84.1 per cent Hindus according to the 2001 Census, and this percentage increased to 97.4 per cent in the 2011 Census. Similarly, 94 per cent of Tharus and 79 per cent of Magars were reported as Hindus in the 2011 Census. In fact, many Adibasi/Janajati groups have claimed themselves as Hindus in various proportions (CBS 2012). In addition, they strictly follow the Hindu model of purity and pollution in day-to-day behaviour and, in no condition, they allow Dalits to enter their houses and share cooked food and water with them.

Historically, many of these Janajati groups used to occupy a particular habitat or territory, and, thus, many of them claim that they are the true 'First Settlers' (Adibasi) of Nepal. The Adibasi/Janajati groups are divided regionally into two distinct cultural groups: Hill Janajati and Tarai Janajati. Some of the Hill Janajati groups are Newar, Magar, Gurung, Rai, Limbu, Sherpa, Sunuwar, Bhote, Raji, Raute and Chepang. Some of the Tarai (Madhesi) Janajati groups are: Tharu, Dhimal, Gangain, Satar/Santhal, Dahngar/Jhangar, Koche and others.

Though Newar is placed under the Adibasi/Janajati category, their case is unique and exceptional. This group not only presents complicated social structure among all groups in Nepal, it also truly reflects the model of four Hindu Varna categories and is clearly divided into two distinct religious groups: Hindu and Buddhist. Newars are divided internally into more than forty distinct cultural groups with different occupational categories, although they share a common language—Newari or Nepal Bhasa.

According to Gellner and Quigley (1995), the Newars of the Kathmandu valley follow a tradition of double-headed caste hierarchy, keeping contested rankings between castes of similar status. Within castes, the ranking of lower order group is also contested. In different localities the same caste may be ranked and treated differently. The Newar caste hierarchy shows that there are two competing priestly heads: the Hindu Brahmans and the Buddhist Vajracharya combine, which is fundamentally different from the regional hierarchy in South Asia. However, their hierarchy is not linear as proposed by Muluki Ain 1854, but a combination of both linear hierarchy and the centre-periphery model.

Newars as a whole are divided into three levels: the caste, sub-caste and caste sub-groups for the purpose of marriage and conducting various rituals. They live in clustered settlements and a have a close-knit kinship network. They had excessive preoccupation with religion, rituals and festivities, which were often backed up with state efforts (Sharma, 1989).

Among the Adibasi/Janajatis, three groups deserve special attention: Kusunda, Chepang and Raute. The Kusunda are very low in number (273 in 2011 Census) and distributed in the western hill and Tarai districts such as Dang, Pyuthan and some other areas. Their language is virtually dying as one linguistic survey reported only two persons speaking Kusunda as their mother tongue. And their culture is basically guided by Hindu faiths and beliefs. If the State does not protect their language and culture, they will gradually disappear from the ethnographic atlas of Nepal.

Though Chepang are quite numerous in terms of population size (68,399 in 2011 Census) and confined mostly in Chitwan, Makwanpur and Dhading districts, they are one of the most economically marginalized indigenous communities of Nepal. Despite their closeness to the economically powerful centres, such as Kathmandu and Chitwan, they barely meet their food requirements from their land for more than six months in one year and almost one-third of their food is directly derived from wild sources such as wild vegetables, shoots, fruits, roots, yams, birds, animals and fish (Rai, 2014). The only hunting semi-nomadic group surviving in Nepal is Raute, who wander in different forest areas from Jajarkot to Achham for their livelihood. Their number is only 618 (2011 Census) and they make wooden tools and exchange them for grains with their neighbours.

Tarai people or Madhesi groups

Although the term 'Madhesi' is a little vague and contested, it is normally understood as the inhabitants of the Tarai region of Nepal, showing a geographical identity of the population living there. But this definition has not been accepted by many Madhesi leaders. They want to be marked separately for their physical and cultural features such as people with a dark brown complexion or those wearing dhotis (loincloth) and speaking primarily Maithili, Bhojpuri and Awadhi languages. For convenience, excluding the hill people (though many have lived in the Nepal Tarai for centuries), Madhesi people of Nepal Tarai can be broadly categorized into four distinct cultural groups:

i. A group of people who have been living in the Nepal Tarai for centuries and who prefer to call themselves 'indigenous' (though many groups have no written history at all) of the Tarai. Some such groups are: Tharu, Dhimal, Gangain, Danuwar, Koche, Meche and so on. These groups are already categorized under the Adibasi/Janajati category by the Janajati Rastriya Utthan Prathisthan. At the same time, many Tharus of Nepal do not want to be labelled as Madhesi as they have a separate cultural identity of their own.
ii. Tarai caste groups of Hindu origin, a broad cultural group with a social structure whereby the Maithil Brahmin group is placed at the top and untouchables, such as Dom, at the bottom.
iii. Indian-origin merchant groups such as the Marwari, Bengali and Sikh, who also do not like to be treated under the Madhesi category.
iv. Muslims (see Dahal, 2013).

The CBS 2011 recorded forty-eight caste-origin Hindu groups in the Tarai (three caste-origin high caste groups, thirty caste-origin middle-caste groups and fifteen low-caste groups or Dalits). The social structure of the caste-origin Tarai-Madhesi groups is complex, reflecting four Varna groups with distinct hierarchical structure within them: three caste-origin Hindu groups, viz. Maithil Brahmin, Rajput and Kayastha, comprise 0.83 per cent of total population but they are the most powerful groups even today in terms of literacy and economic and political status not only in the Tarai but in Nepal as a whole.

In the middle-caste group or the Vaisya category, there are thirty caste groups such as Yadav, Halwai, Koeri, Hajam, Sonar, Lohar, Rajbhar and others. The Yadavs are not only numerous, they are also the most politically powerful groups in entire Nepal. Unlike in the hills, the Lohar of Tarai is the water-acceptable community and is not treated as Dalit or untouchable. Some years ago, cultural groups such as Sudi, Kalwar and Teli (Saha) were not considered as 'water-acceptable community' in the Tarai. Today, they are one of the most powerful communities in the region—socially, economically and politically—and are treated as water-acceptable community in many areas. Many members of these communities own businesses, lend money and many educated youth are employed as engineers, doctors and technicians (Dahal, 2010).

The low-caste groups of the Tarai or Sudra (so-called 'untouchables') represent fifteen groups in the 2011 Census. 'Chidimar' are not treated as Dalits in their traditional habitats such as Banke and Bardiya districts (Dahal and Gurung, 2014), but this group is treated as Dalit by the Rastriya Dalit Ayog even today. The socio-economic status of Tarai Dalit is even worse than that of hill Dalits. There is strict hierarchy within these groups in terms of marriage and accepting food and water in their everyday life. An interesting feature of Tarai Dalits is that the Chamar group of the Tarai sell milk in the market areas, which is acceptable by the high-caste Hindus (Dahal and Jha, 2014). The Chamars of the Tarai also play musical instruments, like Rasan Chowki, during marriages and other social occasions. The women of Chamar caste are also famous as midwives (Chamain or Sudeni) in the Tarai.

These caste-origin Madhesi communities belong to four distinct language groups: Maithili, Bajika, Bhojpuri and Awadhi. More than 99 per cent of these groups follow Hindu religion.

Musalman

Though Nepali Muslims or Musalman are divided into Shia and Sunni sects, Sunni sects are predominant in Nepal as a whole (Sharma, 2004). It is a heterogeneous group consisting of Kashmiri Muslims, Tarai Muslims and Churaute Muslims (Bista, 1967). The larger number of Musalman population lives in the Tarai, the smaller in the western hill districts such as Gorkha and Tanahun and are popularly known as Churaute. The Churaute hill Muslims are greatly influenced by the Hindu cultural traditions. All Muslim boys must undergo circumcision and bury their dead. The nikah (bride price) and Zakat (charity collected during religious festivals) are some of their traditional cultural values practised widely in Nepal as well.

Other cultural groups

The 2011 Census recorded four subgroups with this category: Marwari, Bengali, Punjabi/Sikh and foreigner. Excluding foreigner, most of these cultural groups are relatively recent migrants who came to Nepal from India to do business and other specialized work (Dahal, 1978; Bista, 1967). In total, although they represent only 0.34 per cent of the population, they are the most powerful economic groups in Nepal. For example, Marwari is the most powerful merchant group living in Nepal today and possesses one of the highest literacy rates in the 2011 Census. Similarly, the Bengali population maintains professional positions as doctors, pharmacists, businessmen and politicians. Birgunj was developed as a city and municipality by Pasupati Ghosh, a Bengali Nepali who became a minister during the Panchayat regime (1960–90), and a town, Pasupatinagar, was named after him. Likewise, Punjabi/Sikh came to Nepal as transport businessmen, motor mechanics and repairers and they run auto shops and are employed in government jobs as well. (see Table 2)

Table 2: Some distinct socioeconomic and cultural traits of the Madhesi (Tarai) social structure

Traits	Ethnic/Tribal group	Caste-origin Hindu groups	Indian-origin Nepali merchant groups	Muslim
Tentative history of settlement in the Tarai	Claims to have settled in the Tarai for centuries; indigenous groups; little written history is available about their settlements	Settlement history over the last 100–200 years	For the last 150 years	For the last 100–200 years*
Physical feature	Primarily Mongoloid	Primarily Caucasoid	Primary Caucasoid	Primarily Caucasoid
Language	In general, each group has its own language. Except for the Tharus and Rajbansis who have a Indo-Aryan language, the others belong to Tibeto-Burman language group	Indo-Aryan language group. Three dominant language groups: Maithili, Bhojpuri and Awadhi; also Bajika	Indo-Aryan language group; Marwari, Sikh and Bengali	Urdu, Hindi
Religion	Animism, local Hinduism or folk religion. They have their own priests for rituals and other religious activities	Hinduism of the great tradition; always a Brahmin priest for a ritual except for 'untouchables' who call upon their own priest	Hinduism and Sikhism	Islam

Social structure	Clan organization; no hierarchy within the group, bride price or bride service; sexually more relaxed than the Hindus; age at marriage higher than for Hindu groups; remarriage permitted for both sexes; women have a relatively higher status and more autonomy than Hindu women	Caste organization; distinct hierarchy among various groups; dowry; sexually less permissive society; remarriage of women not permitted; women have relatively lower status and less autonomy than the ethnic/tribal group	Same as the caste-origin Hindu group	Like clan organization; no social hierarchy, Women have lower status than men, divorce is easy
Economy	Relatively poor group, except for a few Tharu and Rajbansi landlords; bonded labour is still present among the Tharus; primarily agriculturists	Relatively better in terms of economy except for the 'untouchables' who are poorest; untouchables are mostly landless; economy: agriculture, service, trade, occupational workers and labourers.	Rich group in the Tarai, many of them are merchants; little agriculture and service as such by groups	Relatively poor group in the Tarai; owns little land, most of them are specialized workers
Politics	Except for a Tharus and Rajbansis, few other groups engage in politics; political culture has yet to emerge	Most sensitive group in the political sphere except for the untouchables; politics in the Tarai is the realm of a few high-caste members of this group	Not involved in current Nepalese political debate	Few are engaged in politics; political culture is gradually emerging

*The settlement history of the Kashmiri Muslims in the Kathmandu valley goes as far back as the sixteenth or seventeenth centuries (Bista, 1967).

Though Nepal was declared a secular state by the interim constitution of 2007, Hinduism is the dominant religion and represents more than 81 per cent of the total population. A number of festivals, fairs and rituals are celebrated in Nepal every year, keeping in the forefront Hindu gods and goddesses of the great tradition. Over the years, other religions are also carving a substantial place in the Nepali society, especially since the 1990s. Christianity has become increasingly reported religious affiliation among various caste/ethnic groups in Nepal. The Kirat religion is also carving its position among the various cultural groups such as the Rai, Limbu and Sunuwar of Nepal. The oral tradition or 'Mundhum' is being kept alive by many of these cultural groups (such as Limbus) to worship their deities and celebrate many rituals.

Though 123 separate language groups are reported in Nepal as the mother tongue of the people, Nepali language is the lingua franca and national language and spoken by more than 44 per cent of the total population.

The Nepali society is not homogenous in term of ethnic/caste structure; rather, it is divided by caste, religion, locality and dialect, thus exhibiting the complexity, reflecting a single homogenous social structure per se. The diversity of ethnicity exhibiting their ethnic/caste structure is more pronounced in the Nepal Tarai today than in the hills or mountains. No doubt, a close juxtaposition between these two large cultural groups—Adibasi/Janajati versus Hindu caste populations—presents a unique social structure, blended with two great civilizations of the north and the south.

Similarities and Differences in Form and Content of the Social Structure

There are fundamental cultural differences between the caste-origin Hindu groups and Adibasi/Janajati groups in terms of their social structure. These are briefly summarized in Table 3.

Table 3: Specific cultural traits of Hindu caste groups vs Adibasi/Janajati groups

Distinct/Social cultural characteristics	Adibasi/Janajati groups	Caste-origin Hindu groups
Division	Horizontal	Hierarchical/vertical
Language	Tibeto-Burman	Indo-European
Origin	Native (claimed); But a lot of people of northern Himalayan region migrated from Tibet	Migrated mostly from the Southern Plains, mostly from India
Social organization	Clan system	Caste system
Religion	Buddhism, Kirat and Animism	Mostly Hindu
Marriage system	Hypogamous or isogamous (ideal)	Isogamous (ideal)
Marriage with mother's brothers' daughter	Permitted in certain groups such as Thakali, Tamang and Magar and so on	Not permitted at all; considered incestuous
Remarriage with widows	Permitted	Not permitted
Marriage practice	Bride price or bride service; viri local	Dowry system; viri local
Divorce	Allowed	Not allowed
Family system	Nuclear (preferred)	Extended or joint (ideal)
Status of women	Medium to High	Medium to low
Societal structure	Open society; one can discuss openly with any member of the society at the household	Close society; women are secluded at home, particularly among the Tarai (Madhesi women
Traditional leadership	Present among many ethnic groups to guide rituals and social customs	Not present

(Adapted and modified from Gellner, 1991)

The caste groups are primarily Hindu and hierarchical in structure, which is based on the principles of purity and pollution within the same linguistic and religious group. Caste forms the basis of social interaction among the majority of Nepal's diverse population. Furthermore, it plays a broad-based model of Nepali social structure to dictate the everyday life of people. Sharma (1989) notes that caste in Nepal is not merely a concern of the individual private social group but a State-protected ideology. The 1854 Old Legal Code of Nepal presented a base for foundation of Hindu caste culture and purity and pollution associated with the Hindu caste values. Bista (1990) criticizes the rigid model of Nepali hierarchical structure of caste which has hindered the country's socio-economic development. Dumont's (1970) Brahmanical model of caste and its hierarchical structure reflected in the Indian society is equally applicable in the Nepali caste society as well. Brahmins are at the apex in the Hindu caste society, this model of caste hierarchy plays a vital role in performing rituals and economic and other social activities in Nepal. Without a Brahman priest, no Hindu ritual can be performed. Rice, grain, flowers, milk and honey are the principal items offered to Hindu divinities.

On the other hand, Adibasi/Janajati division is horizontal or spatial. The Janajati identity is based on specific location, a particular language and they practise Buddhism or animistic religious traditions. The local community customs and laws are present, and if somebody violates these, the person is punished according to the local customs. The clan structure is diverse among various groups, which facilitates marriage and various socio-religious activities. For example, among the Magars of Nepal, there are well over thousands of clans, which separate a group from another for marriage. Blood and alcohol have become a common mode of pleasing divinities among the Adibasi/Janajati groups. Likewise, in the Tibetan Buddhism prevalent in Nepal, Lama is the priest performing rituals but unlike the Brahmin priest, his position is not at the apex in the Buddhist society (Fisher, 1978).

The typical feature of social structure of some Adibasi/Janajati groups such as Limbu is their close association with kipat (a communal form of land tenure) system. Land and cultural relationship of Limbus is closely associated with the kipat land and retains their sense of identity. In 1831, King Prithvi Narayan Shah issued a lalmohar (royal decree) to the traditional leaders of Limbus of Eastern Nepal permitting them to retain their ancient corporate form of land tenure for themselves, paying a nominal tax to the government. Since then, kipat has remained a source of ethnic identity and morale among them.

Though the kipat system was abolished by the government in 1964, Limbus closely tie themselves and their kin network and socio-economic relationship to each other through it. Limbus' land and kin group formation focused on clan, lineage and inheritance pattern through the kipat system (Caplan, 1970). They claim that they follow Kirat religion—a shamanistic tradition—and Faluganada, a saint of Limbu religious ethnic sect, has revitalized the Kirat religion.

Likewise, Newars maintained their cultural identity through their various guthi (religious trusts) such as 'see guthi' (death guthi) and 'lineage guthi'. Through these guthis, Newars maintain their traditional organizations and run various rituals of their everyday life.

Many Adibasi/Janajati groups such as Thakali, Magar, Tamang, Gurung practise cross-cousin marriages. Normally, bhanji (mother's brother's daughter) is preferred in marriage with the son of father's sister's son. This is the most preferred form of marriage among them even today. This type of marriage is not at all permitted among the so-called high-caste Hindu groups of Nepal. This is considered an incestuous relationship among them. The tradition of Rodhi Ghar, a youth dormitory popular among Gurungs where young boys and girls meet and sing and dance together throughout night, has helped young Gurungs to select suitable marriage partners of their choice.

Widow remarriage is common among Adibasi/Janajati groups. A study conducted by CNAS (2004) notes that it is difficult to find widows among the Tharu communities of the far western Tarai. As soon as a Tharu woman is widowed, she is immediately remarried either to her husband's brother or other Tharu men of the community, who easily accept her as the new wife.

Since the majority of Adibasi/Janajati communities have lived together with Hindus for centuries, the process of Hinduization is common among them. Many of them strictly follow the Hindu model of purity and impurity and a Dalit (so-called untouchable) is not allowed to enter their houses.

Changes in Temporal Sequence

For many years, the Nepali society and culture have been defined and depicted in a typical larger Hindu model of the Great Indian Tradition. However, it has been changing gradually over the last twenty-five years, particularly after 1990; though some scholars believe that change began when the nation was opened to the outside world after the revolution of 1950. Time- and place-specific discourses and practices regarding culture, history, notions of selfhood, wishes and desires are increasing in Nepal.

Hinduization, Sanskritization and Westernization

After the unification of Nepal by King Prithvi Narayan Shah in 1768, the Nepali social structure was gradually tied with the Hindu model of Great Tradition, albeit without disturbing the local cultures. This peaceful transition was affected through the implementation of the Old Legal Code 1854, which categorized all the people of Nepal into four distinct orders: Tagadhari; Matwali; Pani Nachalne cho chito halnu naparne; Pani Nachalne cho chito halnu parne (untouchable castes) (Hofer, 2004).

This code embodied certain distinct features: commensality, supremacy of Hindu values and religious orthodoxy and caste as the basis of social mobility (Sharma, 1989). It provided authority to fashion the social organization of various groups from the typical Hindu hierarchical model. The basis of mutual help and relation is also more well-defined by the old code. Though a flexible approach to inter-caste marriage and provision of upward social mobility is encouraged though this legal code, the notion of high and low caste, concept of pure and impure, virtue and sin remained intrinsic in all matters of all caste relations.

Though the Tibeto-Burman-speaking populations are distinct in terms of language, culture and religion, the process of Sanskritization vis-à-vis Hinduization among them has accelerated over the years. Accepting caste norms has become the first step towards Sanskritization among the Adibasi/Janajati groups (Sharma, 1989). The process of Hinduization has also become rampant among them. One of the most Hinduized Adibasi/Janajati groups is Magars. Out of 1,887,733 (7.1 per cent) Magar population in Nepal, the followers of Hindu religion number 1,490,611 (79.9 per cent) (CBS, 2012). Likewise, many Magars do not speak their own language (41.8 per cent, 2011 Census). All Magars observe caste restrictions and claim to be Hindus (Hitchcock, 1966). Conformity to Nepali Hindu norms has become the process of upward social mobility among various groups. The other glaring example is Thakalis who have Hinduized themselves to ensure economic and political relations with the ruling elite of Nepal (Vinding, 1998). Various deities are worshipped together in a lot of festive and religious occasions such as Dashain, Tihar, Teej and so on.

Despite the process of Hinduization vis-à-vis Sanskritization, the traditional social structure of these cultural groups has remained intact. Instead of raising its power of synthesis and assimilation, it has increased the feeling of de-Hinduization and the sense of self cultural identity has increased among them over the years. Likewise, this process of Hinduization has become one of the avenues for social conflict between the so-called high- and low-caste groups and between Adibasi/Janajati and Hindu groups in recent years.

Nepal opened its door to the outside world after the revolution of 1950, encouraging democratization and modernization in the given Hindu framework of social structure. But during the Panchayat regime (1962–90), one of the dramatic changes that took place was promulgation of the Muluki Ain in 1963. According to the new and bold code, nobody is inferior or superior on the basis of race, caste and creed and everybody is equal before the law.

Nowadays, the younger generations are looking towards the

West for their academic career and future. English language and Western culture (in the form of food, dress, music and songs) have not only become essential consumer commodities but also a medium for enhancing social interaction among them. The process of Westernization has become a new model of upgrading oneself in the traditional Nepali society. There is a growing generational divide between farmers versus the urban educated middle-class families in Nepal.

Kinship, family structure, marriage and gender

There is little breach to the patterns of endogamy till today, though inter-caste marriages are gradually increasing over the years. The patriarchal model continues to play a key role in kinship designations. Nepali kinship terms are addressed in the typical hierarchical model and respected accordingly.

In Nepal, changes in economic standards have led to changes in relationships within families, in relationships between families and, ultimately, to emerging redefinitions of the family itself. Parents have increasingly less control over the choices of their children; old cooperation networks between families have become brittle and the cultural models for the extended family are in a flux (Fricke, 1998).

There is a dramatic change of life among many ethnic/caste groups, and changes are observed among many low-caste Dalit groups in the Tarai. A lot of young men go abroad, bring money back home as their remittance and invest in buying land and building new houses. Economic dislocation raised socio-cultural issues, in particular old people are left behind at home and they are forced to live alone without the support of their grown-up children. Because of the increasing flow of remittances over the years, the concept of nuclear family is becoming more and more popular.

Likewise, the number of middle-class families is increasing over the years as these are the people who are teachers, government employees, and work in various NGOs in Nepal today. However, caste-oriented notions of prestige, orthodoxy and property relations have remained intact over the years. The new market-driven, mass-mediated values and desires have increased and the moral logic of caste continues to powerfully inflect the everyday lives of people (Leichty, 2003). Although the Muluki Ain of 1963 abolished the caste-based social customs, marriage laws and rigid hierarchy, caste, as the dominant form of Nepali social structure, is alive even today.

There is little change in the domestic household structure in terms of work. Nepali women must perform household duties unassisted by their husbands and the grandmother still takes the leading part in the socialization of children. But the women of so-called lower caste have louder voices than higher caste women in work and at public places. Cameron (1998) argues that the economic, social and religious agencies of 'low caste' women cannot be understood within the purity and impurity that relegates their caste to a low position. When people emphasize purity, honour, business, occupation or dharma associated with a caste rank, gender boundaries create oppositional difference; the ordering of caste is the ordering of legitimate sexuality (Cameron, 1998; Hofer, 2004).

Today, many women are no longer confined to home. They have entered the workforce gradually. For many non-working women who live in the city areas of Nepal, the television, particularly Indian television channels, shape their lives in many ways. Watching television is not simply the pastime for many of them but also a model of guiding their everyday life. Families are adapting technologies by putting old behaviours into a new context.

Among gender-sensitive groups, the concept of kanyadaan (offering a virgin girl in marriage) is gradually weakening as the girl is not considered simply as an offering to the boy in marriage. Though the concept of empowering women has become an industry in Nepal, it has not helped much to break down the traditional male-dominated social structure.

There is a conflict in value between modernity and tradition. Economic, social and political forces have contributed to an improved lifestyle among people. Computers, Internet and email have revolutionized sources of information and entertainment, altering the nature and speed of communication at work and at home. Urban culture vis-à-vis consumerism culture among various groups of people is increasing throughout Nepal. In Kathmandu, an emerging urban middle class creates itself as a new cultural entity (Leichty, 2003).

Today, there is a tussle between individualism versus collectivism in social principles and hierarchy between the old and young. The younger generation, particularly those who were born after the 1960s, opt for nuclear families and individual culture is gaining ground in work and public places.

Democracy, multiculturalism and forms of ethnic tension

After a long struggle, Nepal was able to form a democratic government in April 1990. But democracy prospers in a society in which people are reasonably conscious and able to participate in and associate with both political and non-political spheres. It works in a society where economic development allows upward social mobility (Hachhethu, 2004). Despite the presence of basic infrastructure and access to schools and other facilities in the Tarai, the Madhesi group as a whole, lags behind the hill groups in many socio-economic indicators.

The democratic political structure provided avenues for people to talk on any issue openly, and this has helped to bring ethnic tensions out on the street. This is more pronounced between Pahade or hill people and Madhesi or plains people, based on regionalism and ethnicity (Gaige, 1975). Also, there is a tussle between high-caste Hindu groups such as Brahmin and Chhetri and Adibasi/Janajati groups for sharing power and resources in a given structure. The upsurge in ethnicity and ethnic identity among various linguistic and regional minorities is increasing, which could pose a threat to the national integration in Nepal. There are several reasons for the ethnic conflicts between the hill and Tarai people, particularly with the Madhesi people, in recent years.

First, the demographics of Nepal Tarai have changed rapidly over the last sixty years. There has been an almost fourfold increase in population—from 2.9 million in the 1952/54 Census to almost 13.3 million in the 2011 Census. In other words, this pattern of demographic change in the Tarai has played a significant role in changing the ethnic structure and composition of the population as a whole. The influx of hill people suddenly increased in the Tarai after the Malaria Eradication Programme in 1958. The percentage of hill people in the Tarai, which was close to 33 per cent in the 1991 Census, increased to almost 37 per cent in the 2011 Census.

Second, the major reason for ethnic tension is the poverty among the Madhesi people. Historically, neglect of Tarai people by the hill-dominated government created an outburst of ethnic tension. Some Tarai leaders, particularly those representing Hindu caste groups such as Madhesi Morcha (United Front of Madhesi, an alliance of seven parties) were not satisfied with the promulgation of the Constitution of Nepal 2014, which was passed by voting more than 85 per cent of the Members of Parliament. Madhesi Morcha, in the name of rights of Madhesi people, has raised the issue of citizenship and demarcation of Tarai land as Madhes as a whole. These leaders also advocate the use of Hindi as the link language of the Tarai, challenging Nepali language, the national language.

Third, the division between the hill people and the plains people also seems to be linked with the uncontrolled flow of Indian migrants crossing the border to settle in the Nepal Tarai over the last fifty years. Because so many groups on either side of the border are culturally identical, it is difficult to differentiate between the Nepali Tarai populations from Indian settlers. Familial, cultural and commercial interactions that take place between these groups daily, as if the border does not exist, further complicate matters. That a problem of national identity should arise among the Tarai people and that hill people question their allegiance seems natural.

There is little success in forging a consensus on the fundamental issues of improving the clauses of the new constitution among the main political forces; the issue of demarcation of seven federal provinces is a case in point. The opposition parties, such as Madhesi Morcha, organized hundreds of rallies and bandhs (shutdowns) against the government during the ethnic movements of Madhes. Even today, the leaders of Madhesi Morcha are against the government and are organizing rallies to sensitize the issue of hill versus Tarai people. The state is playing a weak role in harmonizing and minimizing ethnic tensions.

Fourth, the strategic location of the Tarai has played a crucial role in intensifying the Madhesi movements. This has widened the gap in the understanding between the hill and Tarai people, raising a question on the process of national integration of Nepal (Gaige, 1975). Theories of settler culture where there are conflicts between tradition and modernity have often overlooked the process of demographic change of population and heterogenization of cultures (mixing up the hill and Tarai people with different languages and cultures and multiculturalism has become the way of life) over the years. It should not be forgotten that four main groups of people reside in the Tarai today: the original inhabitants such as the Tharus, Dhimal, Rajbansi and so on; the caste-origin Hindu Madhesi people, people of Indian origin and the hill Nepali people.

The ethnic conflicts between the hill and Tarai people and between high-caste Hindu groups and Adibasi/Janajati groups could develop a new form of social structure in the name of unified Madhesi, Adibasi/Janajati or Dalit. But their arguments are based on rhetorical claims of sharing similarities as if these groups were homogeneous in their typical social structure. They want to create a homogenous culture of a single social structure such as Madhesi, Adibasi/Janajati and Dalits. The issue here is how to demarcate a traditional cultural area in a single social structure such as the Madhesi, Adibasi/Janajati and so on, which is diverse in terms of ethnicity, culture and tradition. Another reason is that it is difficult to demarcate Madhes as a single cultural region or create a homogeneous social structure due to the migration of hill people over the last fifty-five years.

The emergence of indigenous ethnic movement is another example. On the one hand, indigenous groups are organizing movements against the government for their rights in language, culture and religion and part of their traditional territory to be treated as federal provinces such as Limbuwan, Magarat and so on. On the other hand, they want to homogenize their diverse culture into one single social structure in the name of 'Adibasi/Janajati'.

In recent years, religion has become a crucial sociological variable to identify oneself as a person of a particular religious group. No doubt, Hinduism acted as a philosophical guide for the Shah rulers to rule the country for more than 240 years (1769–2006) before Nepal eventually became a secular state in 2007. It should not be forgotten that more than 81 per cent of the total population of Nepal follows Hindu religion even today (CBS, 2012). Nevertheless, various religious groups have been living side by side with the Hindus over the years. Compared with the 2001 Census, two more religious groups were added in the 2011 Census: Prakrit (Animism) and Bon, an old religion of Tibet and Nepal. But Nepal has been declared a secular state since its endorsement in the Interim Constitution of Nepal 2007. However, many Hindu populations of Nepal are not happy with this declaration. No doubt, the State's efforts on secularism simultaneously foster the State neutrality in terms of religious values of people, encouraging all religious groups to live in harmony (Shahu, 2016).

In Conclusion

Since the beginning of the first quarter of the twenty-first century, ethnicity, language and religion have become the most important sociological topics in democratic Nepal. Widespread exposure to different social and political systems around the world through modern media, education and contact with people outside of Nepal has helped to raise serious questions about the traditional values that supported the existing traditional social structure.

It can be said that the Nepali social structure was traditional in nature in the past. It was localized—thriving local or small traditions or indigenous village civilizations hardly crossing the caste, creed and ethnic boundaries.

Even today it is hard to describe the typical Nepali social structure as dictated in the form of food and dress. It is diverse like the material culture of a group in question as it differs from one cultural group to another; one caste order group versus ethnic order and so on. There is a challenge of multiculturalism vis-à-vis the typical Nepali social structure as such. Today, the people of Nepal, regardless of where their territory belongs to, do not live in isolation; eating habits and certain practices of marriage rituals have substantially changed and a blended social structure is gradually taking shape over the years. Today, there is no clear conception of social bounds and cultural reach of this diverse population. Despite deterritorialization or blurring of ethnic boundaries over the years, national conversation about ethnic cultural identity issues and the trend of grouping of various cultural groups in the form of a broad single social structure have become the social facts of Nepali culture today. Nepali society is gradually turning cosmopolitan, with the rise of nuclear families and increasing inter-caste marriages.

No doubt many of the caste strictures such as touching of food and water by the so-called low caste members and religious sanctions against caste behaviour have been weakened after the promulgation of the Muluki Ain in 1963. But the concept of caste continues and, in some cases, it has become a model of distinct social structure separating one group from another. Caste forms the basis of social interaction among the majority of Nepal's diverse ethnic population and there is fairly a uniform order of caste ranking even today. Thus, Brahmanical values have become a model for raising one's socio-economic status and identifying oneself in the existing social structure. This has invariably led to the process of Sanskritization or Hinduization, giving more orthodox and stratified caste hierarchical values even to those who were originally outside the framework of the Hindu caste hierarchy.

The process of Sanskritization or Hinduization of a group (whether Limbu or Thakali or Rai or Dhimal) is, therefore, an affirmation and not a negation of the caste system and their values (Jones, 1976; Iijima, 1977; Sharma, 2004; Bista, 1971). That is why even an educated member of Dalit or untouchable group finds difficulty in locating one's own position within the framework of the Muluki Ain 1963.

Briefly, the system inadvertently provides a new basis for caste exclusiveness, and this has given rise to the creation of ethnic/caste associations, a new form of social structure in Nepal. The objectives of these caste associations, at least theoretically, are to protect one's own language and culture from outside forces, but they see themselves as part of the historical cultural unit which is both exclusive and in opposition to the outside. Cultural identity has taken the shape of political identity in the context of confrontation over issues such as language, religion, economy and culture. Today, a symbol of 'multi-vocal concept of identity' with a new form of Nepali social structure is emerging. The period after 1990 brought renewed focus on the Nepali character focused on caste/ethnicity.

On the other hand, there is little erosion of cultural identities among various groups of people. Myriad of phantasms, images, notions, feelings, desires, among others, are persisting among various groups of people in the name of cultural identity. Family, kinship, caste and village are still the dominant forms of social institutions comprising the social structure of various ethnic or caste groups. However, these structures are gradually losing their lustre and morality because of the changes in education, role of women and improvements in the quality of life of people over the years. Today, the Nepali society has moved towards a structure of tolerance or culture of resilience despite facing serious ethnic tensions over the years.

To conclude, only a functional democracy can lead towards the prosperity of all caste, language and religious groups of Nepal. Cultural pluralism has become the fact of life today and preservation of cultural identity comes as part and parcel of human rights. Burghart (1984) is right in saying that a person's identity based on family, kinship, home and land is more important than any political ties. Even today, there is a strong feeling of common belongingness among various groups of people, suggesting that existing social structure based on caste/ethnicity will persist in the future as well.

Dilli Ram Dahal is Professor of Anthropology and teaches MPhil classes in Anthropology at the Tribhuvan University.

Bibliography

Bhattachan, K.B., et al. 2003. 'Existing Practices of Caste based Untouchability in Nepal and Strategy for a Campaign for its Elimination.' Kathmandu: ActionAid.

Bista, D.B. 1967. *People of Nepal*. Kathmandu: Ministry of Information and Broadcasting.

Bista, D.B. 'Political innovators of the Upper Kali Gandaki.' *Man*, 1971, Vol. VI, No. 1.

Bista, D.B. 1989. 'The Structure of Nepali Society.' In: Malla, K.P. (Ed.) *Nepal Perspectives on Continuity and Change*. Kirtipur: Centre for Nepal and Asian Studies, Tribhuvan University.

Bista, D.B. 1990. *Fatalism and Development*. Calcutta: Orient and Longman.

Burghar, R. 'The Formation of the Concept of Nation State in Nepal.' *Journal of Asian Studies*, 1984, Vol. 44, No. 1, pp. 101–25.

Cameron, M. 1998. *On the Edge of the Auspicious: Caste and Gender Relationships in Nepal*. Urbana: University of Illinois Press.

Caplan, L. 1970. *Land and Social Change in East Nepal*. Kathmandu: Himal Books.

Central Bureau of Statistics (CBS). 2012. 'National Population and Housing Census 2011 (National Report)'. Kathmandu: Central Bureau of Statistics.

Centre for Economic Development and Administration (CEDA). 1981. 'The Status of Women (Five volumes).' Kathmandu: Centre for Economic Development and Administration.

Centre for Nepal and Asian Studies (CNAS). 2004. 'Identification and Analysis of Community-based Care for Orphans and Vulnerable Children in Nepal.' A Report Submitted to the UNICEF, Kathmandu.

Dahal, D.R., et al. 1978. 'Indian Ethnic Groups in the Nepal Tarai.' (A Mimeographed Report). Kathmandu: Centre for Nepal and Asian Studies.

Dahal, D.R., et al. 2002. 'National Dalit Strategy Report Part I Situational Analysis of Dalits in Nepal.' Kathmandu: National Planning Commission.

Dahal, D.R. 2010. 'Hindu Nationalism and Untouchable Reform: The Status of Dalits in Nepali Society.' Kathmandu: SASON.

Dahal, D.R. 2013: 'Cultural Territoriality in the Con text of Modern Nepal: Some Examples from the Adivasi/Janajati and Madhesi Groups.' In: Smada,

J. (Ed.) *Territorial Changes and Territorial Restructurings in the Himalaya.* New Delhi: Adroit Publications.

Dahal, D.R. 2014. 'Social composition of the Population: Caste/Ethnicity and Religion in Nepal'. In: *Population Monograph of Nepal (Volume II).* Kathmandu: National Planning Commission (NPC)/Central Bureau of Statistics (CBS).

Dahal, D.R. and Jha, S.K. 2014. *Chamar of Nepal.* Kirtipur: Central Department of Sociology/Anthropology, Tribhuvan University.

Dahal, D.R. and Gurung, G. 2014. *Chidimars of Nepal.* Kirtipur: Central Department of Sociology/Anthropology, Tribhuvan University.

Dumont, L. 1970. *Homo Hierarchicus: The Caste System and Its Implications.* (2008 Reprint). London: Weidenfeld and Nicolson/New Delhi.

Fürer-Haimendorf, von C. 1964. *The Sherpas of Nepal.* Berkeley: The University of California Press.

Fisher, J. 1978. *Himalayan Anthropology.* Hague: Mouton.

Fricke, T. 'Home work'. *Anthropology Newsletter,* October 1998.

Gaige, H.F. 1975. *Regionalism and National Unity in Nepal.* Delhi: Vikas Publishing House.

Gellner, D. 'Hinduism, Tribalism and Position of Women: The Problem of Newar Identity'. *Man, 1991,* Vol. 26, No. 1.

Gellner, D. and Quigley, D. 1995. *Contested Hierarchies.* New Delhi: Oxford University Press.

Hamilton, B.F. 1819. *An Account of the Kingdom of Nepal.* Edinburgh: Constable.

Hodgson, H.B. 1874. *Essays on the Languages, Cultures and Religions of Nepal and Tibet.* London: Trubner and Co.

Hachhethu, K. 2004. *State of Democracy in Nepal, Survey Report.* Kathmandu: SDA/N and International IDEA.

Hoffer, A. 1997, 2004 (2nd Print). *The Caste Hierarchy and the State in Nepal: A Study of the Muluki Ain of 1854.* Kathmandu: Himal Books.

Hitchcock, J. 1966. *The Magars of Banyan Hill.* London: Holt Rinehart and Winston.

Jones, L.R. 'Sanskritization in Eastern Nepal'. *Ethnology, 1976,* Vol. XV, No. 1.

Iijima, S. 1977. 'Ecology, Economy and Culture Change among the Thakalis in the Himalayas of Central Nepal'. In: Iijima, S. (Ed.) *Changing Aspects of Modern Nepal.* Tokyo: Monumenta Serindica, No. III. CAA.

Kirkpatrick, W. *An Account of the Kingdom of Nepal.* London: William and Miller.

Leichty, M. 2003. *Suitably Modern. Making Middle Class Culture in a New*

Consumer Society. Princeton: Princeton University Press.

Marshall, G. 1994. *The Concise Oxford Dictionary of Sociology.* Oxford: Oxford University Press.

Radcliffe–Brown, R.A. 1952. *Structure and Function in Primitive Society.* London: Cohen and West.

Rai, U. 2014. 'Food security and exclusion among the Chepangs: A Case study from Central Nepal.' PhD thesis submitted to the Faculty of Humanities and Social Sciences, Tribhuvan University.

Shahu, M.B. 2016. 'Discourses on Secularism in Nepal.' Paper presented at Second Anthropology Conference on Earthquake, Post-disaster Reconstruction and the State in Nepal (16–18 December 2016). Kathmandu.

Sharma, P.R. 1989. 'Nepali Culture and Society: Reflections on Some Historical Currents.' In: Malla, K.P. (Ed.) *Nepal Perspectives on Continuity and Change.* Kirtipur: Centre for Nepal and Asian Studies, Tribhuvan University.

Sharma, P.R. 2004. *The State and Society in Nepal*. Kathmandu: Himal Books.

Sharma, S. 2004. 'Lived Islam in Nepal. In: Ahmad, I. and Reifield, H. (Eds.) *Lived Islam in South Asia*. Delhi: Social Science Press.

Vinding, M. 1998. *The Thakali: A Himalayan Ethnography*. London: Serinda Publications.

3

SUCCESSIVE CONSTITUTIONS AND GEOPOLITICAL PINCHES

Bipin Adhikari

Nepal started ushering in modern democracy in 1951 (Joshi and Rose, 1966). That year it kicked off the process of transition to a modern political system—choosing and replacing the government through free and fair elections; active participation of people, as citizens, in politics and civic life; protection of the fundamental rights of all citizens; and a system of the rule of law, in which laws and procedures apply equally to all citizens (Diamond, 2004). The process had its ideological origin in the revolution that was accomplished in the same year. It was grounded in the call for democratic representation and public accountability on the basis of a new constitution finalized by an elected CA. It aimed at achieving legal equality, political freedom and rule of law as the basic principles of change (Joshi and Rose, 1966).

However, the effort to establish democracy in Nepal, a country situated between two Asian giants—India and China—has remained unfulfilled even after experimenting with six written constitutions one after another (Dhungel, et al., 1998). This involved a broad spectrum of political system and choice about the norms and standards and institutions and procedures. Even after almost seven decades, Nepal has not been able to institutionalize constitutional democracy of any form and achieve the objective of change. The country is in long transition and remains under protracted instability.

There is so much difference in opinion among analysts about the root causes of Nepal's unsuccessful constitutional experiments and what needs to be done to sort them out (Riaz and Basu, 2007). Obviously, the problems of Nepal, as the contributors to this book attempt to show, are manifold, interrelated and multidimensional. The inability to achieve political stability by institutionalizing constitutional democracy and a level of socio-economic development is one of the causes, and perhaps, the most vital of all the problems that the country faces today. This chapter, in particular, argues that Nepal's major problem in institutionalizing constitutional democracy is more external geopolitical than internal.[1] It is the neighbourhood that has been the cause of Nepal's plight than her internal problems.

Most of the internal problems of Nepal exist because it has not been able to fix this geopolitical vulnerability, which always comes in the way (Wariko, 2009; Athwal, 2008; Goldstein, 2010; Meredith, 2008; Lal, 2006). The political institutions in Nepal, notwithstanding the frequent change in the constitution to adapt to the changing requirements of the country, failed to play a key role in averting this vulnerability by creating a strong national perspective of the situation and defending the national interest through appropriate methods.

Over the years, democracy has been criticized for not offering enough political stability, but it is not democracy which is the reason behind this deplorable situation. Even though the governments are frequently elected or formed (even without elections) on and off to respond to the people's voices, they fail to deliver, feel helpless and, in the end, get manipulated on their decisions. The mass media are often enough to force sudden, unexpected political change. The people have hardly any role in the crucial political decisions in the country by way of a participatory process.[2]

Any functioning constitutional democracy worth its name empowers people, ensures their right to participate in the affairs of the state, enables them to raise their voice and gives the people an opportunity to defend their personal and nationalist inspirations for organization and development. These realities, in turn, revitalize the social, economic and political institutions in the country, and enable the people to reassert power and self-actualization as individuals or groups. This process has always collided in Nepal with the geopolitical ambitions of its neighbouring countries, particularly India and China (Meredith, 2008). And Nepal's leaders have been unable to deal with the challenges. As an effect, democracy has not been able to achieve its basic purpose, including the objective of economic development. The chapter also argues that the solution to Nepal's problem of institutionalization of constitutional democracy is not only possible, but also inevitable. But the major fault lines of Nepal's constitutions are not constitutional; rather they are geopolitical. As long as India and China have problems with each other, Nepal will remain unstable, impacting its constitutional democracy.

Movement for Democracy and Change

Nepal was a 'closed' ancient country till 1950. Ruled by monarchs for most part of its written history, the country remained under the grip of hereditary Rana prime ministers for 103 years until 1950–51. The last Rana prime minister was Mohan Shamsher, who assumed office in 1948. This was the time when King Tribhuvan was attempting to work with the opposition forces and assert himself.

Till the 'revolution' of 1950–51, Nepal had virtually no system of constitutional democracy, which enforced the limits of political authority through clearly stated provisions, including protected rights, and the people were not defined as electorate with the power to remove poorly performing governments (Dhungel, et al., 1998).[3] Although the country had a legal system, with written rules of law and jural traditions, it had no system of democracy, with or without a legal framework, such as a written constitution, by which to rule over the country. The system, if at all it existed, was a feudal system. This enabled the rulers to rule the country with hereditary powers based on a combination of legal and military customs. It flourished historically and as a way of structuring society around relationships derived from the holding of land in exchange for service or labour. Although the Ranas were able to keep the country safe, united and independent while the rest of the South Asian subcontinent was under the British rule, they were not governing according to the popular will or the principles of an accountable government. The kings of Nepal throughout the Rana period (1846–1951) were reduced to figurehead, with no real powers, while the Ranas ruled the country with absolute powers.

The Ranas started facing noticeable resistance since the beginning of 1940s. There was pressure on them to liberalize the polity and accommodate dissenters. Padma Shamsher (1945–48), who was the eighth hereditary Rana prime minister, assuming power in November 1945, was considered a liberal ruler when compared with his predecessors. Aware of the internal and external situations, the 66-year-old prime minister wanted to tackle the challenge by introducing political reforms. The Government of Nepal Act, 1948, which he issued in response, was the first political document defining power in the country. The objective of this Act was to start the process of democratization in Nepal, even though it had structural limitations, while keeping the titular monarchy and hereditary prime ministerial system intact. As it happens with most of the oligarchs, there was resistance to concede meaningful power to the people. Nevertheless, Prime Minister Padma Shamsher tried to diffuse the pressure by issuing the constitution, giving clear indications that change was coming up.

However, the Government of Nepal Act, 1948, was a skeletal document (Singh, 1970/71).[4] It did not say that it was the supreme law of the land, but provided for the executive, legislature and judiciary to exercise the powers of the state. Together with monarchy, the position of the hereditary prime minister was kept intact as a 'non-amendable' feature of the Act.[5] The executive power was vested in the prime minister, who was to exercise the power either directly or through officers subordinate to him.[6] The council of ministers formed by him as its chairperson was to help and advise him to exercise the executive power of the state. Its members were to be appointed from among the members of the Legislative Assembly (Section 7 of the Government of Nepal Act, 1948). At least two of the members were to be from the elected members of the House. All the members of the council were accountable to the prime minister. He could dismiss any or all of them on his discretion. The prime minister could also suspend or modify this Act by issuing special ordinances. These ordinances were to be effective for six months. A chief government legal advisor was to be appointed by the prime minister to give advice to the government in legal matters (Section 12 [a] of the Government of Nepal Act, 1948).

The legislative power was to be exercised by the bicameral parliament of Nepal, called Legislative Assembly (Part IV of the Government of Nepal Act, 1948). It was to comprise the prime minister, the National Assembly (Rastra Sabha) and the Advisory Assembly (Bhardari Sabha). The National Assembly was to consist of no fewer than sixty and no more than seventy members, both elected and nominated, as per Schedule A of this Act. The ratio between nominated and elected members was to be in the proportion of 2:3, as approximating to that proportion as much as possible. The Advisory Assembly was to consist of no fewer than twenty and no more than thirty members, nominated by the prime minister keeping in mind inclusion of all organizations, professions, employment and personalities who contributed towards the national pride, as far as possible. One-fourth of the members of the legislature thereof were to retire every year and new members were to be elected or nominated in their places.[7]

On the judicial side, Section 49 stated that justice shall be administered by judges in public courts established for the purpose. It stated that the court shall comprise courts of first instance and also courts of appeal. Section 53 created a Supreme Court known as Pradhan Nyayalaya. A judicial committee was to be appointed consisting of two outside members and ten members of the legislature. It was to act as the Supreme Court of Appeal in special cases and was authorized to frame rules and regulations for administration of justice (Section 52 of the Government of Nepal Act, 1948). The prime minister retained power to appoint or dismiss any Supreme Court judge. The offices of Auditor General and Public Service Commission were also created.

The Act guaranteed freedoms of personal liberty, speech, press, assembly and organization, freedom of religion, complete equality before the law, affordable and speedy justice, universal free compulsory elementary education, universal and equal suffrage for all adults and security of private property as defined by the prevailing laws. All these guarantees were subjected to 'the principles of public order and good practices' (Section 4 of the Government of Nepal Act, 1948). There were no special procedures to enforce these guarantees under the Act.

The Government of Nepal Act, 1948, was issued by the prime minister by virtue of the 'Supreme power vested [in him] through the instruments of their sacred *Panjapatras* by His Majesty King of Nepal, dating from the year 1903BS [1846] onwards, delegating all powers of the State upon the contemporaneous Shree 3 Maharajas [meaning Rana Prime Ministers]'(Singh, 2013). The Act did not use words like 'democracy' or 'republic' being the basic purpose of the change.

Prime Minister Padma Shamsher refused to accept the utility of a parliamentary democracy that the leaders in the opposition wanted, allegedly for fear of 'multiplicity of leadership' (Dhungel, et al., 1998). The Act, however, asserted the resurrection of Nepal's ancient ideals of the Panchayat and other similar self-government institutions, which were connected with the Legislative Assembly, and the prime minister's declared policy to provide for increasingly closer association of the people in every branch of administration. He believed that the 'giving effect of this policy can only be achieved by successive stages and must be guided by the cooperation received from those to whom new opportunities have been offered and by the extent to which further confidence can be reposed upon their sense of responsibilities.' Answering potential critiques, Prime Minister Padma Shamsher pointed out:

> The Government of the day was so enamoured of the British system that it desired to introduce the same kind of parliamentary institutions here, in which the people's will might find expression. But the people showed energetic disapproval, because they thought that Nepal which had previously been brought to the verge of catastrophe by the multiplicity of leadership was again being led on the same path.

However, the Act could not be implemented as proclaimed. Mohan Shamsher took over as the next prime minister in 1948 and he was not keen to implement the Act immediately. Rather he was quick to ban the Nepali National Congress that was posing a challenge to him as an opposition group. On the one hand, there was some resistance from the members of the Rana family in the implementation of this Act. A new party, Nepal Democratic Congress, was formed by some of them. Similarly, a third party, Nepal Praja Panchayat (Nepal People's Council), was also formed after this. The latter was ready to function under the 1948 Act, and was insisting on its implementation. Other pro-change forces were not keen on this document as it did not provide for an elected and accountable executive. Even the jurisdiction of the legislature was 'severely restricted.'[8] Its democratic credential was in question.

It is around this time that B.P. Koirala entered Kathmandu with some of his associates to establish contact with the Praja Panchayat leaders, who were organizing civil disobedience, and got arrested within two months. It was his second arrest. According to Bhuwan Lal Joshi and Leo Rose, 'Koirala was released in June [after six months in prison], and his talk with Mohan Shamsher probably led him to persuade the Nepali National Congress leadership in India to call off the further agitation which had been planned.' In April 1950, Nepali National Congress and Nepal Democratic Congress merged with each other, giving birth to the NC. The new party gave up non-violence and started building a liberation army. Bhuwan Lal Joshi and Leo Rose explain the further strategy:

> The Nepali Congress quickly began preparations for revolution. In its main outlines, their plan called for (1) the abduction of King Tribhuwan, who would be taken from Kathmandu to western Nepal, presumably to Palpa; (2) the establishment of a constitutional government under the King; and (3) a revolt against the Rana government by sections of the Nepal Army. The abduction of King Tribhuvan was to take place in September, during the week-long Indra Jatra festival (held at the old royal palace and traditionally attended in person by the kings of Nepal),

and the revolt in the army was to be sparked by several Rana and Shah family officers.

The change was imminent because a movement was going on in the country, which would eventually culminate in the revolution of 1950-51. The king was on the side of NC. There were external factors as well, which forced the Rana prime minister to act. The revolution was imminent. However, the turn of events was not exactly what was planned by the revolutionaries. They also limited the potential for change and future constitutional development.

Geopolitical environment

The 1940s was a decade of instability in the region. It was the decade of World War II (Beevor, 2014). Nepal, as an independent country, stood with Great Britain during the war. It had no war policy, but wanted to help Britain as its only ally in South Asia. During the Rana regime, Nepal developed a mutual relationship with Britain, which helped not only the Ranas but also the British on terms of mutual non-interference. This also gave stability to the relationship between the two countries. The British standing in World War II mattered most to Nepal as it had no meaningful mutual relationship with any princely state or British territories on the eastern, southern or western side of its border.

The geopolitical environment of the immediate South Asian region further explains the scenario. This region remained a leading civilization for most part of its history, although it faced colonization again and again. The Quit India Movement began in 1942, further weakening support of the British rule in India. Indian independence was getting momentum, but the religious sentiments between Hindu and Muslim leaders overwhelmed Indian politics. In 1945, the newly elected British government led by Clement Attlee wanted to push ahead with its plan to leave India. Early in 1947, he announced that Britain would leave India no later than June 1948. Lord Mountbatten, who was appointed new viceroy for India, concluded that peace could only be achieved if partition was effected.

But the partition of the British Indian Empire into India and Pakistan was a disaster. It led to the creation of the sovereign states of Pakistan (which later split into Pakistan and Bangladesh) and the Union of India on 14–15 August 1947. The civil war raised anti-British feelings to a new height. No undue interest of the Soviet Union and the USA was seen. However, as an imperial country, Britain remained disgruntled with the situation, but it was not able to dictate its terms.

Quick changes were being observed in China as well. Although a leading civilization in the past, outpacing the rest of the world in the arts and sciences, China faced hard times during the nineteenth and early twentieth centuries. It had to face civil unrest, major famines, military defeats and foreign occupation. While the Japanese, who were at war with China, surrendered in 1945, China saw the resumption of the civil war between Chiang Kai-shek's Nationalist Party (Kuomintang) and Mao Zedong's Chinese Communist Party. This brought in not only military deployments and clashes in North China and Northeast China (Manchuria), but also undue interest of the Soviet Union and the USA. This finally resulted in a full-scale civil war, accompanied by severe economic problems and intense internal social and political struggles. By the end of 1949, Chiang was forced to withdraw to Taiwan. China remained disturbed throughout the next few decades.

A weak China worried about Tibet as well. It was not able to assert its power as it would have wanted, in the context of Indian Independence and end of the British Tibet Policy in 1947. At the time when the NC was busy negotiating the terms of change in Nepal, the military campaign of the People's Republic of China (PRC) against a de facto independent Tibet in Chamdo region was being fought. The purpose of the campaign was to capture the Tibetan army in Chamdo, discourage the Lhasa government and exert pressure to get Tibetan representatives to agree to attend negotiations in Beijing and sign terms recognizing Chinese sovereignty over Tibet. Nepal always had a close relation with Tibet, but it had no say in the changing situation there.

The 1940s is the decade of the troubled world. While the global context of World War II and Cold War has been neglected in historical writings about the 1940s Nepal, their significance for the Nepalese situation has not attracted attention. In this scenario, the effort towards political change, though very inspiring, were certainly fragile moves.

Concerns of Nepal in the given geopolitical scenario

The situation that the rulers of Nepal—Ranas in particular—were in, was obviously critical. Realistic of the situation around them, the rulers including the king, certainly wanted to remain an independent nation with its own peculiarities nurtured through centuries of carefully planning its destiny.[9] The relationship with Britain did not work as efficiently as before and there was little time to develop a new balance of power in the region.[10] The Ranas knew that they could not pull on as absolute rulers in the changing scenario anymore, but they were not able to strike meaningful interactions with the opposition forces—the NC and the elite—whom they had marginalized. The country remained in a very deplorable socio-economic and political shape. This limited their manoeuvrability in the political domain.

The revolution led by NC against the Rana system was already at its peak in 1950. There were several anti-Rana activities going on in the kingdom from several quarters. But the NC commanded more visibility in its campaigns than other institutions due to its organizational strength. The people were with the NC, which had agenda for change. By now they believed that the agitation based on non-violence cannot give results anymore. The NC wanted immediate change. The Ranas were fatally divided and had no strategy to cope with the situation by acting on necessary democratization. They were failing to reach out. Notwithstanding its strengths, the Congress was basically based on the other side of the Nepal-India international border. It decreased their security risks vis-à-vis Ranas. They gained certain strength in the organization of the revolution, but the movement created certain vulnerabilities quickly.

As soon as the revolution started gaining momentum, the NC's activities came under the close scrutiny of the Indian government and its security agencies. They were being monitored and were under the strategic control of the Indian establishment. Most of the leaders of the revolution were young people, educated and aspiring, but lacked maturity and strategic understanding of the situation. They had a plan to overthrow the Rana regime and had somewhat of a capacity to organize, but no plan on how to succeed on their own strength and eventually lodge themselves in the seat of power. The king largely stood with the democratic forces, but had little critical understanding of the revolution that was taking place. There was a lacuna in his approach when he encouraged the NC and other opposition forces to fight against the Ranas. He lacked capacity for foreign relations. The movement was in effective control of neither the NC nor the king. They thought of Mahatma Gandhi and his fight for national independence, but had no clue about how the emerging establishment in India must have been thinking about their manoeuvres.

There were some geopolitical issues that should have been properly understood and addressed in the 1950–51 revolution by all the parties involved. The hitherto closed Nepali state being represented by the Rana elite nurtured a mutually beneficial relationship with the British ever since the Rana rule was established. The Ranas maintained an effective alliance with the British, which guaranteed not only safety to them and to their regime but also independence to their land. However, the balance of power created by the Ranas was no longer effective to ensure autonomy in Nepal's dealing with India's emerging establishment. They were under severe stress because the British in India had started to withdraw following the independence movement.

The departure of the British from the subcontinent was an opportunity to regain Nepal's territories lost to the British 131 years ago. The situation of the Ranas became vulnerable to the extent that they were not even able to ask the outgoing British in 1947 to return their territories.[11] The last Rana prime minister, Mohan Shamsher, was already old and fragile for any such manoeuvring. It was impossible for them to speak of anything that could further put them at risk. Aware of such vulnerabilities, he even supplied ten battalions of NA to maintain law and order in India for waging military campaigns against the princely state of Hyderabad in 1949, which was not at all necessary (Joshi and Rose, 1966). The Ranas rather wanted Indian assurances and were ready to not raise any issue in this regard. Meanwhile, the NC, based in India and under the de facto control of Indian authorities, was not able to say anything about this vast territory that had now become liberated and Nepal had the right to claim back.

The negotiating capacity of the Ranas and the NC conducting the movement was not as strong as was necessary. It must be noted here that, after the Indian independence and the partition of India, the original ten Gurkha regiments consisting of the twenty pre-war battalions were split between the British Army and the newly independent Indian Army under a tripartite agreement between Nepal, Britain and India. Six Gurkha regiments (twelve battalions) were transferred to the post-Independence Indian Army, while four regiments (eight battalions) were transferred to the British Army. The NC was a silent spectator in the move. It was not able to call the Gurkhas back to the country, or send all of them under the British command.

It was, therefore, not surprising that, seeing the NC and the imminent challenges, India pressurized Prime Minister Mohan Shamsher to sign the controversial India–Nepal Treaty of Peace and Friendship on 31 July 1950. The treaty allowed free movement of people and goods between the two nations and also contained provisions that affected Nepal in a precarious way.[12] From that day on, India started insisting on open international borders for Indians and eventual planned settlement of Indian immigrants in Nepal.

The NC was mostly silent on the treaty provisions despite the public outcry; as a revolutionary force, it could have warned India to wait until they had taken over the reign of the state.

The NC partnered with the then King Tribhuvan to dethrone the Ranas from the seat of power, rather than the new establishment of the liberated India. Obviously, the idea was to recognize each other in the new Nepali state—king as the traditional and historical legitimacy, and democratic forces as the modernity and voice of sovereign people.

They wanted to move the king to Palpa to run the affairs of the state from there.

However, in a very dramatic turn of events, on 6 November, the king took refuge in the Indian embassy with his whole family, except for his four-year old grandson, Gyanendra. The NC was not consulted either by the king or the Indian embassy. The king was kept in the Indian embassy for four days. The Ranas were not given access to him. What happened during these four days or the nature of negotiation between the king and the Indian authorities has never come out to the public. Whatever the story given,[13] the king, often taken as a gullible Rana prisoner, was outsmarted by the Indian ambassador to Nepal. The move was a big surprise for the NC and the Ranas. At once, the king found himself in the hands of Indian authorities.

There was a sea change in the situation of the NC and its political power. It was no longer the leader of the revolution, but it had formed a revolutionary government under its liberation army and launched armed attacks on the Rana outfits from 10 November. This continued through December. India negotiated the terms of change in Nepal with both the Ranas and the NC separately; the king was not the decision-maker. The proposal for final settlement came from India on 8 December. The king accepted it. After sometime, even the Ranas agreed.

On 10 January, King Tribhuvan issued a public statement in favour of what the prime minister had agreed, appealing to the NC's liberation army to lay down its arms. The settlement reached was: (1) that a CA composed entirely of properly elected members should be brought into being as soon as possible to draw up a constitution for Nepal; (2) pending the meeting of the CA, an interim government which will include persons representative of popular opinion and enjoying public confidence should be established. This body should also include members of the Rana family, one of whom should be prime minister. This body should act as a cabinet on the principle of joint responsibility and should frame its own rules of business; and (3) King Tribhuvan should continue as king in the interest of the realm.

Bhuwan Lal Joshi and Leo Rose say:

> The Nepali Congress, which had not been a participant in the negotiations, at first reacted negatively to the royal appeal. M.P. Koirala characterized the political compromise reached at New Delhi as a 'disillusionment' and observed that no interim arrangement could be acceptable to the people unless there was 'an effective transfer of power to the people of Nepal.' He defined the aims of the Nepali Congress as the liquidation of the feudal regime rather than a compromise with it.

The revolution was over with the so-called 'Delhi compromise.' The king returned to Nepal after that. It created dissension within the revolutionary party, weakening it further and India became a key player in the politics of Nepal.

Succeeding Experiments: Struggles and Failed Efforts

Apparently, the Government of Nepal Act, or Padma Shamsher's Constitution of 1948, was not able to ensure the sanctity of a constitutional system worth its name. It did not either ensure democracy or an accountable government or protect the rights of citizens, as proclaimed. Moreover, the constitution came only as a lollipop, and was not implemented fully and with sincerity. Following the revolution, the Interim Government of Nepal Act 1951 was promulgated by the king after discussion with, and with the approval of, the Council of Ministers. During the eight years of its existence between 1951 and 1959, seven amendments were made to the Interim Act. However, the political situation remained unstable. In 1959, King Mahendra promulgated a new constitution which was modelled on the British parliamentary tradition. It was built on the failures of the past as far as Nepal is concerned, and the British experience, as Ivor Jennings perceived, applied to the Nepalese situation. King Mahendra dissolved the NC-led government that came to be elected under it and imprisoned B.P. Koirala for eight years without charge (Adhikari, 2012). According to B.P.:

> In fact, the Chinese had made a special effort to develop our relationship, and this is why I do not believe that they had a role in our ouster in 1960. The Indians insisted that the Chinese were involved, but I believe they had absolutely no hand in it (Koirala, 2001).

Referring to dealings between him and Nehru, he noted:

> Jawaharlalji had already come here once upon my invitation, before my visit to India. At that time, we had argued over each word of the joint communiqué we had released. Nehru would show me the paper and ask, "So, is this draft okay?" I stayed with him till 11 at night, before we came out with the final text. Our emphasis was on independence, whereas his was on a 'special relationship' between the two countries (Ibid.).

In December 1962, Mahendra announced a new constitution, which created a system more reminiscent of the 104-year Rana rule rather than a move towards democracy as contemplated by the 1959 constitution. It could not sustain itself again. A new democratic constitution was drafted in 1990 by a Constitution Recommendation Commission representing the main opposition parties. Whatever the motive and the role of geopolitics (Sharma, 2000), the systemic changes introduced by the 1990 constitution were largely positive. But the new democracy did not have time to mature with the Maoist movement to establish 'Naulo Janbad' (New people's democracy) beginning in 1996. And on 2 June 2001, the Nepalese woke up to the news of the royal massacre. King Birendra and several other members of the royal family had been assassinated in the Narayanhiti Palace the night before. The dead king's son, Crown Prince Dipendra, was said to have opened fire on his extended family before shooting himself in the head (for different versions, see: Shah, 2011; Gregson, 2002; Shrestha, 2001).

The ceasefire between the Maoists and the government and the commencement of the peace process led to the passage of the interim constitution on 15 January 2007 and adoption by the new interim legislature on 16 January. The constitution prescribed, among others, the procedure for holding CA elections. The elected body was to draft a permanent constitution for Nepal, which was to be promulgated by 28 April 2010. However, the CA postponed promulgation by a year because of a disagreement. Since 29 May 2011, the CA repeatedly extended the Interim Constitution. And on 28 May 2012, the CA was dissolved after it failed to finish the constitution after the latest extension, ending four years of constitution drafting and leaving the country in a legal vacuum. New elections were held on 19 November 2013 to the second CA and political leaders pledged to draft a new constitution by 22 January 2015. However, even this time around, due to continued differences on key issues, including system of governance, judicial system and federation issues such as number, name and areas of the states to be carved, the constitution could not be finalized and promulgated on time.

The question of why the constitution was not completed on time during the first CA is a complex one. Rather than constitution-drafting, the psychology of codifying political slogans, keeping in mind the next elections for political gain was dominant. Parties, rather than forming consensus, were trying to tire out other parties.

There are several factors behind the breakdown of the constitution-drafting process and failure of the constitutional machinery. To begin with, the CA was a huge project. It would have been a very challenging process in any country in the world. The most important reason behind the CA disaster, obviously, was the lack of effective political leadership in the country which could instil belief in the CA and its process. The other problem was the opportunism and shifting positions of the major parties. Democratic and rule of law considerations were never invoked or believed in. While the Maoists generally had a clear position on federalism and related issues, even though they were often at odds with modernity, the NC and CPN (UML) had a poor performance on this score.

The parties also did not trust each other and were unwilling to compromise on certain values. The leaders refused to sit with their internal dissenters and make compromises. The fear of crossing the floor on caste, ethnicity and religious/cultural issues became rampant.

The consensual process that the interim constitution envisaged was not possible without charismatic leadership and a dominant party with a clear agenda for change. Intraparty squabbles were also a major cause of the lack of leadership and vision. Each major party had internal threats to be managed. These parties were helpless and could not tackle these threats. This weakened the leaders' grip on the cadres.

Thirdly, the Assembly was attempting to battle with several difficult constitutional issues. These included fundamental differences between key stakeholders on whether the country should go for single identity or multiple identity provinces, the number of provinces and their boundaries, and failure to discover a compromise solution. There were geopolitical sensibilities as well. The proposed provinces like Jadan, Tamsaling and Sherpa on the northern borders of Nepal were sensitive security issues for China. Similarly, India is said to have its own perceptions of the Tarai. This marred the prospect of federalization of Nepal, a key issue for many. Factionalism along ethnic lines did not help the process.

The fourth problem was the size of the CA. Although it was an inclusive body ensuring diversity and ethnic representation, the leaders were not able to get the best out of it. Only the leading parties played decisive roles. The capacity of many of the members of the CA was not utilized. The size made the House unmanageable at times. It was also difficult to separate the job of the CA from that of the normal parliament. The proceedings of the CA were obstructed several times because the parliament remained unsettled on the issue of formation of government. The CA was not assisted by anything like a constitutional experts commission. This flaw helped create controversial constitutional formulations.

The CA process, as set out in the CA Rules, was underused. While the Reports Study Committee made a serious effort to trace out grey areas in the constitution-drafting process, it was not able to forge a consensus on all issues. This led to the formation of the High-Level Political Taskforce. Subsequently, a Dispute Resolution Sub-committee was formed under the Constitutional Committee of the House. But even these efforts could not solve all contentious issues. The leaders could have taken some risks, but none of the major parties or the Front was able to rethink their positions. Even though there was enough room for that, they feared backlash from their supporters. The idea of buying time, thus, came to be a political tool to deal with the situation.

On a positive note, in the final hours of 27 May, the factions developed along ethnic lines were ready to strike out a compromise in the new constitution, but the House was not called for deliberations. For example, the chairperson of the Janajati caucus, Prithvi Subba Gurung, who was interviewed by Kantipur Television, along with a Tharu activist, Surendra Prasad Chaudhari, and this author as a constitutional expert, acknowledged that they were ready for multiple-identity provinces rather than to let go the prospect of having a new constitution. But neither the speaker nor the government coalition was able to ensure a sitting of the CA session.

The most tragic part of the final day was that the House was not allowed to assemble and think of the future. Only the leaders of the major political parties were meeting outside the CA.

Many people at that time thought that the Khas community dominated politics, bureaucracy, army, and the judiciary was also a problem. The party bosses did not do enough during the constitution-making in 'equalizing' these structural matters. There was in fact enough time to speed up the process of 'de-structuring' the structural limitations and dealing with immediate grievances of the Janajatis, Madhesis and Dalit communities. There has certainly been improvement in terms of the participation of Janajatis and Madhesis in major parties like NC and CPN-UML. But their internal decision-making process is still not inclusive. This has only fanned extremism in posturing and articulating demands by marginalized communities. Furthermore, a certain section of Hindus in Nepal considered the CA II years to be a golden age for Christian missionaries. They were accused of nurturing during these instabilities.

When going back to hard politics, it must not be ignored that the CA would have been successful had the CPN-M tried to find solutions to contentious constitutional issues from the liberal discourse of constitutionalism and the rule of law. Instead, the Maoists tried to mould the concept of constitutionalism to the parameters of the 'People's War' and state-capturing theories. Even though the they were able to get to state power through democratic elections, their transformation to lead the mainstream forces with necessary modifications was not easy. The Maoists even had trouble accepting an individual's right to property, coupled with the right to get reasonable compensation where the state claims eminent domain. They were further unable to accept phrases such as diversity and pluralism in the text of the constitution.

Significantly, the Maoist dialogue on federalism was excessively focused on 'autonomy' and 'self-determination' and paid little attention to creating a balance between self-rule and shared rule. It is the deteriorating political situation emerging from these failures that has led to discussion of reviving the 1990 constitution. There are calls to revert to the system, which included constitutional monarchy, parliamentary system of government and executive prime minister, with just a few additional changes to introduce federal features. This line of thought is an acknowledgement of the failure of the present political actors and the forces which backed them.

None of the parties—revolutionary or conservative—had done any homework on what type of reform they wanted. The Madhesi parties had generally only Madhesi agenda. The media was also not able to generate opinions on necessary reforms. The problem began in 2006 with the 12-point understanding reached between the Seven Party Alliance (SPA) and CPN-M, considered a bizarre agreement. It swiftly changed the conflict between the Maoists and the state into a conflict between the monarchy and democracy. The demand of the king that political parties make their position clear as to the threat to democracy and sovereignty from the Maoists led the parties to shake hands with the insurgents. The erratic behaviour of the monarch and his unwillingness in handing over power to the parties added fuel to the movement.

The 12-point understanding highlighted an inevitable need to implement the concept of full democracy through a forward-looking restructuring of the state. It was destined to resolve the problems related to class, caste, gender and region of all sectors, including political, economic, social and cultural, by bringing the autocratic monarchy to an end and establishing full democracy. In order to pacify the nationalists, it said that the people and their representative political parties were the real guardians of the nation.

The understanding expressed a firm commitment to protect the independence, sovereignty, geographical integrity and the national unity of the country. The obligation to maintain friendly relations based on the principle of peaceful co-existence with all countries of the world, especially with India and China, were also emphasized. They requested all the patriotic people to remain cautious against the false attempt of the king and the monarchists to create confusion by projecting fake nationalism to prolong an autocratic and illegitimate rule. Yet, the 12-point understanding had no explanation for why the 1990 constitution had failed. Nor did it have any vision for the newly formed alliance in the country.

The significance of regional politics cannot, however, be ignored even if one is realistic about internal failings. It must be emphasized that the government never had an appropriate mechanism to engage Nepal's powerful neighbours with their distinct security perceptions. In turn, these neighbours generally had limited faith in the process that had been started. Both the neighbours never came out openly on this issue, never sat with each other and so dealt with the constitution-drafting process in their own way.

Apparently, it was not a transparent process. It would be a serious mistake to ignore the ways in which the power rivalry between China and India in Nepal affected the constitution-drafting process. For instance, many of the internal party struggles were said to have been supported by external actors. All leaders are either pro-India or pro-China. India is high-handed and seeks influence in all aspects of Nepali politics. In response, China attempts to protect its interests in Nepal. The usual Chinese comment has always been that it wants Nepal to take decisions on its own. This is a diplomatic way of saying that India is taking decisions in Nepal and it is not acceptable to the Chinese.

India and China do play a great game of sorts, competing for economic and military influence in Nepal, Bangladesh, Myanmar and Sri Lanka. But these places are generally within the South Asian subcontinent. While Indian authorities pretend that Nepal is a virtual colony, giving it the right to interfere, it is increasingly obvious that China has some major strategic interests in Nepal. The first is to constrain Tibetan refugees south of the Himalayas and halt their anti-China activities as much as possible lest they inflame the already tense situation in Tibet. Secondly, Beijing is interested in degrading India's increasing influence in Nepal and contributing to a China-friendly regime there. As part of that effort, China, in the past few years, has focused on upgrading its engagement policies, including soft diplomatic measures such as people-to-people contacts, cultural relations, student scholarships and increased economic aid. They want Nepal to remain non-aligned and independent. The next pillar of Chinese policy on Nepal is increasing investments in strategically important infrastructure projects such as airports and highways. This is for China's own safety and not just for the purpose of catering to Nepal's development needs. Thus, China is essentially taking the struggle to India's backyard.

The role of international actors behind factionalism around constitutional issues is an obvious secret. It has never been transparent. The situation of the major political parties is precarious. Growing political factionalism, especially on the basis of caste, ethnicity and region, has led to further weakening of the political parties. A strong sense of popular disenchantment with the political class has already been building up with the recurrent delays. These are now likely to explode with the recent developments. There could be further social, economic and political ramifications of the current impasse. The problem with factions is that they are neither broad-based nor driven by clear-cut political principles. The democratic culture is fading. The regional power rivalry is said to be the main factor behind this.

The tensions that developed since the success of the mass movement of 2006 and the ensuing uncertainties have all subsided with the events of 27 May. Even though the country has lost much, people in the political class neither gained nor lost anything out of the constitution-building process. Many people, especially those active in politics, slept late on Monday. The Kathmandu Valley looked deserted on the next day. There were no demonstrations, no mass meetings, and no incidents of violence and skirmishes that characterized the last two months. The Republic Day, 28 May, was also quiet. It appeared as if nothing had happened. The expected dramatic response to 27 May did not appear. For experts and students of constitution-building, Nepal's failed process shows how not to build a constitution. But there are other lessons as well.

Constitution of Nepal 2015: Does It Deal with the Real Problems?

On 28 May 2012, as stated above, the CA I was dissolved after it failed to finish the constitution-drafting process despite repeated extensions, ending four years of constitution-drafting and leaving the country in a constitutional vacuum. There was no provision in the interim constitution for a situation when the CA failed to deliver a new constitution, and could not as well amend it to provide for a fresh election. As a result, new elections were held after a delay of one and a half year to elect a new CA. This was made possible by a special arrangement agreed by the political parties and approved by the President who acted on the power of constitutional presidency.[14]

The political leaders then pledged to draft a new constitution within a year. The new Assembly, also known as CA II, expressly committed that the new constitution would be promulgated on 22 January 2015. Due to continued differences on key issues, including a system of governance, judicial system and federation issues such as number, name and areas of the provinces to be carved, the constitution could not be finalized and promulgated in time. Only on 20 September did it become possible to finalize a new constitution and adopt it.

The new constitution is a document of significant political compromise between the democrats, communists, royalists and ethnocentric forces. It is a compromise between the nationalists, whether democrats or communists, and pro-Indian or pro-Chinese forces. At

CA II, a total of 507 votes were cast in favour of the Constitution Bill, while twenty-five votes went against it. The three major political parties of Nepal, viz. NC, CPN-UML and CPN-M (now UCPN-Maoist), and a majority of the fringe parties voted in support of the Bill at a meeting of the CA. Those voting against the Bill were members of Rastriya Prajatantra Party-Nepal (RPP-N). Some Tarai-based parties boycotted the constitution finalization and adoption process. Of the total 598 CA members, 532 were present at the meeting. About sixty members from the Madhesi and Janajati communities also boycotted the voting.

The first President under the republican polity, Ram Baran Yadav, announced the promulgation of the Constitution of Nepal 2015 at a special meeting of the CA on 20 September 2015. He announced the commencement of the new constitution endorsed by the CA and as authenticated by CA Chairperson Subash Chandra Nembang. With this, It has become the seventh constitution to have been adopted by Nepal in the last sixty years and the first by democratically elected representatives. Just four months later, articles 42 and 286 were amended according to the Constitution of Nepal (First Amendment) Act 2016, making some minor changes on a couple of provisions as demanded by some Madhesi parties.

The new constitution has thirty-five parts, 308 articles, nine annexes, which aim to achieve the 'preambular' pledges by way of necessary norms and values, and institutions and procedures. At the outset, it must be emphasized here that the constitution builds on the anatomy of the past and has many new and progressive provisions. It provides the Fundamental Rights of Nepalese citizens, the Directive Principles, Policies and Obligations of the State, the principal organs of the government, the scheme of separation of powers, different independent constitutional functionaries outside the control of the Executive, political parties, Emergency power, constitutional amendment, etc. as the past constitutions of Nepal, with a separate chapter on each. New chapters that appear in the constitution are mostly on restructuring of the state, distribution of state power and three-tier federal arrangements, which are new to Nepal's constitutional experiment. Even the chapters which have been inherited have been adjusted, modified and refurbished. For example, independent constitutional functionaries of some types and modalities have been existing in Nepal ever since the country ushered in modern democracy. The new constitution has, however, left all the past editions behind in terms of the number of constitutional bodies created and their expected role.

The new constitution is somewhat a lengthy document, and there are several reasons behind it. The first and foremost is obviously political. There was no party in the House which could command a simple majority, not to mention a two-thirds majority by itself that the Article required for the passage of the draft. All political forces, especially the largest few among those in the House, struggled with internal factions. The efforts of the leaders were aimed at striking a compromise document that did not offend any. Efforts were also made to dispel distrusts between each other and persuade women, Dalits, indigenous people, Madhesis, Tharus, Muslims and other minorities. Each of these groups wanted their identity protected, visibility ensured and rights guaranteed. A lengthy document was thus inevitable.

Apart from the fundamentals, the framers of the constitution tried to cover many details that could have been conveniently left to the future government and the parliamentary legislative process. However, due to the distrust between the major parties, they discussed, negotiated and settled everything that they considered important, offering it a rightful space in the constitution. These compromises have been unnecessarily elaborated in the constitutional corpus. For example, all issues relating to the right to equality could have been addressed by one article without being scattered in different articles of the constitution. Similarly, one human rights and inclusion commission could have catered to all the interests that wanted different commissions created by this constitution. Many matters, like Directive Principles, Policy and Obligations of the State, which were not very contentious, were given significant space to show that the future State will remain more committed to the people than before. These matters have been dealt with in the constitution extensively. They should better have been addressed in ordinary laws.

As such, the constitution does not seem to be the basic law, which usually only sketches the basic principles of the statehood and concerns on the fundamental rights and limitations of power. It includes laws on citizenship, municipality and, to a certain extent, even the civil service. It would have been better if the constitution had been limited to regulate the principles, leaving the details for ordinary legislations because it is easier to reform these. The details of the legislation on citizenship do not require constitutional guarantee. All these features could not be avoided in the new constitution. The framers could not dispense with the legacy of the past constitutions which carried forward these features.

The new constitution is not the constitution of a unitary state. It is not only a constitution of the federation but also of all provinces and even the fundamental law of municipalities, village assemblies and special autonomous structures that the constitution provides for. One may question, if, under the flag of decentralization, would it not have been better if the constitution had not laid down some basic principles for the internal structure of the provinces, leaving the more detailed shaping of the statute to the provinces, thereby strengthening their autonomy, or to a federal law which could be amended to the requirements. But this is here already.

Salient features of the Preamble of the new constitution:

1 The constitution has been adopted and proclaimed in the name of 'We, the people of Nepal, in exercise of the sovereign powers inherent in us.'
2 The people of Nepal have the sovereign power and the right to autonomy and self-rule, by maintaining Nepal's independence, sovereignty, geographical integrity, national unity, freedom and dignity.
3 It recalls historic people's movements and armed struggles and the sacrifices made by the people for national interest, democracy and progressive change.
4 It recognizes the martyrs, the disappeared and the victims.

5 It declares ending all forms of discrimination and oppression created by the feudal, autocratic, centralized and unitary system of government in the past.

6 It notes its commitment to Nepal's multi-ethnic, multilingual, multicultural and diverse geographical specificities and end of discriminations on grounds of class, ethnicity, region, language, religion and gender, including all forms of racial untouchability, in order to protect and promote unity in diversity, social and cultural solidarity, tolerance and harmonious attitudes.

7 It also expresses the determination to create an egalitarian society on the basis of the principles of proportional inclusion and participation, to ensure equitable economy, prosperity and social justice.

8 There is a commitment to create bases of socialism by adopting democratic norms and values, including people's competitive multi-party democratic governance system, civil liberty, fundamental rights, human rights, adult franchise, periodic elections, complete press freedom and an independent, impartial and competent judiciary, and the concept of rule of law.

The new constitution has introduced many changes. Apart from federalism, which is a new feature in Nepal, it tries to make the state inclusive and the democratic system more participative than before. It tries to further consolidate people's competitive multiparty democratic governance system, civil liberty, fundamental rights, human rights, adult franchise, periodic elections, complete press freedom, an independent, impartial and competent judiciary and the concept of the rule of law. The state embraces multi-ethnic, multilingual and multicultural characteristics and policies based on diverse geographical specifics. It ends discrimination relating to class, caste, region, language, religion and gender, including all forms of racial untouchability, in order to protect and promote unity in diversity, social and cultural solidarity, tolerance and harmonious attitudes. These are all lofty principles. It is in the implementation of the constitution that the process of change will depend. This is not a process that can be accomplished very quickly. Obviously, there is a long way to go.

Issues and Options for the Political Class

The constitutional politics in Nepal has strong geopolitical dimensions. At the top of the world, lying on the Himalayas and the mountains, Nepal has been a place which is important for both China and India, the two rising great neighbours, which are jealous of each other. Both these countries take an expansive view of their roles and responsibilities in their respective geographic neighbourhoods. Both these countries consider pressing interests at stake in Nepal.

An average Nepali of the hill or Himalayan origin has strong feelings against Indian hegemony of all sorts in Nepal. The effort of all Indian governments in the past has been to pressurize Nepal to make its market and territory open to Indians. It also wants monopoly or significant control on harnessing Nepal's natural resources, including water, hydropower potentials and other resources. It has forced Nepal to keep its international borders open. Additionally, India has also pressurized the Nepal government to periodically offer Nepalese citizenship to fresh immigrants from India. The Nepalese consider the population influx as dangerous to their sense of nationalism. India has forced change of government and regimes to get things done. This is also one of the main reasons for instability in Nepal.

During the constitution-drafting process, Indian Home Minister Rajnath Singh, who visited an Indian township along the Nepal-India international border, was quoted as saying that ten million Indians live in Nepal, and India is concerned about their stake in constitution-drafting. The report states:

> Although the Madhesi problem is an internal issue of Nepal, the Indian government will protect the interests of the *one crore* [ten million] Indians living there,' Singh said, during his visit to Maharajganj on Sunday. He was there to unveil an outpost of the Sashastra Seema Bal (SSB) and lay the foundation stone of

> its proposed new building. The home minister's visit is being considered crucial at this point of time because the entire Tarai area along the UP-Nepal border is caught in violent clashes between the natives and Madhesis. Madhesis are Indians who had migrated to Nepal years ago. While many have received Nepali citizenship, majority of them are still without a nationality. The Madhesis have alleged that several political and militant organisations have been targeting them and inflicting atrocities to force them to leave Nepal. However, the BJP has been supporting the Madhesis for long.
>
> Yogi Adityanath, BJP, Chief Minister of UP (as of April 2018) and Mahant of Gorakhnath Temple, has often been alleged for providing logistic support to the movement of the Madhesis against the Nepal government.
>
> The southern region of Nepal, running along UP, Bihar and West Bengal [provinces of India], is known as Madhes. Madhesis, who constitute 30 per cent of Nepal's population live in the Tarai area. But 40 per cent of these Madhesis still don't have a citizenship or the right to vote. They claim that the Nepal government deliberately ignores the Tarai area to relegate them (Srivastava, 2015).

The Chinese are not so keen to speak on Nepal's internal issues. They have been vocal about its independent decision-making in its affairs. They are concerned about the security of Tibet and don't want to see anything in Nepal that affects the stability of Tibet. They want peace in Nepal for peace in the Tibetan region. China is desirous to invest in Nepal and work in all business sectors to the mutual advantage of both countries. The Belt and Road Initiative of President Xi Jinping is lucrative for Nepal as well as the rest of South Asia (Wei, et al., 2016).

In recent years, they have even shown willingness towards tripartite arrangements among Nepal, India and China in order to invest in Nepal. China is clear about the historical role of Nepal as a transit country between India and China, and looks upon Nepal as the gateway to entire South Asia. Yet, they are jealous of the extended role of India or any other country in Nepal. Obviously, the Chinese are as alert in Nepal as in any of the sixteen countries that surround them, and believe the West is trying to pursue a policy of containment. As such, China also has vestiges of power in Nepal. Apparently, India competes with China in Nepal in all sectors.

Over the years, Nepal has tried to maintain a relation of confidence with both its neighbours. These neighbours have fought with each other in the past. While they both understand Nepal's situation, each of them is concerned about its narrow national interest. On the part of Nepal, it is clear about its difficult geographical location. As an India-locked country from three sides, it has faced consistent encroachment by India of its lands. There is increasing interference as well. It has created problems in Nepal's access to the sea and it has also managed to be the monopoly supplier of fossil fuel and cooking gas in Nepal. Needless to say, the Indian government is looked on cautiously in Nepal.

Unlike India, China is taken in Nepal as a friendly, caring country. There are no outstanding controversies. But the cooperation between China (Tibet) and Nepal faces geographical barriers, Indian intimidation and other limitations. However, the situation is expected to improve in a couple of years.[15]

India and China are in competition in many economic sectors. As of now, China is considered more competitive than India. Both neighbours operate with their own preoccupations about their security interests vis-à-vis Nepal Himalayas, water resources, hydropower, minerals and military use. There can be real issues or perceived clash and miscalculations when two adjacent powers are doing things in waters, skies and territories where they both have pressing interests at stake. India surely reckons that it is losing influence to China everywhere. Its weak civilian political elite have a clear anti-Chinese tilt. The military establishment has become stronger but nurtures the same feeling. As far as China is concerned, though it has done remarkably well, the process of democratization back home has a long way to go. India has the advantage of tested democracy. But both these countries have a strong military point of view. Until the Chinese and Indian powers mature, the possibilities of Nepal flourishing will remain limited, unless it shows exceptional ability to outsmart both. The latter scenario is fairly unlikely.

When asked how China sees the promulgation of the new constitution of Nepal, the Chinese Foreign Ministry spokesperson, Hong Lei, said at a regular press conference on 21 September 2015: 'China sincerely congratulates Nepal on promulgating the new Constitution, and hopes to see that Nepal can take this opportunity to realize national unity, stability and development. China attaches great importance to relations with Nepal, and stands ready to further deepen bilateral friendly cooperation and provide assistance for Nepal's economic and social development to the best of her capacity.' (Lei, 2015)

And in December 2015, Chinese Foreign Minister Wang Yi, who was visited by Nepal Foreign Minister Kamal Thapa, said that, 'China has all along believed that countries, irrespective of their size, are equal. China and Nepal have always treated each other sincerely and as equals. We hope that the same policy and practices will also be adopted by India.' He added that, 'A stable Nepal enjoying development fully serves the interests of both China and India. So, in other words, I would like to say that Nepal is a great place for mutually beneficial cooperation between China and India, not a boxing arena for China and India.' (PTI, 2015)

The adoption of Nepal's constitution, however, triggered alarm in India (Rawat, 2015). No sooner was the constitution promulgated that India came out expressing its displeasure about its content. New Delhi had reportedly asked Nepal to make as many as seven amendments to address the concerns of the Madhesis. The *Indian Express* published this report with much emphasis. These amendments, the report suggests, were conveyed to Nepal's leadership through official channels. However, the Indian Ministry of External Affairs denied handing a list of amendments. In an official statement, it said: 'This article is incorrect. Government of India has not handed over any list of specific constitutional amendments or changes to the GoN. We continue to urge that issues on which there are differences should be resolved through dialogue in an atmosphere free from violence, and institutionalized in a manner that would enable broad-based ownership and acceptance.' The newspaper maintained that it 'has confirmed from its sources that these amendments/changes were communicated by New Delhi to Kathmandu. It stands by the report.'

A critique in India states: 'A review of India's response to the constitution supports the *Indian Express.* Indian Foreign Secretary S. Jaishankar was sent on a diplomatic mission to ensure that India's concerns are amicably addressed. His visit was a failure. Immediately after Nepal adopted the 2072 (2015) Constitution; India recalled its ambassador in Kathmandu for a briefing. New Delhi expressed its displeasure without much impact.'

Nepali disapproval of India's reaction intensified when New Delhi imposed an unofficial blockade of critical goods and supplies across its border with Nepal. India claimed that it was not a 'blockade.' Rather, to India, the problem was created by the Madhesis on the part of Nepal affecting the movement of goods. To the Nepalese, this was the third time a blockade had been imposed by India in an attempt to control them.

The impact of the blockade was enormous on the economy of Nepal and post-earthquake reconstruction. To the common Nepalese, however, it was also an opportunity to understand India and its agenda. As an Indian critique said, 'India's reaction to the crisis may actually have had the ironic effect of uniting Nepalese interest groups that traditionally disagree with one another. The NC, CPN-UML and UCPN-M, who together represent a majority in Nepal's CA, have come together to oppose New Delhi's approach. India's move to support Nepal's disenfranchised Madhesis has cost it goodwill and political capital with the country's traditional elites and power-brokers.' (Ibid).

Prime Minister K.P. Oli (who was also the Prime Minister in 2016) paid a week-long visit to China to cure the problems of an ailing nation. A 10-point agreement was signed between the two nations, including a trade and transit treaty, which Nepal needed desperately. This treaty has ensured Nepal's right to access sea as a landlocked nation and transit freedom through the Chinese land. The prime minister also talked with the Chinese to expand land and air connectivity and improve land transport infrastructure.

Madhesi Remarks on the Constitution

The 2015 Constitution was welcomed by the majority of the people of Nepal. However, some aspiring ethnic Madhesi (plains based) parties with regional roots were not happy with both the process of finalizing the constitution and its final contents. Even on the first anniversary of its promulgation, protests were going on in the country.

The main comments of the Madhesi parties have been mainly attributed to the issue of delineation of provinces, the provision of carving out constituencies on the basis of geography and population, representation of provinces both in the Lower House and in the Upper House of the federal parliament, the theme of proportional representation and certain issues related to new citizenship provisions.

As their significant demand, these parties want the entire Tarai region, extending from the east to the west, to be divided into only two provinces. The initial proposal, which has now been taken back, was to carve one state from Parsa to Saptari and another extending from Nawalparasi to Bardiya. Now, there is a province from Parsa district to Saptari district. At that time, there were three disputed districts in the east and two in the west. Now, all the districts that lie to the west of Nawalparasi are disputed because they have been mixed with hill districts. In the east, Jhapa, Morang and Sunsari districts are also part of a province that includes the hills. The Madhesi parties want to carve only two provinces in the plains.

Thus, the Constitution of Nepal (First Amendment Act) tried to address some issues, including the issue of proportional inclusion. The government also registered at the Legislature-Parliament the second amendment bill dealing with redrawing of provincial boundaries, recognition of languages, citizenship and representation in the National Assembly in the new constitution (*China Daily*, 2016).

According to the proposed amendment, the demarcation of provinces 4 and 5 will be changed by swapping some plains districts with the hills. New languages will be given the national language status and included in the constitution's schedule in line with the report given by the Language Commission formed by the government. According to the amendment proposal, any foreign woman married to a Nepalese male can obtain naturalized citizenship after she starts abandoning her citizenship of the country of her birth. To make the Upper House of Parliament more inclusive, the proposal has sought representation of one member each from Dalit, woman and marginalized community categories and the remaining five to be elected on the basis of the population of each province, eight members from each of the proposed seven provinces. Meanwhile, the CPN-UML, the then main opposition party, warned to launch massive protests against the constitution amendment proposals tabled by the government. It thought the proposed amendment would jeopardize the country's territorial integrity and sovereignty and invite communal violence in the country. Ultimately, the amendment failed to secure the required number of votes in the parliament. It would be interesting to see how the CPN-UML which is in power at present (April 2018) would take the proposals it rejected and whether or not come back with the same type of amendment to satisfy the demands of the Madhesis.

There is a widespread realization in Nepal that India has been using Madhesi parties to further its strategic interests in Nepal.

Recommendations: 'Hope for the Best, but Prepare for the Worst'

Nepal is in a difficult situation (Riaz and Basu, 2007). The people want genuine democracy that protects the national interests of Nepal as well as their feeling of nationalism. Its experiment with the succeeding constitutions shows that the process of democratization is only an alibi to create instability and space for India and Indian interests. There is every possibility that the new constitution will also fail.

There are possibilities for democracy and prosperity in Nepal. It is possible to make the constitution matter. For this to happen, Nepal's processes must be autonomous, especially vis-à-vis India. If relations between the countries are to improve, it must be changed from an oppressor-oppressed one to one based on sovereign equality and principles of justice. As a point of departure, India needs to understand Nepal as an independent and equal country, with its own national ego and plans and priorities and not a client country. This understanding must follow with certain other actions (Adhikari, 2016):

- The Nepal-India international border, which India has forced Nepal to keep open, needs to be closed so that there is no free and unrestricted movement across the border for either the Nepalese or Indians. Nepal wants this country to remain a home of Nepalese people. An open border is certainly a lasting threat.
- Immigration services need to be established in place so that both the neighbouring countries are better able to record and limit the flow of populations across the border.
- All immigrant Indians working in Nepal (who do not have citizenship certificates yet), should immediately attain time-bound work permits according to the law so that the GoN is well-aware of the number of Indians working here and create adept policies to control that number as is necessary. All Indians who do not register but serve as labourers, vendors, merchants, professionals and ghost professionals in major industries and trading groups need to return to India in a given period. There should be an end to unauthorized work to Indians in Nepal under Indian pressure. Of course, the same policy should apply to the Nepalese working in India.
- Stemming from this point, the GoN should encourage Nepalese working abroad (one could call them Nepalese economic refugees) in countries in the Arab world, Malaysia and Singapore, among others, to return and fill these jobs so that the priceless labour of Nepal is rightfully utilized within its own borders. As a good neighbour, India should help to rehabilitate them as they had to escape due to lack of opportunities within their own country owing to competition by Indians.
- The Indian government should offer citizenship certificates to all Nepalese who have been working and living in India the same way

that the Nepali government was forced to do for Indian immigrants and working people in Nepal during the last few decades. The natives of Nepal know how even the constitution was sidelined to allow for easy naturalization (claiming a mostly fake theory that they were Madhesis of Nepal who were denied citizenship). This is so that the rights and responsibilities of the Nepalese in India are protected, and they are granted the same sort of privileges and attention that were afforded to the Indians in Nepal.

- It is never possible to build mutual trust when many of the past bilateral treaties signed between these neighbouring countries benefit one at the cost of the other. Coexistence and mutual benefits are simple concepts. The treaties need to be revisited, rectified and implemented as soon as possible.
- India should not try to involve with the people who already have Nepalese citizenship as people of India. This will never help create an integrated Nepali identity.
- The Nepalese expect India to withdraw from Kalapani in western Nepal and return all encroached lands along the Nepal–India international border.

In Conclusion

The points mentioned above are not new suggestions. The Harka Gurung Report on the Internal and International Migrations in Nepal (1983) is still the best document to rely on to leave Nepal for the Nepalese and improve the situation here. Nepal needs to prosper, and prosper with its own peculiarities as a people in terms of their age-old demography, sociopolitical institutions, the Himalayan identity, religion, culture and economic potentials. What comes as new development in recent years is the sharp increase in the effort to change Nepal in an 'un-Nepali' way, and interference in making or unmaking the government, nomination of political appointees, transfer and promotion of senior employees and even charging somebody with corruption. Along with the sufferings as above, this all means that Nepal cannot even function within a democracy and the system of the rule of law.

Currently, India pretends that Nepal is under its security umbrella. It is unwarranted. Nepal is certainly struggling with natural disasters, increase in poverty, environmental degradation, and law and order challenges. But they are Nepal's problems. The Himals, mountains, rivers and streams in Nepal have been gifts of god. Nepal did not create them to bring rains or create flood, or other natural calamities in the downstream countries. They should not be taken as a security issue for Indian interference. Nepal is a Nepalese responsibility.

By no means should India compromise its security; indeed, it should tighten its border security, build fences, mobilize army and police and install facilities of whatever type that befits its security needs along its side of the international border or anywhere in its territory. It may also do many other things to assure its citizens that they are protected. Nepal should not want India relaxing its security for any purpose. What it does not mean is for India to meddle in Nepal's internal affairs through actions in the government or attempts to influence its constitutional functionaries, or act for Nepal in its territory under its security perception. This will never be acceptable. The educated Nepalese will continue to take it as security threat for their country.

Nepal has remained overwhelmed with neigbourhood demands and pressures, and has been turned into a laboratory (Sharma, 2016). It has never had enough time and resources to attend to its own constitutions and the people having legitimate claims on the government. The political controversies will never settle in Nepal unless there is genuine national reconciliation between all Nepalese stakeholders keeping geopolitics out. A constitution alone is not enough for this purpose. This is not possible until there is an external game plan to keep Nepal under control, or use it against one country or the other. All alternative scenarios will eventually lead to extremism in Nepal, sooner or later, that may not be in the interest of any of the stakeholders. Preparing for the worst is, therefore, also a compulsion.

***Bipin Adhikari** is a constitutional law expert and Dean, School of Law, Kathmandu University.*

Bibliography

Government and Allied Publications

Constitution and Laws

The Government of Nepal Act, 1948.

Other Publications

Adhikari, B. 2012. *Nepal Constituent Assembly Impasse: Comments on a Failed Process* 6. Kathmandu: Nepal Consulting Lawyers Inc.

Adhikari, B. 2013. *Constitutional Crisis in Nepal: Ensuring democratic governance during the transition to a new constituent assembly.* Kathmandu: Nepal Constitution Foundation.

Adhikari, B. 1997. 'Nation Building Sub-cultures and Constitutionalism: Nepal's Case'. In: *Journal of Behavioral and Social Sciences, Special Issue on Nation Building and Sub-Cultures III: Asian Countries' Cases,* 1997, No. 1, Research Institute of Social Sciences, Tokai University, Japan.

Beevor, A. 2014. *The Second World War.* New York: Little, Brown and Company.

Dhungel, R.K. 2012. 'Pandhra Salko Sambidhan Mashyaudaka Gopya Patra haruko Khulasa' (Disclosure of Confidential Papers related to Draft Constitution 2015 (1959), In: *HURON Annual Publication,* 2012, No. 15.

Dhungel, S., et al. 1998. *Commentary on the Nepalese Constitution.* Kathmandu: DeLF & Lawyers, Inc.

Duff, A. 2015. *Sikkim: Requiem for a Himalayan* Kingdom. Gurgaon: Random House.

Fairfield, P. 2008. *Why Democracy.* Albany: State University of New York Press.

Flinders, M. 2012. *Defining Politics: Why democracy matters in the twenty-first century.* Oxford: Oxford University Press.

Goldstein, M.C. 2010. *The Snow Lion and the Dragon: China, Tibet, and the Dalai Lama.* Berkeley: University of California Press.

Gregson, J. 2002. *Massacre at the Palace: The Doomed Royal Dynasty of Nepal.* New York: Talk Miramax Books.

Gurung, H., et al. 1984. *The Main Report of Nepal's Internal and External*

Migration. Kathmandu: Migration Study Task Force/National Population Commission.

Joshi, B.L. and Rose, L.E. 1966. *Democratic Innovations in Nepal: A Case Study of Political Acculturation.* Berkeley and Los Angeles: University of California Press.

Khanal, G. 2016. *Bhurajniti: Nepali Rajnitima Bharat ra Chin (Geopolitics: India and China in Nepal's Politics).* Kathmandu: Phoenix Books.

Koirala, B.P. '2007 Salko Shahi Ghosanako Pristhabhumi (Background of Royal Declaration of 2007 (1951)'. In: *Rajtantra ra Loktantra*, 1974, Vol. 1. Baranasi: Samajbadi Bidya Sadan.

Koirala, B.P. 2006. *Raja, Rastriyata ra Rajniti (King, Nationalism and Politics).* Kathmandu: Jagadamba Prakashan.

Koirala, B.P. 'Hamro Dhyeya (Our Intention)'. In: Giri, P. (Ed.), *Bishweshwar Prasad Koirala: Rajnaitik Abhilekh (Bishweshwar Koirala Political Archive).* Kathmandu: Bidyarthi Pustak Bhandar.

Koirala, B.P. 'Bishesh Adalatama Diyeko Bayan (Statement given to Special Court)'. In: *Rastriya Ekatako Avhan.* Kathmandu: Nepali Congress.

Koirala, B.P. 2001. *Atmabrittanta: Late Life Recollections.* Lalitpur: Himal Books.

Lal, R. 2006. *Understanding China and India: Security Implications for the United States and the World.* Westport: Praeger Security International.

Lim T.W., et al. (Eds.) 2016. *China's One Belt and One Road Initiative.* London: Imperial College Press.

Mathema, D.B. 2016. *Anubhava ra Anubhuti: Jivan Yatraka Aitihasik Mod [Experience and Perceptions: Historical Turns on the Journey of Life].* Kathmandu: Daya Foundation.

Meredith, R. 2008. *The Elephant and the Dragon: The Rise of India and China and What It Means for All of Us.* New York: W.W. Norton & Company, Inc.

Oldfield, H.A. 1880. *Sketches from Nipal.* Vol. 1 and II. London: W.H. Allen and Co.

Rawat, M. 'Nepal's Constitution and Lessons for India'. *The Diplomat*, 7 October 2015.

Riaz, A. and Basu, S. 2007. *Paradise Lost?: State Failure in Nepal.* New York: Lexington Books.

Shah, B.K. 2011. *Maile Dekheko Durbar: Sainik Sachib ko Sansmaran (Palace Observed: Reminiscence of a Military Secretary)* Kathmandu: Yeti Publications.

Sharma, G.R. 'Nepal ko Sambaidhanik Paddhati: Abhyas ra Parimarjan' (Constitutional System of Nepal: Experiment and Improvement), *Kanoon*

Bi-Monthly, 2000, No. 22.

Sharma, S. *Prayogshala [The Laboratory]*. Kathmandu: FinePrint.

Shrestha, A.M. *The Dreadful Night: Carnage at Nepalese Royal Palace.* Kathmandu: Ekata Books.

Singh, Tope Bahadur. 2070/71. *Nepalko Sambidhan ra Sambaidhanik Kanoon [The Constitution of Nepal and Constitutional Law].* Kathmandu: Indra Rajya Laxmi Malla.

Thapa, D. and Sijapati, B. 2005. *A Kingdom Under Siege: Nepal's Maoist Insurgency 1996–2004.* London: Zed Books.

Upadhya, S. 2008. *The Raj Lives: India in Nepal.* New Delhi: Vitasta.

Uprety, B.R. 2004. *The Price of Neglect.* Kathmandu: Bhrikuti Academic Publications.

Wariko, K. (Ed.). 2009. *Himalayan Frontiers of India: Historical, Geo-political and Strategic Perspectives.* New York: Routledge.

Articles, Newspapers and Websites

Articles and comments

Panda, A. 'India, China React to Nepal's Constitutional Crisis'. *The Diplomat*, 8 October 2015, http://thediplomat.com/2015/10/india-china-react-to-nepals-constitutional-crisis/

Athwal, A. 2008. China–India Relations. London: Routledge.

Newspapers

Brown, S. and Felbab-Brown, V. 'Nepal, on the Brink of Collapse', *International Herald Tribune,* 5 June 2012.

Sharma, G.R. 'The Middle Way the Only Way' (Interview). *New Spotlight,* 4 May 2012. (Excerpts of 28 October 2005 interview taken)

Websites

http://www.china-embassy.org/eng/fyrth/t1298582.htm

http://www.chinadailyasia.com/asia/2016-11/30/content_15534318.html; accessed on 12 January 2017.

Foreign Ministry Spokesperson Hong Lei's Regular Press Conference on 21 September 2015; http://www.china-embassy.org/eng/fyrth/t1298582.htm

http://thehimalayantimes.com/nepal/nepal-must-not-be-a-boxing-arena-for-india-china/:

Press Trust of India. 'Nepal not to be a boxing arena for India, China'. *The Himalayan,* 27 December 2015. Also available at: Mukesh Rawat, 'Nepal's

Constitution and Lessons for India.' *The Diplomat*, 7 October 2015.
'PM Oli returns home from China.' *The Himalayan*, 27 March 2016; http://thehimalayantimes.com/kathmandu/kp-sharma-oli-returns-home-china/ :
'Nepal government tables second amendment to constitution.' *China Daily*, 30 November 2016; http://www.chinadailyasia.com/asia/2016-11/30/content_15534318.html
http://www.bipinadhikari.com.np/notes_ind.php?id=107; accessed on 12 January 2017.

Endnotes

1 This article is a part of the bigger research project that the author intends to undertake on geopolitical influences on the constitutional experiment of Nepal.

2 While things continue to happen, the winner in the process remains India, Nepal's southern neighbour. Referring to the plight of Nepal following 2006, a Nepalese analyst noted: 'The rapidity of political developments in Nepal since April 2006 has, among other things, reinforced the traditional centrality of India in the affairs of its tiny northern neighbour. For the third time in fifty-six years, New Delhi almost singlehandedly led the initiatives to pull the Himalayan nation from the precipice.' (See Upadhya, S. 2008. *The Raj Lives: India in Nepal*. New Delhi: Vitasta, Preface.)

3 See Surya Dhungel, Bipin Adhikari, et al., *Commentary on the Nepalese Constitution*, (arguing that 'from ancient times, therefore, right up to the revolution of 1951, the homegrown, indigenous and autochthonous dharmik arrangements and common laws of society encapsulated the political state').

4 For the basic features of the Act, see Tope Bahadur Singh, *Nepalko Samvidhan ra Samvaidhanik Kanoon* (Kathmandu: Indira Rajya Laxmi Malla, 2027 BS)

5 Section 3 of the Government of Nepal Act 2004 (1948) stated: 'The rule of succession relating to succession of throne of His Majesty the King and His Highness Sri 3 Maharaja shall continue as hereto force in accordance with the laws, customs and usages on their behalf and shall, for all time, be inalienable and unchangeable.'

6 Section 6. Section 11(a) of the Government of Nepal Act, 2004 (1948) defined the ambit of executive power as follows: 'The Council of Ministers shall perform all executive business of the State. It shall, however, be its

special responsibility to give particular attention to all matters not falling within the purview of the legislature, to lay down the general policy of the State, to scrutinize the budget of the various departments, to give final consideration to the Government bills to be placed before the legislature, and to bring about-coordination and cooperation.'

7 Section 22. Section 13 of the Government of Nepal Act 2004 (1948) envisaged a committee system in the Assembly. It stated: 'His Highness [Prime Minister] shall set up different Governance Committees among the members of the Legislative Assembly to help and give advice to the various departments of the executive and associated thereby with the intention that to be functioned of government policy also with opinion of the Legislative Assembly.'

8 According to Bhuwan Lal Joshi and Leo E. Rose, '[i]t could not discuss the list of expenditures charged upon the revenues of the state, nor could it consider a demand for a grant without the permission of the Prime Minister... The Prime Minister reserved to himself discretionary powers to stop or veto any legislation contemplated or approved by the legislature if he deemed it harmful to the public welfare. All bills approved by the legislature were to be enacted into law only after the Prime Minister's seal had been affixed' (See: Joshi, B.L. and Rose, L.E., *Democratic Innovations in Nepal: A Case Study of Political Acculturation.* Berkeley and Los Angeles: University California Press. 1966)

9 In his book, Henry Kissinger recognizes this fact in the following words: 'For centuries, Nepal skillfully balanced its diplomatic relation between the ruling dynasties in China and those in India—offering letters and gifts that were interpreted as tribute in China but recorded as evidence of equal exchanges in Nepal, then holding out special ties with China as a guarantee of Nepal's independence vis-à-vis India.' (See Kissinger, H. 2014. *World Order: Reflections on the Character of Nations and the Course of History.* London: Allen Lain).

10 At the time of Indian independence in 1947, the British India was divided into two sets of territories: one under direct British rule and the other under the suzerainty of the British Crown, with control over their internal affairs remaining in the hands of their hereditary rulers. In addition, there were several colonial enclaves controlled by France and Portugal.

11 The war ended with the signing of the Treaty of Sugauli in 1816, which ceded around a third of Nepal's territory to the British. Nepal came to be confined between the Mechi River in the east and the Mahakali River in the west and lost Sikkim (including Darjeeling), the territories of Kumaon

and Garhwal and Western Tarai. The Tarai lands, however, were returned to the kingdom later (See: Oldfield, H.A. 1880. *Sketches from Nipal,* Vol I and II. London: W.H. Allen and Co.)

12 Some of such provisions are as follows: Article 2 [The two Governments hereby undertake to inform each other of any serious friction or misunderstanding with any neighboring State likely to cause any breach in the friendly relations subsisting between the two Governments]. Article 5 The Government of Nepal shall be free to import, from or through the territory of India, arms, ammunition or warlike material and equipment necessary for the security of Nepal. The procedure for giving effect to this arrangement shall be worked out by the two Governments acting in consultation]. Article 6 [Each Government undertakes, in token of the neighbourly friendship between India and Nepal, to give to the nationals of the other, in its territory, national treatment with regard to participation in industrial and economic development of such territory and to the grant of concessions and contracts, relating to such development]. Article 7 [The Governments of India and Nepal agree to grant, on a reciprocal basis, to the nationals of one country in the territories of the other the same privileges in the matter of residence, ownership of property, participation in trade and commerce, movement and other privileges of a similar nature].

13 The story given is as follows: 'On the morning of 6 November, King Tribhuwan and his entire family, with the exception of his four-year old grandson Gyanendra, departed by automobile from the Royal Palace on what was ostensibly a hunting trip. The Indian Embassy was on the road the royal party was supposed to follow. On reaching the gates of the Embassy, the King and his sons, who were all driving their own cars, suddenly swung through the gates and into the grounds, to the surprise and consternation of those Rana guards who had not been apprised of the King's plan. Thus, the royal family took sanctuary and escaped from the Rana ruler's control.' (See Joshi, B.L. and Rose, L.E., *Democratic Innovations in Nepal: Political Acculturation, op cit.)*

14 See Bipin Adhikari. 2013. *Constitutional Crisis in Nepal: Ensuring democratic governance during the transition to a new constituent assembly.* Kathmandu: Nepal Constitution Foundation. (Professor Cheryl Saunders notes in her preface to the book that it 'explains how the original CA was conceived and structured; how, in the view of the author, the impasse leading to the stalemate arose; and the difficult choices that political leaders then faced in organizing a transitional administration

that did least violence to the principles of democracy and the rule of law.’)

15 Once the Qingzang railway of China reaches Zhangmu (Khasa) on the Nepalese border in 2020, the trade and tourism between the two nations will reach a new height.

4

THE UNREMITTING STRUGGLE FOR ECONOMIC SURVIVAL AND GROWTH

Madan Kumar Dahal

Nepal's economic development is a challenging proposition. The economy has been struggling for survival and growth for the last six decades of planned economic development experience. Currently, the Nepalese economy is passing through a critical phase of low-level equilibrium trap circumscribed by poverty and stagnation.

Current Status of the Economy

Nepal's economy has been suffering from a sluggish growth with average annual growth rate confined to 3.5 per cent during the last five years. The growth declined to 0.77 per cent due to the devastating earthquake, prolonged agitation and economic impasse in 2015–16. Subsequently, the growth rate increased to 6.9 per cent in 2016–17 (MoF/GoN), resulting in Nepal becoming one of the poorest countries in the world. Nepal's commitment to upgrade the economy from the status of LDC to a developing economy with 8.0–9.0 per cent growth rate is extremely challenging. Although available data shows that the population below the absolute poverty line is estimated to be 21.6 per cent (NPC, 14th Plan Approach Paper, 2016), a study organized by the United Nations Development Programme (UNDP) and Oxford projected that around 65 per cent of the population lives in abject poverty in Nepal (UNDP/Oxford, 2015). The economy, which is primarily based on imports, remittances and foreign assistance, is extremely vulnerable.

The current macroeconomic indicators exhibit that the size of GDP is extremely diminutive (approximately $20.4 billion) with inordinately low GNI per capita ($862) (Economic Survey, 2017) and inflation rate hovering at around 4.5 per cent as of July 2017 (NRB, 2017), followed by conspicuously growing unemployment likely to move towards 'stagflation'. The contribution of the agriculture sector to GDP is estimated to be as high as 33.0 per cent, of the industry sector at 14.0 per cent, of the manufacturing sector at 6.0 per cent, and the contribution of the services sector is projected to be as high as 53.0 per cent (WDR, 2016).

The consumption expenditure levelled at 89.7 per cent, Gross Domestic Savings (GDS) lowered down to 10.3 per cent, export of goods and services confined to 9.8 per cent, import of goods and services increased to 42.0 per cent, the total fixed capital formation is estimated to be 33.8 per cent and the resource gap is projected to be around 1.3 per cent during 2016–17 (NRB, 2017).

The macroeconomic data reflects that the magnitude of exports declined to NPR 73.05 billion against the growing size of imports equivalent to NPR 990.11 billion, with a huge trade deficit of NPR 917.06 billion in 2016–17 (Annexure 1). Exports to India, China and other countries account for 56.7 per cent, 2.3 per cent and 40.9 per cent, respectively. Similarly, imports from India, China and other countries account for 64.0 per cent, 12.9 per cent and 23.1 per cent, respectively, during the same period. The share of export and import in total trade is found to be 6.9 per cent and 93.1 per cent and the total export is unable to sustain the imports of petroleum products. The workers' remittances went up to NPR 695.5 billion, which is 26.9 per cent of GDP, and the size of the population in foreign employment is estimated to be 4.3 million in 2016–17 (NRB, 2017).

The total magnitude of expenditure levelled at NPR 793.9 billion (30.5 per cent of GDP), while the size of recurrent expenditure increased to NPR 501.6 billion (19.3 per cent of GDP). The size of capital expenditure (NPR 189.5 billion) remained conspicuously low at 7.3 per cent of GDP, and the extent of financial management expenditure marked NPR 102.8 billion (3.9 per cent of GDP) in 2016–17.

Similarly, the total government revenue went up to NPR 609.2 billion, the tax effort ratio being as high as 23.4 per cent of GDP during the same period (Annexure 1). The tax structure is heavily dominated by indirect taxes. The major sources of internal revenue are direct taxes, indirect taxes and non-tax revenues. Indirect taxes such as VAT (26.3 per cent), customs duties (18.6 per cent) and excise duties (13.9 per cent) constitute 58.8 per cent of the total revenue, while the contribution of direct taxes like income tax (24.3 per cent), registration fees (3.2 per cent), vehicle tax (1.2 per cent) and other taxes (2.4 per cent) accounted for 31.1 per cent of the total revenue, and the share of non-tax revenues was 10.1 per cent in 2015–16 (NRB, 2017).

The extent of foreign grants levelled at NPR 14.5 billion and foreign loan amounted to NPR 47.8 billion. Deposits of banks and financial institutions significantly increased to NPR 2,660 billion. The NEPSE Index is regularly fluctuating due to the imperfect market. This is attributed to a sharp fall in investment due to the earthquake, agitations and economic impasse, which is likely to encourage capital flight from the banking to the non-banking sector. Despite trade deficit, current account was in surplus by NPR 10.1 billion and balance of payments (BoP) situation was favourable at NPR 82.15 billion during 2016–17, which is attributed to remittances (NRB, 2017).

The International Monetary Fund (IMF) has projected that Nepal would remain one of the poorest countries in South Asia till 2021 (IMF, 2016), and, more recently, the World Atlas ranked Nepal 17th in the list of twenty-five poorest countries in the world (World Atlas, 2016). The decelerating economy comprising 'development of underdevelopment', if not improved with speedy recovery within the time frame, may lead Nepal to becoming a 'Banana Republic.'

The budget for 2017–18 estimated total expenditure to be NPR 1,278.99 billion, which is a whopping 49.1 per cent of GDP (Budget, 2017/18). The staggering magnitude of expenditure is necessary to successfully accomplish reconstruction and rehabilitation activities within the time frame. However, the economy has been suffering from the 'under-spending syndrome' for a long time due to the effects of transition, followed by inefficiency, mounting corruption and poor governance.

The international comparison refers to a very disgusting situation where that Nepal's performance is trailing behind other countries in terms of Global Competitive Index (3.38/World Economic Forum, 2014), Doing Business Index (59.56/The World Bank Group, 2014), Human Development Index (0.54/HDR, 2014), Fragile State Index (90.5/ FSI, 2014), Corruption Perception Index (29.0/TI, 2014) and World Happiness Index (4.15)/WHI, 2013) (See Annexure 3).

Measuring Performance and Trends (2007/08–2016/17)

Let us take a detailed look at the country's economic performance in the past ten years. As shown in Table 1, GDP increased steadily from NPR 816 billion in 2007–08 to NPR 2,600 billion in 2016–17 (CBS, 2017), which is estimated to be equivalent to $20.4 billion (at the exchange rate of $1=NPR 110.26 on 29 November 2017). Despite tremendous economic potential, it is unfortunate that the quantum of Nepal's GDP is extremely small and, therefore, the major challenge is how to expand its size by effectively mobilizing and utilizing internal as well as external resources within the given time frame. A quantum jump in the economic front is virtually impossible with a diminutive size of GDP.

Table 1: Size of GDP (at producer's price in NPR billion)

Financial year	GDP
2007/08	816
2008/09	988
2009/10	1,193
2010/11	1,367
2011/12	1,527

2012/13	1,695
2013/14	1,965
2014/15	2,120
2015/16	2,249
2016/17	2,600

Source: CBS, 2017

Table 2 provides a time series annual real growth rate of the agriculture, industry and services sectors and the real GDP growth rates of overall economy for the period 2006/07–2015/16. The annual growth rate of the agriculture sector was almost constant (1.0–1.3 per cent), indicative of a dismal performance of the sector. Despite the considerable size of subsidies provided by the government to farmers on fertilizer, interest on credits (including other incentives) and productivity and production of both food and cash crops have remained low, as investments from both government and private sectors have conspicuously been minimal, turning Nepal from a rice exporter country till a few years back to a rice importer one. The expenditure earmarked for the agriculture sector was estimated to be 6.4 per cent of the total expenditure and 2.9 per cent of GDP in 2016–17 (Budget Speech, 2016/17). Agriculture is the mainstay of life and more than two-thirds of the population still derive their livelihood from it directly. The sector suffers from a high incidence of poverty and huge rural indebtedness with a considerable size of disguised unemployment.

The real GDP growth rate of the industry sector substantially declined from 4.0 per cent in 2006–07 to –6.30 per cent in 2015–16 and the contribution of the manufacturing sector to GDP has also been minimal in recent times. The low growth rate of the industry sector is attributed to a critical shortage of electricity and the lack of comparative advantage and competitive edge in export promoting industries. Most of the industries are running below capacity (Economic Survey/MOF, 2016). Similarly, the performance of the services sector has not been satisfactory in recent times as compared to the previous period. The share of the tourism sector is less than 3.0 per cent of the GDP and the contribution of the financial and other services sector improved relatively in recent times.

The overall growth rate moderately increased at the initial stage but rapidly declined to 0.77 per cent in 2015–16. Despite moderately higher level of investment, overall growth rate is discouraging not only due to natural catastrophe, agitations and economic deadlock, but also due to growing inefficiency, mounting corruption and poor governance.

Table 2: Real GDP growth at basic price

Financial year	Agriculture	Industry	Service	Overall
2008/09	3.00	0.60	6.00	3.90
2009/10	2.00	4.00	5.80	4.30
2010/11	4.50	4.30	3.40	3.90
2011/12	4.60	3.00	5.00	4.60
2012/13	1.10	2.70	5.70	3.80
2013/14	4.50	7.10	6.20	5.70
2014/15	0.80	1.50	3.60	2.32
2015/16	1.30	-6.30	2.70	0.77
2016/17	5.30	7.70	6.90	6.90

Source: Macroeconomic Indicators of Nepal, Nepal Rastra Bank (NRB/GON), November 2017.

Table 3 provides the trends in GNI per capita of Nepal in terms of dollars, which is the lowest in South Asia, next to Afghanistan. Unfortunately, GNI per capita increased steadily at a snail's speed, from $496 in 2007–08 to $862 in 2016–17. As of 2014, the GNI per capita income of Bangladesh (1,080), Pakistan (1,410), India (1,610), Bhutan (2,390) and Sri Lanka (3,400) have remained fairly higher compared with Nepal and Afghanistan in the South Asian region (Annexure 2). Therefore, Nepal's commitment to upgrade its status from that of an LDC to a developing economy by 2022 with 8.0–9.0 growth rate is a challenging proposition, considering the diminutive size of its GDP, inordinately low GNI per capita and galloping inflation.

Table 3: GNI per capita (current price in dollar)

Financial year	GNI per capita
2007/08	496
2008/09	502
2009/10	614
2010/11	718
2011/12	708
2012/13	714
2013/14	737
2014/15	775
2015/16	766
2016/17	862

Source: Economic Survey, 2016/17.

Inflation hovered between 6.7 per cent and 4.5 per cent during the period 2007/08–2016/17 (Table 4). The incidence and impact of rapidly increasing inflation is acute on daily-wage earners, the fixed income bracket and marginal groups. Since the purchasing power of the Nepalese currency is very low in comparison to the Indian currency and other hard currencies, a moderately higher level of inflation without corresponding increase in the income of the average people adversely hit the economy of households, resulting in a fall in living standards. Not only have the prices of food, clothes, medicines, petroleum products and fertilizer increased substantially but also the cost of education, health, transportation, electricity, water and Internet systems have remained extremely exorbitant in recent years. However, the inflation rate was suppressed to 4.5 per cent in 2016–17 not due to increase in production but because of the rising level of imports.

Nepal is listed in the group of high inflation countries in South Asia. Unfortunately, inflation is not under the control of the GoN, for productivity and production of the agricultural and non-agricultural sectors are conspicuously low, resulting in huge import bills and trade deficit. Moderate inflation with gradual increase in growth rate is justified to some extent in the context of economic development, but rising inflation with sluggish growth and lack of employment opportunities at home have led to 'stagflation'.

Table 4: Inflation in Nepal (year-to-year change in per cent based on CPI)

Financial year	Inflation
2007/08	6.7
2008/09	12.6
2009/10	9.6
2010/11	9.6
2011/12	8.3
2012/13	9.9
2013/14	9.1
2014/15	7.2
2015/16	9.5
2016/17	4.5

Source: Economic Survey, 2016/17.

Table 5 shows that the quantum of total exports increased very slowly from NPR 59.57 billion in 2007–08 to NPR 73.05 billion in 2016–17, and total imports increased rapidly from NPR 221.95 billion to NPR 990.11 billion and total trade went up from NPR 281.52 to NPR 1,063.16 billion 2016–17 (Annexure 1). The export–GDP ratio sharply declined from 7.30 per cent to 2.81 per cent, import–GDP ratio increased from 27.20 per cent to 38.08 per cent and the total trade/GDP ratio increased from 34.50 per cent to 40.89 per cent during the same period.

The time series data on direction of trade for the last ten years clearly exhibits that Nepal's dependence on India has been increasing alarmingly over the years due to lack of adequate trade diversification with China and other overseas countries over the period. The trade deficit with India alone is as high as 64.6 per cent of the total trade deficit. The share of exports confined to 6.9 per cent and the share of imports in total trade conspicuously increased to 93.1 per cent in 2016–17 (Annexure 1).

Although trade is the engine of growth, low comparative advantage and poor comparative edge have been factors constraining growth in Nepal. In addition, Nepal is extremely disadvantageously placed in the context of international trade. However, more recently, the provision of duty-free access to more than 8,000 Nepalese products to China is a significant initiative to help improve the economy of LDCs. Similarly, the USA has provided duty- and quota-free export facility for sixty-six goods from Nepal, which would be valid for the next ten years.

Table 5: Direction of trade (in NPR billion)

Financial year	Export	Export % GDP	Import	Import % GDP	Total	Total Trade % GDP
2007/08	59.57	7.30	221.95	27.20	281.52	34.50
2008/09	68.17	6.90	284.54	28.80	352.72	35.70
2009/10	60.84	5.10	374.60	31.40	435.45	36.50
2010/11	64.25	4.70	396.43	29.00	460.68	33.70
2011/12	74.82	4.90	461.15	30.20	535.98	35.10
2012/13	76.28	4.50	555.96	32.80	632.24	37.30
2013/14	92.36	4.70	715.26	36.40	807.62	41.10
2014/15	84.80	4.00	773.80	36.50	858.60	40.50
2015/16	70.10	3.11	773.60	34.40	843.70	37.51
2016/17	73.05	2.81	990.11	38.08	1,063.16	40.89

**Source:* Economic Survey 2016/17 (MOF/GON).

As shown in Table 6, the share of Gross Domestic Savings (GDS) in GDP witnessed a marginal increase from 9.8 per cent to 10.30 per cent during 2007/08–2016/17, whereas the share of Gross National Savings (GNS) in GDP moderately increased from 33.20 per cent to

43.80 per cent of GDP. Similarly, the contribution of the Gross Fixed Capital Formation (GFCF) to GDP slowly increased from 21.90 per cent in 2007–08 to 33.90 per cent in 2016/17. Nepal conspicuously suffered from a sluggish growth rate with considerable size of Gross Fixed Capital Formation in the past.

Table 6: Gross Domestic Savings (GDS), Gross National Savings (GNS) and Gross Fixed Capital Formation (GFCF) (NPR billion)

Financial year	GDS	GDS as % of GDP	GNS	GNS as % of GDP	GCFC	GFCF as % of GDP
2007/08	79.97	9.80	270.91	33.20	178.70	21.90
2008/09	92.87	9.40	354.69	35.90	210.44	21.30
2009/10	136.00	11.40	428.29	35.90	264.85	22.20
2010/11	191.38	14.00	505.79	37.00	292.54	21.40
2011/12	167.97	11.00	603.17	39.50	317.62	20.80
2012/13	179.67	10.60	689.87	40.70	383.07	22.60
2013/14	233.84	11.90	898.01	45.70	461.78	23.50
2014/15	186.56	8.80	930.68	43.90	587.24	27.70
2015/16	119.20	5.30	964.82	42.90	562.25	25.00
2016/17	267.80	10.30	1,138.80	43.80	878.80	33.80

Source: CBS, 2017.

The size of remittances grew from NPR 142.70 million to NPR 695.50 billion, which is 26.80 per cent of GDP, during the last ten years. Remittance has been one of the major sources of foreign exchange earnings in Nepal for a relatively long period and, according to a crude estimate, more than six million people are in foreign employment. It is estimated that every day more than 1,500 workers migrate to Gulf countries, Malaysia and other nations in quest of employment. Despite the huge and widening trade deficit, current account and BOP situations have remained positive during the last several years, which is attributed to remittances.

Unfortunately, Nepal sells more than 53.0 per cent of hard

earned total remittances to the Reserve Bank of India (RBI) in order to meet the demand for Indian currency in Nepal. The shortage of Indian currency in Nepal is alarming, especially after the recent demonetisation in India. However, remittance is one of the significant instruments to sustain the economy and is only next to increasing the size of imports and dwindling foreign aid.

The World Economic Forum forecasted in 2016 that the next global economic meltdown will occur any time from now, which will be more dangerous than that of 2008. Its implications will be more severe and will hit hard the economies of not only developed countries but also of developing countries, resulting in drastic cut-down in the flow of remittances with increasing current account deficit and negative BOP situations. Since Nepal has no capacity to absorb external shocks, the fall of aggregate demand in the global market will lead to substantial cuts in foreign employment and hence there will be a drastic fall in the size of remittances, resulting in macroeconomic instability. The major sources of foreign exchange reserves are remittances, merchandize exports and foreign aid and the share of remittances in foreign exchange reserves is estimated to be as high as 67.0 per cent in 2016/17 (Table 7).

Table 7: Remittance flow in Nepal (in NPR billion)

Financial year	Remittance	% GDP
2007/08	142.70	17.49
2008/09	209.70	21.22
2009/10	231.70	19.42
2010/11	253.60	18.55
2011/12	359.60	23.55
2012/13	434.60	25.64
2013/14	543.30	27.65
2014/15	617.30	29.12
2015/16	665.00	29.60
2016/17	695.50	26.80

Source: Nepal Rastra Bank, 2017.

Table 8 shows the status of foreign exchange reserve in Nepal, which increased from NPR 212.6 billion to NPR 1,079.5 billion during 2007/08–2016/17. The major sources of foreign exchange reserve are remittances, merchandize exports and foreign aid. The share of remittances in foreign exchange reserve was estimated to be as high as 67.0 per cent and of merchandise export at 7.0 per cent of total foreign exchange earnings in 2016/17, which can sustain the imports of goods and services for about 10.5 months.

Table 8: Foreign exchange reserves and sufficiency of equivalent months for imports of goods and services (G/S)

Financial year	Foreign exchange reserves (NPR billion)	Months for imports of G/S
2007/08	212.6	9.4
2008/09	286.5	10
2009/10	268.9	7.4
2010/11	272.2	7.3
2011/12	439.5	10.3
2012/13	533.3	8.7
2013/14	665.4	10
2014/15	824.1	11.2
2015/16	1,009.5	13.2
2016/17	1,079.50	10.5

Source: Nepal Rastra Bank, 2017.

Table 9 shows the size of total revenue for the last ten years. The total revenue went up from NPR 107.71 billion to NPR 609.20 (Annexure 1) during the period under consideration and it was buoyant even during the period of conflict (NPR 482.70). The tax effort ratio was as high as 23.4 per cent.

The burden of taxation (R/Y) is relatively high in Nepal as compared to other countries in South Asia. The tax structure primarily comprises VAT, customs duties, excise duties (indirect taxes) and other related taxes, which together constitute around 58.9 per cent of total revenue, while income tax, property tax (direct taxes) and other related taxes comprise 31.3 per cent, and non-tax revenues contribute to around 10.1 per cent of total revenue in recent years. Around 8,00,000 people are under the jurisdiction of taxation and the income from the agriculture sector is exempted, for this is a subsistence sector. Massive business exemptions and standard deductions have been provided to the manufacturing sector, resulting in an extremely low tax base. The elasticity coefficient of overall taxation is found to be below the unity (Dahal, 2015). Although revenue mobilization is encouraging, it is not adequate to supplement the capital expenditure. The capital expenditure suffers from 'under-spending syndrome' attributing to administrative hassles, inefficiency, poor governance and rampant corruption originating from top to bottom.

Table 9: Total revenue and revenue/GDP ratio (tax effort ratio)

Financial year	Total revenue (NPR billion)	Revenue-GDP Ratio (tax effort ratio)
2007/08	107.71	13.20
2008/09	143.26	14.50
2009/10	177.76	14.90
2010/11	200.95	14.70
2011/12	244.32	16.00
2012/13	296.63	17.50
2013/14	357.63	18.20
2014/15	404.92	19.10
2015/16	482.70	21.50
2016/17	609.20	23.40

Source: Economic Survey 2015/16, MoF/GoN.

Table 10 shows the size of total government expenditure and its share in GDP. The magnitude of government expenditure increased from NPR 161.57 billion in 2007–08 to NPR 793.90 billion in 2016–17 (Annexure 1). The share of total expenditure in GDP went up from

19.8 per cent to 30.5 per cent, almost at par with the middle-income countries in the last ten years. It is crucial that the growth rate remains low despite satisfactory increase in government expenditure during the period under consideration, which is attributed to growing inefficiency, rampant corruption and poor governance.

Table 10: Total government expenditure and expenditure (NPR billion) as % of GDP

Financial year	Government expenditure (GE)	GE as % of GDP
2007/08	161.57	19.80
2008/09	219.34	22.20
2009/10	260.07	21.80
2010/11	295.27	21.60
2011/12	338.99	22.20
2012/13	359.34	21.20
2013/14	398.90	20.30
2014/15	532.12	25.10
2015/16	569.60	25.30
2016/17	793.90	30.50

Source: Economic Survey 2016/17, MoF/GON.

As shown in Table 11 recurrent expenditure increased from 11.20 per cent of GDP in 2007–08 to 19.29 per cent in 2016–17, while capital expenditure marginally remained between 6.6 per cent and 7.29 per cent of GDP during the ten-year period and the share of expenditure on financial services marginally declined from 4.80 per cent to 3.95 per cent. It is unfortunate that the size of capital expenditure is significantly below the demand and the actual capital expenditure is estimated to be minimal in Nepal, resulting in poor growth.

It is, therefore, imperative to identify the growth-stimulating capital expenditure headings and increase the quantum of capital expenditure in priority sectors, which would be instrumental to achieve a robust growth. There is also need for reordering of priorities in the changing context to restore normalcy and make a breakthrough in the economic front for a take-off from underdevelopment to development.

Table 11: Total expenditure, recurrent expenditure, capital expenditure and expenditure on financial services (NPR billion and as % of GDP)

Financial year	RE	RE as % of GDP	CE	CE as % of GDP	FS	FS as % of GDP
2007/08	91.39	11.20	53.86	6.60	39.17	4.80
2008/09	127.45	12.90	73.11	7.40	45.45	4.60
2009/10	151.51	12.70	90.67	7.60	46.53	3.90
2010/11	210.52	15.40	47.85	3.50	47.85	3.50
2011/12	242.79	15.90	51.92	3.40	54.97	3.60
2012/13	247.47	14.60	54.24	3.20	84.75	5.00
2013/14	267.24	13.60	66.81	3.40	94.32	4.80
2014/15	339.20	16.00	89.04	4.20	137.80	6.50
2015/16	434.06	19.30	159.68	7.10	148.43	6.60
2016/17	501.60	19.29	189.50	7.29	102.80	3.95

RE = Regular Expenditure, CE = Capital Expenditure, FS = Financial Services.
Source: Economic Survey 2016/17, MoF/GoN.

Quantitative Targets as Envisaged in the 14th Plan, 2016/17–2018/19

Table 12 provides the quantitative targets set for 2016/17–2018/19 as envisaged in the 14th Plan (NPC, 14th Plan, Draft Approach Paper, 2016). Although the growth rate shrunk to 0.77 per cent during 2015–16, attributed to aberrant situations comprising the earthquake, agitations and economic impasse, it went up to 6.9 per cent in 2016–17. The growth rate target is estimated to be 7.2 per cent during the 14th Plan and, subsequently, the growth rates for the agriculture and non-agriculture sectors are estimated to be 4.70 per cent and 8.30 per cent, respectively. Inflation rate would be limited to 7.5 per cent, annual GDP per capita per annum would increase from NPR 80,000.90 to NPR 105,000.70 and the size of population below poverty line will climb down from 21.6 per cent to 17.0 per cent of total population during the period.

Similarly, the Human Development Index (HDI) would increase from 0.54 to 0.57; average life expectancy would improve from 71 years to 72 years; population with access to drinking water would increase from 83.60 per cent to 90.20 per cent; net enrolment at higher secondary level would increase from 37.60 per cent to 45.0 per cent; literacy rate among 15–24 years age group would increase from 88.6 per cent to 91.0 per cent; the number of VDCs connected with road would increase from 2,739 to 3,062; electricity production at installed capacity would increase from 829 MW to 1,500 MW; population with access to electricity would rise from 74.0 per cent to 87.0 per cent; land under irrigation would increase from 1,396,000 hectares to 1,520,000 hectares; and population with access to the Internet would increase from 46.40 to 65.0 per cent.

Table 12: Major economic, social and physical targets as envisaged in 14th Plan (2016/17–2018/19)

	Target	Status as of 2015–16	Targets for 14th Plan
1.	Annual average growth rate (in %)	0.77	7.2
2.	Annual average growth rate of agriculture sector (in %)	1.33	4.70
3.	Annual average growth rate of non-agriculture sector (in %)	0.63	8.40
4.	Inflation (In %)	9.5	7.5
5.	GDP per capita (NPR in '000)	79.37	116.50
6.	Size of population below the absolute poverty line	21.6	17.0
7.	HDI	0.54	0.57
8.	Gender Empowerment Index (GEI)	0.56	0.58
9.	Average expectancy of life (Years)	69	72
10.	Population with access to drinking water facility (in %)	83.60	90

11.	Net enrolment rate at Higher Secondary level (in %)	37.70	45.0
12.	Literacy rate among 15–24 years age group (in %)	88.6	91.0
13.	Number of VDCs connected with road	2,739	3,062
14.	Electricity production (installed capacity MW)	851	2,301
15.	Population with access to electricity (in %)	74.0	87.0
16.	Irrigation (in lakh hectare)	13.92	15.20
17.	Population with access to Internet (in %)	46.40	65.0

Source: 14th Three Year Plan, 2016/17–2018/19, Final Approach Paper, National Planning Commission (NPC), GoN, 8 January 2017.

The 14th Plan is relatively ambitious and, therefore, it is imperative to galvanize not only domestic investment in potential areas and priority sectors but also effectively mobilize bilateral cooperation, especially from the two neighbouring economic powers, including regional as well as multilateral cooperation at a greater quantum in future.

Binding Critical Constraints and Major Bottlenecks to Economic Development

The economy suffers from structural as well as several binding critical constraints comprising:

i. **High-cost economy:** Nepal's economy is a high-cost one, attributed to its landlocked position, absence of direct access to sea, inadequate transit facilities and exorbitant transportation cost, as a result of which consumption goods, as well as intermediate, capital and luxury items are extremely expensive. Not only the prices of food, clothing, medicines, petroleum products, fertilizer, public utilities such as water, electricity and telephone, have increased but also education, health, transport and Internet services have been extremely costly. The prevailing fixed exchange regime, especially between Nepalese and Indian currencies, and a series of devaluation of Nepalese currency vis-à-vis other hard currencies have also excessively fuelled rise in general price levels, for Nepal imports everything. Sixty-four per cent of total imports are from India and nearly 13 per cent from China, and the remaining 23 per cent from other countries. In addition, the unwarranted profit margins of wholesalers, dealers and retailers have also helped to exorbitantly increase prices. Nepal also falls in the group of countries with high level of inflation in the world.

Also, Nepal is disadvantageously placed vis-à-vis international trade due to rise in the prices of all items. It imports almost all items from India, including rice and paddy, for production is insufficient to meet the local demand, leading to excessive price rise. The value of Nepalese currency would appreciate only when the terms of trade can be improved by increasing the size of exports to India and other countries.

ii. **Subsistence agriculture sector:** Agriculture is the biggest and a priority sector, engaging more than two-thirds of the population and contributing 33 per cent to GDP; however, this is a subsistence sector and, therefore, there is no taxation on the income derived from agriculture. The investment in the sector by the government is a mere 3 per cent, which is extremely low. The private sector is also indifferent towards investment in agriculture. Nepal imports rice from India, which accounts for NPR 24 billion in 2016–17. The land reforms programme has not been instrumental in increasing productivity and production of both food and cash crops. Modernization and mechanization of agriculture to move towards a green revolution like in the states of Haryana and Punjab in India is not possible due to fragmentation of holdings in Nepal.

iii. **Increase in dependency:** Trade deficit has alarmingly increased over the years, which surpassed the size of annual budget, which was estimated to be 35.3 per cent of GDP in 2016–17. Trade deficit with India alone went up to 64.6 per cent, followed by that with China (13.7 per cent) and other countries (21.7 per cent) during the same period (Annexure 1). Nepal accomplished sixty years of planned economic development with dismal performance, resulting in increasing dependency with India. This is a serious disequilibrium, which can be corrected only by improving productivity and production and increasing exports of agriculture and non-agriculture products in potential areas such as high-value cash crops and medicinal herbs to international markets and export of surplus hydropower to India.

iv. **Inadequate and poor physical infrastructure:** The 14th Plan projects that Nepal requires 2,300 MW of electricity during the plan period, whereas only 961 MW of electricity has been generated so far (Economic Survey, 2017). Total production of electricity as of 2016–17 is less than 1 per cent of theoretical hydropower potential (83,000 MW) of Nepal and commercial potential is estimated to be 40,000 MW. Currently, the deficit in power sector is very acute and crucial. Nepalese people have been facing as many as 14–19 hours of load-shedding for the past twenty-five years. Kathmandu Valley is now free of load-shedding, but how long this commitment continues is yet to be seen.

This is the era of energy, and without adequate supply of energy there can neither be industrialization nor economic prosperity with robust growth. The private sector is apprehensive of poor infrastructure, which is detrimental to the industrialization of the country, and private sector investment would be mobile only when investment is safe and profit is assured. All developing economies have followed the model for higher, sustainable and inclusive growth with huge spending on infrastructure development by attracting Foreign Direct Investments (FDIs) in mega projects and mobilizing domestic investments in priority projects in recent years.

The status of roads (29,157 km) is also vulnerable with rising number of accidents each year. Of the total roads, blacktops occupy 42.20 per cent, gravelled cover 23.55 per cent and fair-weather comprise 34.25 per cent in 2016–17 (Economic Survey, 2017). Roads, especially those connecting China in the north through Tatopani, Rasuwagadhi and other corridors, have not been rebuilt and become operational after the 2015 earthquake. Furthermore, there is acute shortage of water in the capital and the water supply situation all over the country is very poor.

v. **Rampant corruption:** As of the Corruption Perception Index (CPI) 2017, Nepal is the second most corrupt country in South Asia and mostly concentrated in the political sector (Report of Transparency International, 2017). According to a report published by the Office of the Auditor General (OAG)/GoN), the size of arrears is as high as NPR 396 billion, which is estimated to be 15.2 per cent of GDP, comprising all government offices in 2016–17 (OAG/GoN, 2017). The local bodies are also no exception to rampant corruption, for local resources are being misused at a large scale due to absence of elected representatives since the last twenty years.

vi. **Inefficiency and poor governance:** Inefficiency and poor governance are the factors responsible for economic backwardness of Nepal. A Secretary, the top-level administrator in government bureaucracy, is transferred within four months from one ministry to another at the personal whims of politicians in power. Good governance is antidote to corruption. The extremely slow progress in reconstruction and rehabilitation is a glaring example of inefficiency, corruption and poor governance. The capital expenditure is extremely minimal, which is another bitter example of the 'under-spending syndrome' afflicting the economy and inefficiency and poor governance in Nepal. The private sector is also no exception. The future of the Kathmandu–Hetauda tunnel road, initiated by the private sector, is unknown and there is no indication when construction work will start. The prime reason attributed to inefficiency and poor governance is the lack of meritocracy and excessive politicization in all spheres of statecraft.

Issues and Challenges Facing Nepalese Economy

The target of 6.0 per cent growth rate envisaged in the budget for 2017–18 will be extremely challenging to attain due to floods, landslides and fall in the production of cash crops and, therefore, international agencies like the World Bank, Asian Development Bank (ADB) and UNDP have confined it to 4.5 percent (Budget Speech, FY 2017/18). The economy is encapsulated by crucial structural constraints on economic development comprising extremely inadequate physical infrastructure, low investment and productivity in the agriculture sector, poor comparative advantage and fragile competitive edge in trade and manufacturing sectors.

The major issues facing Nepalese economy are:

- How to effectively expedite and accomplish reconstruction and rehabilitation activities with recovery and return of the economy to normalcy within the next two years and promote a 'self-reliant' economy to sustain economic catastrophe attributed to natural disasters, agitations, economic blockade and global economic meltdown in the future.
- How to transfer a population excessively dependent on agriculture to more productive non-agriculture sectors, especially manufacturing, with comparative advantage and competitive edge by creating employment opportunities and thereby reducing the extent of poverty.
- How to integrate the Nepalese economy with the neighbourhood economies, especially those of India and China, as well as regional and global economies, for a take-off and maximize the benefits from globalization and liberalization, ensuring a high, sustainable and inclusive growth.
- How to mobilize external assistance and effectively utilize economic cooperation from donor communities, such as India, China, USA, European Union, UK, Organisation for Economic Co-operation and Development (OECD) countries, Asia Pacific region (Japan, Australia and New Zealand), Scandinavian countries (Denmark, Sweden, Norway, Finland and others),

regional groups like SAARC, BBIN and multilateral financial institutions like the World Bank, ADB and other agencies such as World Trade Organization and UNDP, to spur robust growth with social justice.

- How to upgrade the economy from the status of LDC to a developing economy with 8.0–9.0 per cent growth by 2022.
- How to increase the GNI per capita at par with the level of middle-income countries by 2030.
- How to make Nepal the Switzerland of Asia by 2040 by improving efficiency, competitiveness and governance.

Underpinnings of the Nepalese Economy

Nepal's strategic location between two giant countries offers a great opportunity to spur robust growth by improving efficiency and competitiveness in potential and priority areas.

1. **Agriculture, especially farming of high-value crops:** Agriculture is the mainstay of life in Nepal and latest data shows that the sector contributes as high as 33.0 per cent of GDP, which is a common characteristic of underdeveloped economies. Theoretically, whenever an economy moves from low-income to a middle- or high-income one, the share of agriculture in GDP gradually declines and, subsequently, the contribution of the industry sector to GDP increases. However, agriculture is the prime sector instrumental in promoting a 'self-reliant' economy in Nepal, which is vital to sustain the economy even during internal or external crises.

   Although productivity and production of major food crops, i.e. paddy (rice), maize, wheat, maize, barley, buckwheat and pulse, have not been encouraging over the period, the production of cash crops like potato, vegetables and fruits has shown a moderately increasing trend. The trends in productivity and production of major industrial crops such as oilseeds, tobacco, sugarcane, jute, tea, coffee, cotton, honey, mushroom, silk cocoon, floriculture, and spices like ginger, garlic, turmeric, chilly and cardamom have been relatively satisfactory with tremendous export potential.

There are good prospects for setting up agro-based industries, especially high-value crops such as cash crops and spices, in Nepal to promote export, increase foreign exchange earnings and create employment opportunities at home, in cooperation with the private sector by mobilizing domestic investment. It is also necessary to implement the recommendations of the Agriculture Development Strategy (ADS), formulated by the ADB in partnership with GoN (ADS/ADB-GoN, 2015), to improve the fragile situation through modernization, mechanization and commercialization of agriculture. Since land reforms programmes were not associated with increasing productivity of the agriculture sector in the past, it is important that a new and scientific land reforms programme be implemented to augment productivity. Although mechanization demands large estate farming and, subsequently, supports the idea of higher land ceiling, small farming has also proven to increase productivity.

2. **Water resources and hydropower:** Nepal possesses abundant water resources and is the second biggest country in the world next to Brazil in terms of per capita hydropower potential. Nepal's theoretical hydropower potential is estimated to be 83,000 MW and its commercial potential is 50 per cent of total potential, i.e. 41,500 MW. Nepal's hydropower potential is adequate not only to meet domestic requirements, but also help speed up industrialization and reduce the widening trade gap with India. Furthermore, the Bangladesh, Bhutan, India, Nepal (BBIN) subregion in South Asia will benefit immensely from hydropower development in Nepal.

   Water resource is the lifeline of Nepalese economy, for altogether thirty big- and medium-sized hydropower projects are under construction, which is likely to produce 12,766 MW of electricity within the next few years. The ten big hydropower projects under construction have the capacity to produce 11,460 MW, which comprise: (1) Seti West: 750 MW,

(2) Budhi Gandaki: 600 MW, (3) Kali Gandaki: 600 MW, (4) Arun (total): 643 MW, (5) Karnali (total): 1,380 MW, (6) Mahakali–Pancheswar–Tanakpur: 6,480 MW, (7) Dudh Koshi: 300 MW, (8) Adhi Khola: 180 MW, (9) Langtang: 218 MW; and (10) Upper Tamakoshi: 456 MW. Twenty other big, medium and small projects with a total combined production equal to 12,766 MW are likely to generate additional 1,306 MW within the next few years (NEA, 2016).

While delivering a public lecture—'Sustainable Development in an Uncertain World'—on 4 December 2016 in Kathmandu, Jeffrey David Sachs, economist and senior UN adviser, recommended speeding up work to harness at least 10 GW of hydroelectricity out of the potential 40 GW within the next fifteen to twenty years. Sachs categorically emphasized that this will not only substitute the import of petroleum products, expand industrial base, increase agriculture output, provide quality life to people through proper electrification in households but also supply clean energy to India, Bangladesh and other countries in the region. He also said that, 'Harnessing hydroelectricity is critical from the perspective of energy security and also to improve the quality of air because air is highly polluted due to excessive use of fossil fuels and Nepal can also convert to an all-electric transport system within the next fifteen to twenty years by utilizing the electricity generated over the period because the world is moving forward towards electric vehicles.' (*The Himalayan Times*, 5 December 2016).

3. **Tourism:** Although the contribution of foreign exchange earnings from the tourism sector has been confined to a mere 2.9 per cent of GDP in recent times, this is one of the potential and priority areas with comparative advantage and competent edge to spur economic growth and prosperity. The total number of tourist arrival increased to 753,002; the average length of stay per tourist is 13.4 days and per tourist spending per day was $70 during 2016/17. The National Tourism Strategic Plan (NTSP) has set the target of attracting 2.5 million tourists to Nepal and create

employment opportunities for 0.9 million Nepalese by 2022 by protecting and promoting natural, cultural, biodiversity and human-made heritage, apart from developing Nepal as one of the attractive and secure international destinations for tourists from all over the world (Economic Survey, 2017). However, the tourism sector is a highly competitive one, which requires developing the capacity of human resources engaged in it and offering quality services at par with international standards for tourists from the region as well as around the globe. The budget for 2016/17 envisaged that a National Tourism Strategic Action Plan 2016–2025 would be implemented at the earliest possible to maximize benefits from the tourism sector (Budget Speech/MoF, 2017).

4. **Biodiversity, wealth of nation:** Nepal is rich in biodiversity, including subterranean resources, which are instrumental in accelerating the pace of economic development. However, the wealth of the nation has not yet been fully exploited and its economic value not yet fully estimated. Nepal's wealth could be described as follows: (a) Its geophysical setting and time zone location assume strategic significance in South Asia. (b) Rich biodiversity with three ecological regions comprising mountains, hills and the Tarai experiencing tropical, mesothermal, microthermal, tiga and tundra climates that provides 60–80 per cent of the rainfall. Nepal is bestowed with 6,000 rivers and rivulets, 5,000 species of vascular plants, 175 species of mammals and 850 species of birds. Some herbal and medicinal plants are used for the treatment of cancer (Shrestha and Gupta, 1993). (c) Nepal possesses 2.3 per cent of the world's hydro resources attributable to four principal river systems, the lifeline of Nepalese economy, viz. Koshi (east), Gandaki (central), Karnali (far west) and Mahakali (far west) (Dahal and Inoue, 1994). (d) One of the most popular tourist hubs and a global destination for tourists from all over the world. (e) Preliminary geological surveys indicate that subterranean resources are available in the country. However, the extent and commercial potential of mineral deposits are not yet known.

5. **Human resources, foreign employment and remittances:** Human resource is the prime wealth of the nation. Of its thirty million population, the economically active population comprising ages 15–59 years is estimated to be 54.2 per cent (NLSS III, 2010). Annually, more than 5,00,000 youth enter domestic labour market and around 1,500 youth migrate to foreign countries every day in search of employment for livelihood and better life. According to crude estimates, approximately 6.0 million people (20.0 per cent of total population) are in foreign employment, mostly engaged in blue collar jobs with contribution to remittances as high as NPR 695.5 billion (NRB, 2017), which is 26.8 per cent of GDP in recent years. Since this is the era of globalization and liberalization and foreign employment remittances are a global phenomenon, not only Nepal but also many developing countries are competing in the international labour market to gain substantial amount of remittances from foreign employment. It is, therefore, necessary that quality of human resources is improved, especially for those aspiring for foreign employment. It is also important to create employment opportunities within the country in cooperation with the private sector in agriculture, small and cottage industries, medium enterprises and other potential and priority areas.
6. **Export potential:** Nepal Trade Integration Strategy (NTIS) 2016 identifies key commodities and services that have priority export potential. These are: agro-based products (cardamom, ginger, tea, medicinal and aromatic plants); craft and manufacturing products (all fabrics, leather, footwear, pashmina, carpets); services (skilled and semi-skilled professionals at various categories—remittance-generating services); Information Technology & Business Process Outsourcing (IT & BPO) and IT engineering and tourism, including leisure, business, education and medical.

Vision/Mission and Strategic Objectives

The vision or mission of Nepalese economy should be to build a strong 'economic nation state' through active participation of the people ensuring a high quality of life to each individual and household within given time frame (Dahal, 2004).

And, the strategic objectives of the Nepalese economy should be to:

1. Bring back the economy to normalcy for a take-off during the initial stage, especially after the devastating earthquake, prolonged agitations and economic impasse;
2. Upgrade the economy from the status of an LDC to a developing economy with 8.0-9.0 growth rate by 2022 and increase the magnitude of GNI from $20.4 billion to $100 billion and transform the economy from an inordinately low GNI per capita ($862) to a higher GNI per capita ($3,764), at par with the average of middle-income countries, by 2030;
3. Provide employment to each economically active population for reducing absolute poverty from 21.4 per cent to 0 per cent by 2025;
4. Control inflation by increasing productivity and production of both agriculture and non-agriculture sectors, especially manufacturing sectors in the long-run;
5. Check rampant corruption by improving efficiency, competitiveness and good governance in all spheres of the statecraft and also strengthen the capacity of constitutional organizations such as the Commission for Investigation of Abuse of Authority (CIAA), OAG, Office of Comptroller General (OCG), Election Commission (EC), Special Court and the Supreme Court to effectively deal with corruption; and
6. Ultimately, make Nepal the 'Switzerland' of Asia by 2040.

Recommendations: A Roadmap for Economic Prosperity

At this critical juncture it is important that the nature of federalism as envisaged in Nepal's new constitution (2015) must be urgently reviewed. This would help create all provinces economically viable units with an admixture of economic resources, population and geography comprising mountain, hill and Tarai having north–south axis territory adjoining each province with China in the north and India in the south, with the number of provinces not exceeding five. This would be instrumental in strengthening the economy through integration and mobilizing of the economic potential of mountains, hills and the Tarai.

Top priority must be accorded to promote a 'self-reliant' economy by utilizing the 'wealth of nation', including subterranean resources, mobilizing potential areas, and improving the productivity and production of the agriculture sector, especially high value crops, including medicinal herbs like Yarsagumba, to sustain the economy even during critical situations.

Since incidence of disguised unemployment, poverty and rural indebtedness is very high in the agriculture sector, top priority must be accorded to increase bumper production of both food and cash crops. A fertilizer factory must be established in the Tarai on a priority basis under the Public Private Partnership (PPP) model, for each year farmers are struggling to get fertilizers in time and at reasonable prices and also the import bill for fertilizers is very high. Since agriculture is a subsistence sector that requires subsidy to sustain, it is extremely urgent to review the subsidy policy provided to state-owned enterprises (SOEs), which have been a big burden to the exchequer, and the extent of subsidy should not exceed 2.0 per cent of GDP.

Similarly, the 'cooperative sector' is a reliable tool for poverty alleviation with great success through micro credit and it is a vital instrument to sustain the economy during the internal as well as external crises. Although the Nepalese economy does not have the capacity to absorb external shocks, it is the 'cooperative sector' that helps the economy to survive during a global economic meltdown that is likely to occur any time from now onwards (WEF, 2016).

A new 'master plan' for tourism development must be designed in cooperation with and active participation of the private sector and in conformity with the spirit of globalization and liberalization to create Nepal as an international tourism and biodiversity hub. It is imperative to improve the efficiency and competitiveness of the tourism sector by attracting private sector investment through adequate incentive packages, including development of trained human resources, upgrading facilities, especially those of hotels, flights and infrastructure development, providing safety to tourists and advertising on the international media.

This is the era of interdependence and, therefore, it is also important to attract FDI in priority mega projects, especially for infrastructure development (hydropower, roads and airports) and industrialization, ensuring robust growth with social justice. It is also imperative to promote domestic investments in small, cottage and medium-sized industries. This requires establishing Special Economic Zones (SEZs) and dry ports in industrial corridors and developing energy, especially hydropower, with adequate transmission lines connected to the national grid to spur industrialization. This is the epoch of energy and, therefore, without energy neither economic development will accelerate nor will the economy sustain, ensuring prosperity to the people of Nepal. In this context, there is a need to improve efficiency and competiveness to maximize the benefits from globalization and liberalization by integrating the national economy with neighbourhood, regional and global economies, ensuring a high, sustainable and inclusive growth.

At the initial stage it is imperative to expedite the efforts towards restoring the economy to normalcy and moving towards achieving the target of 7.2 per cent growth rate within the next two years (Budget Speech, 2017/18). Secondly, the government must work in tandem with the private sector to fulfil its commitment of upgrading the status of the economy from that of LDC to a developing economy with 8.0–9.0 per cent growth rate by 2022. Furthermore, the state must also improve economic performance, ensuring the per capita income at par with middle-income countries ($3,764) by 2030 and make Nepal a Switzerland of Asia by 2040 (Dahal, 2013). The strategy for economic development must shift from excessive dependence to self-reliance and thereby towards interdependence, from protection to competition, from aid to trade, and from agriculture to industrialization with massive use of modern technology.

It is significant to encourage private sector export-led growth with amendments of the Acts, regulations and policies, especially the Industrial Policy 2010, Foreign Investment Policy 2015, Foreign Employment Act 2007, National Agriculture Policy 2004, Hydropower Policy 2006, Tourism Policy 2011, Trade Policy 2009 and Banking and Financial Institution Act (BAFIA) 2006 so that they are compatible with the national requirements and in the changing context of economic development. The legislature-Parliament has recently endorsed the Industrial Enterprises Act 2016, and the Special Economic Zone Act 2016, and the Foreign Investment and Transfer of Technology Act (FITTA) 2016 are likely to be placed before it for approval. Private sector investment can be mobilized only when investment is safe and profit is ensured. In the changing context, there is need for reordering of priorities, as well as formulating a 'National Economy Policy' in conformity with the need of the hour, ensuring prosperity and a dignified life.

A package of incentives must be designed to attract private sector investment and FDI for establishing export-oriented and import substituting industries in potential and priority areas with comparative advantage and competitive edge against targets to increase the quantum of production and export, increase foreign exchange reserves and internal revenue and augment employment opportunities during the next three years. The fragile industrial relations should be improved through tripartite agreements between the government, trade unions and the private sector. There is also need to speed up the process of privatization.

The burden of taxation or 'tax effort ratio' is very high in Nepal, employing per capita criterion and, therefore, there is need for developing a competitive tax structure to attract both FDI and domestic investments. The agreements signed with China and India must be speedily and effectively implemented, especially in the field of infrastructure such as hydropower, highways and expressways, railways, regional and international airports, construction of bridges, SEZs and dry ports and connection of pipelines.

Since the future of South Asian Association of Regional Cooperation

(SAARC) is uncertain with increasing mistrust and conflicts between member countries, the importance of subregional cooperation such as BBIN is getting momentum and, accordingly, Nepal should move towards reordering of priorities to maximize benefits from regional cooperation. The prospects for regional cooperation are tremendous, especially with reference to tourism and biodiversity, attributed to the rich ecosystem and species. The quality of human resources must be improved to match the demand for international labour market, which would be instrumental in expanding the opportunity for foreign employment and increase the magnitude of remittances. Although trade is an engine of growth, it depends on the prospect for industrialization, nature and size of investment and the status of industrial relations.

The past experiences suggest devising a stringent housing policy to resist 9.5 magnitude earthquakes, especially after the one in 2015. Unfortunately, reconstruction and rehabilitation works are moving extremely slowly due to political wrangling between the ruling and opposition parties.

There is urgent need to liberalize imports of petroleum products to ensure quality of petroleum products and sustain regular supply by inviting private sector and multinationals to take part. Furthermore, it is important to initiate stern action against corruption by effectively activating Commission for Investigation of Abuse of Authority (CIAA) with provisioning of adequate human resources and budget backed by relevant institutions such as the Special Court and the Supreme Court. It is imperative to induct 'meritocracy' in all spheres of statecraft which would certainly help combat corruption by improving efficiency and governance.

There is a need to introduce the doctrine of 'interdependence' while designing annual budgets and periodic plans in conformity with the spirit of globalization and liberalization (Rana and Dahal, 2013). It is also significant to create an international financial services centre in Nepal and mobilize capital investment to accelerate economic development for the whole South Asia region (Collins, et al., 1996). It is urgent to induct the policy of skill development to eliminate poverty, especially of the families and households living below absolute poverty line for employment.

More importantly, economic relationships need to be strengthened with both the economically powerful neighbouring countries, India and China. India ranks 5th in the world in terms of nominal GDP, which was estimated to be $2.44 trillion in 2017 (CIA World Fact Book/ Wikipedia, 2018). Although Nepal–India economic cooperation has a wide spectrum, it is important to focus on five priority areas: (1) harnessing of water resources and developing hydropower; (2) review of existing trade treaty, especially with induction of 'zero tariff regime'; (3) mobilizing FDI from India to Nepal; (4) increasing India's aid to Nepal; and (5) the open border.

In this context, the Mahakali–Pancheswar–Tanakpur Treaty, held in 1995 between Nepal and India with a view to generating 6,500 MW of electricity must be speedily implemented within the time frame. The existing trade treaty with India should be reviewed to boost Nepal's export to India by reducing the value added component, relaxing quantitative restrictions and reducing the items in the negative list. This is not adequate and, therefore, there is need to induct a 'zero-tariff regime', ensuring free trade between Nepal and India. Although this would reduce the magnitude of internal revenue available to Nepal from customs duties at the initial stage, this could be offset by establishing a 'revolving fund' in cooperation with India at par with the size of loss from customs duties to invest in priority projects mutually beneficial to both countries.

Nepal's advantage to increase the size of exports to India with the implementation of the 'zero tariff regime' would also be instrumental in appreciating the value of Nepalese currency and move towards determining exchange rate at par with India in the long run. With Nepal's accession to the WTO, SAFTA and BIMST-EC, FDI is entirely opened to Nepal, except in the context of small and cottage industries and a few other areas under the sensitive list. Although India was a premier donor country to Nepal during 1950s, 60s and 70s, previous locus standi of India as a leading donor country has been relegated to the tenth position in rank order with shift in priority to smaller projects (Pyakuryal, Dahal & Adhikari, 2009). This situation must be reviewed and efforts should be made to expedite India's economic cooperation to Nepal on a greater quantum.

Although the open border between Nepal and India has both positive and negative ramifications, it is important to minimize the bottlenecks disrupting smooth flow of goods and services and free mobility of people from both sides. However, both governments should stringently regulate deflection of trade and cross-border terrorism. The open border between the two countries would be of great help to minimize the cost of trade. There are other priority areas such as tourism, agriculture and biodiversity, education, health and IT sectors, easy access for transfer of remittances through banking channels, construction of the East–West railway lines, extension of transmission lines to connect at national grid and connection of pipeline for smooth supply of petroleum products that require India's cooperation on a greater scale.

Similarly, the economic relationship with China must be further strengthened. China is the second largest economy in the world in terms of nominal GDP, which surpassed $13.3 trillion in 2017 (CIA World Fact Book/Wikipedia, 2018). The provision for exporting more than 8,000 products with zero customs duty from Nepal to China as a privilege to LDCs is another significant trade facilitation to promote Nepal's export to China in the future. The announcement of developing an 'Energy Silk Road' in this region and, more recently, establishment of Asian Infrastructure Investment Bank (AIIB) on China's initiative is a path-breaking development effort that will yield benefits to Nepal to spur its growth. The AIIB was envisaged to promote interconnectivity and economic integration in the region and cooperate with existing multilateral development banks. Interestingly, the USA has offered duty-free and quota-free access for sixty-six Nepali products to the American market for the next ten years and Nepal government must improve efficiency and capitalize on the opportunities to maximize the benefits from these facilities.

Nepal and China signed a 10-point agreement comprising agreements on transit transport; construction, management and maintenance of boundary river bridge at Hilsa, Humla; economic and technical cooperation, including a framework agreement to implement the Pokhara regional international airport project; feasibility study for exploration of oil and gas resources; Memorandum of Understanding (MoU) on the provision of goods for addressing climate change; MoU to strengthen intellectual property right; MoU on launching a joint feasibility study of China–Nepal Free Trade Agreement; MoU between China Banking Regulatory Commission and Nepal Rastra Bank; and Concessional Loan Agreement on Pokhara Regional International Airport (MoFA: Joint Press Statement, 2016).

Since China has initiated the historical proposal of One Belt One Road (OBOR), the Ninth Wonder of the World under the dynamic leadership of President Xi Jinping, the efforts towards developing China–Nepal economic cooperation is, indeed, a path-breaking event in the development of the Trans-Himalayan region. This calls for implementation of agreements and MoUs between Nepal and China held in Beijing in March 2016. It is also necessary for Nepal to enter into agreements with China separately on trade, transit, scientific cooperation, peace and friendship in the changing context of liberalization and globalization. Nepal, as a 'transit economy', has the great opportunity to foster economic growth by mobilizing 'trilateral cooperation'. It has been the gateway for India–China Trans-Himalayan trade since time immemorial.

Although Nepal is a landlocked country, this concept does not hold true today. It is now gradually shifting towards a 'land-linked nation' having direct land links with the two economic powers of the world, India and China. Nepal serving as a transit economy between them can derive various types of benefit ranging from monetary to creation of employment opportunities, and setting up of various infrastructures. This scenario helps create 'win-win' effects for all three countries by expanding trade and investment in potential areas and promoting biodiversity and tourism. It would be highly cost-effective. Nepal, as a transit economy, would not only strengthen connectivity within the China–Nepal–India economic corridor but also ensure peace, stability and prosperity in the region.

In Conclusion

Nepal's economic development is a challenging proposition. The country is struggling for survival and growth for the last six decades of planned economic development. This calls for a breakthrough in the economic front for both survival and growth. The economy is suffering from the under-spending syndrome for a long time due to transition-effects, followed by inefficiency, corruption and poor governance.

As of data for the last ten years, it is most unfortunate that the quantum of Nepal's GDP is extremely small despite tremendous economic potential and, therefore, the major challenge is how to expand the size of GDP by effectively mobilizing and utilizing both internal and external resources within time frame. A quantum jump in the economic front is virtually impossible with the diminutive size of GDP. Although the growth rate squeezed to 0.77 per cent during 2015/16 due to aberrant situations comprising devastating earthquake, protracted agitations and economic impasse, it was optimistically projected to be 7.2 per cent during the 14th Plan, 2016/17–2018/19.

The economy suffers from structural as well as several binding critical constraints comprising high-cost economy, subsistence agriculture, alarming increasing dependence, inadequate and poor status of physical infrastructure, rampant corruption, followed by inefficiency and poor governance. The major issues and challenges facing Nepalese economy is struggling for survival and sustaining the economy even during the crisis by ensuring robust growth with social justice. The underpinnings of the Nepalese economy are extremely confined to agriculture, especially high-value crops, hydropower, biodiversity, tourism, foreign employment and remittances and limited exportable items.

The vision or mission of Nepalese economy should be to build a strong 'economic nation state' through active participation of the people, ensuring a high quality of life to each individual and household within a time frame. The road map for Nepal's economic development suggests speedily accomplishing reconstruction and rehabilitation activities. In addition, it is imperative to promote a 'self-reliant' economy in potential areas, upgrading the status of the economy from an LDC to developing economy by 2022, ensuring a high, sustainable and inclusive growth with social justice by maximizing benefits from globalization and liberalization, and, finally moving towards achieving the target of GNP per capita at par with middle-income countries by 2030 and making Nepal the Switzerland of Asia by 2040. Investment is not a critical binding constraint on growth in Nepal, it is the lack of enlightened leadership to forcefully drive the economy, ensuring economic prosperity (ADB, 2009). Despite numerous limitations, Nepal's strategic location between India and China, abundance of biodiversity comprising both ecosystem and species, vast prospects for tourism and a large size of economically active population (gigantic 'wealth of nation') will be instrumental in ensuring economic prosperity of its three million people.

Annexure 1: Nepal: Annual Data 2016–17

	Particulars	**Amount**	**in % of GDP**
1.	GDP NPR (in billions)	2,599.23	
2.	GDP growth rate (in %)	6.0	
3.	Inflation rate (in %)	4.5	
4.	Total exports (NPR in billions) Exports to: India 56.7%; China 2.3%; Others 40.9%	73.0	2.8
5.	Total imports (NPR in billions) Imports from: India 64.0%; China 12.9%; Others 23.1%	910.11	38
6.	Total trade deficit (NPR in billions) India 64.6%; China 13.7%; Others 21.7%	917.0	35
7.	Share of export and import in total trade	Export 6.9%; Import 93.1%	

8.	Imports of selected commodities from India: Petroleum products, NPR 118.9 billion; Rice, NPR 23.6 billion; Vegetables, NPR 10.6 billion; Vehicles and spare parts, NPR 71.8 billion, Medicines, NPR 21.5 billions		
9.	Imports from India against payment in US Dollar (in NPR billion)	95.0	3.6
10.	Remittances (in NPR billion)	695.5	26.7
11.	Foreign Direct Investment (in NPR billion)	695.4	26.7
12.	Balance of payments situation (in NPR billion) Surplus	82.15	3.2
13.	Total expenditure (in NPR billion)	793.9	30.5
14.	Current expenditure (in NPR billion)	501.6	19.3
15.	Capital expenditure (in NPR billion)	189.5	7.3
16.	Financial management expenditure (in NPR billion)	102.8	3.9
17.	Total revenue (in NPR billion)	609.2	23.4
18.	Foreign grants (in NPR billion)	14.5	0.6
19.	Foreign loans (in NPR billion)	47.8	1.8
20.	Revenue collection (in NPR billion): VAT, 26.3%; Customs, 18.6%; Excise, 13.9%; Income Tax, 24.3%; Registration fee, 3.2%; Vehicle tax, 1.2%; Educational service tax, 0.1%; health service tax, 0.1% other tax, 2.2%; Non-tax revenue, 10.1%.		
21.	Deposit details of bank and financial institutions (in NPR billion)	2,660.0	
22.	Purchase of foreign currency IC NPR. 435.8 billion	US$4.1 billions	
23.	Foreign exchange reserves (in NPR billions)	1,079.5	41.5
24.	Current account deficit (in NPR billions)	10.1	0.4

Source: www.nrb.org.np, 2017

Annexure 2: GNI Per Capita (Nominal) of South Asian Countries and China (Atlas Method)*

Rank	Country	GNI per capita in $	Year
Upper middle-income group			
84	China	7,380	2014
86	Maldives	7,290	2014
Lower middle-income group			
127	Sri Lanka	3,400	2014
139	Bhutan	2,390	2014
151	India	1,610	2014
155	Pakistan	1,410	2014
163	Bangladesh	1,080	2014
Low income group			
175	Nepal	730	2014
179	Afghanistan	680	2014

Source: Wikipedia, 2016. According to World Bank classification (197 countries)

Annexure 3: International Comparison as of 2014

Name of index	Score	Score value range	Rank
Global Competitive Index[1]	3.38	1-7, 7 is best	102/144
Doing Business[2]	59.56	In %, 100 % is good	109/189
Human Dev. Index[3]	0.54	0-1, 1 highest	145/193
Fragile State Index[4]	90.5	higher value is worse	143/178
Corruption Perception Index[5]	29	0-100, 0 being very corrupt	126/175
World Happiness Index[6]	4.15	0-10, 10 being highest	135/156

Source: (1) Global Competitive Index 2014, and World Economic Forum 2014; (2) Doing Business Group 2014 and The World bank Group; (3) Human

Development Report (UNDP) 2014; (4) Fragile State Index 2014; (5) Corruption Perception Index 2014 (TI); and (6) World Happiness Index 2013 (Sustainable Development Solutions Network)

∽

Madan Kumar Dahal *is former Head and Professor of Economics at Tribhuvan University, and is a member of the Board of Directors, Institute for Strategic and Socio-Economic Research (ISSR) and Revenue Advisory Board, Ministry of Finance, Government of Nepal.*

Bibliography

Government and Allied Publications

Ministry of Law, Justice, Constituently Assembly and Parliamentary Affairs (LBMC). *Constitution of Nepal 2015*. Kathmandu: Law Book Management Committee.

Ministry of Commerce, Government of Nepal (MoC/GoN). *Nepal Trade Integration Strategy, 2016*.

Kathmandu: Ministry of Culture, Tourism and Civil Aviation, Government of Nepal (MoCTCA/GoN). *National Tourism Strategic Action Plan, 2016-2025*.

Ministry of Finance/Government of Nepal (MoF/GoN). *Budget Speech, FY 2016/17*.

Ministry of Finance/Government of Nepal (MoF/GoN). *Budget Speech, FY 2017/18*.

Ministry of Finance/Government of Nepal (MoF/GoN). *Economic Survey, FY2015/16*.

Ministry of Finance/Government of Nepal (MoF/GoN). *Economic Survey, FY 2016/17*.

Ministry of Foreign Affairs/Government of Nepal (MoFA/GoN). Joint Press Statement between the People's Republic of China and Nepal. 23 March 2016.

Nepal Electricity Authority (NEA). *Report of Nepal Electricity Authority, 2016*.

Nepal Stock Exchange, 30 September 2016.

National Planning Commission/Government of Nepal (NPC/GoN.) 2016. 14th Three Year Plan, 2016/17–2018/19, Draft Approach Paper.

National Planning Commission/Government of Nepal (NPC/GoN). 14th Three Year Plan, 2016/17–2018/19, Final Approach Paper, 8 January 2017.

Nepal Rastra Bank (NRB). *Macroeconomic Indicators of Nepal.* November 2017.

Office of the Auditor General–Nepal (OAG–N). Annual Report of the Office of the Auditor General, 2017.

Other Publications

Asian Development Bank. 2009. *Strengthening Country Diagnosis and Analysis of Binding Development Constraints in Selected Developing Member Countries.*

Asian Development Bank. 2012. *Agriculture Development Strategy, 2012.*

Central Bureau of statistics/Government of Nepal (CBS/GON). *Statistical Data, 2017.*

Central Bureau of Statistics/Government of Nepal (CBS/GON). *Nepal Living Standard Survey III, 2010.*

Collins, J.H., et al. 1996. *A Financial Future for Nepal: Creating an International Financial Services Center (IFSC).* Boston: Collins and Associates.

Dahal, M.K. and Inoue, K. 1994. *A Profile of Industrial Development in Nepal.* Tokyo: Institute of Developing Economies.

Dahal, M.K. 2004. *Nepalese Economy: Towards Building A Strong Economic Nation-State.* Kathmandu: Central Department of Economics, Tribhuvan University.

Dahal, M.K. 2013. 'Nepalese Economy and the Road to Development'. In: Rana, H.S. and Dahal, M.K. *Politics and Economy of Nepal.* Kathmandu: Nepal Nagarik Samaj.

Dahal, M.K. 2015. 'Fiscal Reforms for Sustainable Growth'. In: Pyakuryal, B. (Ed.) *Macro Economics: A Radical Thinking in Growth, Inequality and Inclusiveness in Nepal.* Kathmandu: Mandala Book Point.

International Conference of Nepal's Reconstruction (ICNR). 2015. Kathmandu: Ministry of Finance (MOF).

International Monetary Fund (IMF). 2016. *Report of International Monetary Fund, 2016.* Washington, D.C.: International Monetary Fund.

Pyakuryal, B., Dahal, M.K. and Adhikari, D. 2009. *India's Aid Policy to Nepal.* New Delhi/Kathmandu: India Nepal BPK Foundation.

Shrestha, T.B. and Vimal N.P. Gupta. 1993. 'Biodiversity Profile and Conservation Strategy for Nepal'. In Dahal, M.K. and Dahal, D.R. (Eds.) *Environment and Sustainable Development: Issues in Nepalese Perspective.* Nepal Foundation for Advanced Studies (NEFAS) and Friedrich Ebert Stiftung (FES).

Transparency International. 2016. *Report of Transparency International, 2016.*

United Nations Development Programme (UNDP). 2011. *Oxford Poverty and Human Development Initiative (OPHI).* New York: United Nations Development Programme.

United Nations Development Programme (UNDP)/Oxford, 2015. *Multidimensional Poverty Index (MPI).*

United Nations International Strategy for Disaster Reduction (UNISDR). 2015. *The UN Disaster Risk Reduction Situation Report.* http//:preventionwb.net/g0/44170

World Bank. 2016. *World Development Report, 2016.* Washington, D.C.: World Bank.

World Economic Forum (WEF). 2016. *Report of World Economic Forum, 2016.* Davos.

Newspapers and Websites

'Commitment of donors' assistance to Nepal equal to US$4.4 billion', *Republica,* 26 June 2015.

Himalayan Times, 2 March 2016.

Himalayan Times, 5 December 2016.

http://www. nrb.org

http://www.worldatlas.com

www.aiib.org

www.en.wikipedia.org

CIA World Fact Book/Wikipedia, 2018.

5

TRYST WITH DEMOCRACY: ELUSIVE STABILITY AND LOST OPPORTUNITIES

Dwarika Nath Dhungel
Jan Sharma

Nepal's tryst with democracy remains as elusive as its political stability ever since the collapse of the Rana oligarchy in 1951 and the advent of democratic innovations after the promulgation of a written constitution. The first abortive attempt at a constitutional order and constitutionalism was made in 1948 to replace the 'hukumi sasan' (the rule of the thumb) of the then rulers, viz. Rana oligarchy. The constitution of Nepal, promulgated in September 2015, is the country's seventh constitution. The hope is that it will institutionalize a Federal Democratic Republic, provide political stability and propel economic growth to catch up with its neighbours—China and India. It has already been three years since the promulgation, yet Nepal seems to be back to 'mangalman' (back to square one). The form of government is deeply contested. Governance has deteriorated rapidly and power remains concentrated in the hands of the syndicate of a few individuals running the country as if it were their fiefdom. Favouritism, nepotism and 'chakari' (sycophancy) remain entrenched in the society.

Since the promulgation of a new constitution, four prime ministers have changed already. The current Communist Alliance-led government, headed by Prime Minister Khadga Prasad Sharma Oli, enjoys the support of more than two-thirds of majority in Parliament but the alliance of the two communist parties is highly fragile. Internally, the economic situation has gone from bad to worse as the agriculture sector has declined, industrial sector left in ruin and remittance inflow has triggered imports and trade deficit to surge. The World Bank said the economy will grow by 4.6 per cent this year, lower than the projected growth of 7.5 per cent in fiscal year 2016-17. It said the country must create 2,40,000 jobs a year to maintain its employment rate.[1]

The social fabric in the country, once known for its tolerance and harmony, remains disturbed. Despite the creation of powerful local governments, power remains firmly under the control of Singha Durbar—the Central Secretariat. Externally, the country's image has been tarnished. Relations with most countries, including China and India, and major donors, are marked with mistrust and suspicions. With every single political innovation in the 2015 constitution being challenged and contested, political stability remains an illusion. What went wrong? We are examining Nepal's obscure democratic order, including recent political developments, political fissures and the future prospects in the following portions.

Political Development: 1951–2015

Since the overthrow of the Rana oligarchy in 1951, Nepal's political system has basically revolved around one form of Westminster model of parliamentary democracy or the other. The Interim Nepal Government Act 1951 promulgated by King Tribhuvan after the overthrow of the Rana oligarchy had enshrined the idea of a CA for drafting a new constitution through representatives of the people. It was, however, largely inspired by the nationalist movement in India rather than being a product of the emerging ground realities. In addition, it had provided a political system in which the king was to act as a constitutional head and the government was to be run by the people through political leaders. However, Tribhuvan amended the Act in February 1954, which some think laid the foundation for an absolute monarchy. Although the Act had promised an election for a CA, no assembly was ever elected.

Instead, a new constitution, the Constitution of the Kingdom of Nepal 1959, was promulgated by King Mahendra on 12 February 1959. This constitution provided for a Westminster parliamentary form of government with a constitutional monarch equipped with discretionary power, two houses of parliament—the House of Representatives (HoR) and the Upper House—and an independent judiciary. The country's third constitution, thus, came as a gift from the monarch, who described it as 'suitable to the genius of our country.' Within a week, elections were held for parliament. The NC, with a two-thirds majority, emerged as the largest party in the HoR and the Gorkha Parishad as the main opposition party. Bisheshwor Prasad Koirala, the leader of the NC, was appointed as prime minister. The responsibility of running the country, for the first time, was passed on to an elected prime minister.

A royal proclamation, on 15 December 1960, dismissed the government, dissolved parliament, and scrapped the constitution of 1959. A new constitution was promulgated two years later in 1962. The democratic experiment was short-lived, mainly because of mutual bickering among political parties and their leaders, as well as due to King Mahendra's ambition of not remaining as a constitutional head but instead to rule the country and his thinking that he was no less a personality than Koirala—a well-known personality in the then socialist world. Had these two persons realized the importance of each other and worked together, Nepal's destiny would have been completely different from what it is now.

The new political system was a 'party-less' one. It banned all political activities and political parties and restricted the freedom of the press and speech. The main feature of the new political system, also called the Panchayat polity, was a departure from the Westminster model, with a strong and decisive role for the monarchy in the political process. The king was the supreme leader and source of all powers—legislative, executive and judicial. The Rastriya Panchayat—a unicameral legislature—was elected indirectly through an electoral college comprising district and zonal assemblies. The king selected, from among the legislature members of cabinet who were accountable to him, and not to the national legislature. In addition, a four-tiered political structure starting from the lowest level, i.e. village or Town Panchayat, District Panchayat, Zonal Panchayat (later abolished) and National Panchayat (national assembly), which were all interlinked for the purpose of election, was also established.

Since political parties were banned, the election to all these bodies was held on a non-party basis, meaning candidates had to file nomination on individual capacity and not as nominees of political parties. In order to keep control over different sections of society, six officially sponsored class and professional organizations were established, viz. Nepal Youth Organization, Nepal Ex-servicemen Organization, Nepal Peasants Organization, Nepal Women's Organization, Nepal Labour Organization, and Nepal Students' Organizations. The new political system, King Mahendra explained, was 'rooted in our soil and suited to our conditions' (HMG/N 1965). But, as per lawyer and constitutional expert, Shambhu Prasad Gyawali (1998/1999), the king was considering to introduce democratic reforms by lifting the ban on political parties through an amendment in early 1970s. Unfortunately, this did not take place, as King Mahendra died of a massive heart attack in 1972.

The Harvard and Eton-educated King Birendra took over as the new king, sparking widespread hopes that he would carry forward the reforms his father was contemplating. After several false starts such as the Back to the Village National Campaign (BVNC), which was essentially an attempt at building a centrally controlled communist model of the politburo, Birendra somewhat reluctantly gave the people of Nepal the right to decide whether they wanted a reformed Panchayat system or switch to multiparty democracy through a national referendum in May 1980. The Panchayat option won with a razor-thin majority. After the referendum, a number of reforms such as direct election to the national legislature, appointment of the prime minister elected by its members from amongst themselves and accountability of the council of ministers to the national legislature were instituted through the third amendment of the constitution in 1980. The outlawed political parties continued to oppose the system, calling for lifting the ban on political parties and activities.

Critics of the reforms argued that the changes were too little and too late. Frustrations began to grow, sparking demonstrations against the Panchayat regime. Popular protests in April 1990, with the political and moral support of India, forced King Birendra to lift the ban on political parties, revive the multiparty parliamentary system of government with constitutional monarchy, guarantee independent judiciary and fundamental rights and name a commission to draft a new constitution (Sharma, 1990) based on these elements.

Coming as it did at the end of the Cold War and the collapse of the Soviet Union and other communist regimes in Eastern Europe, Nepal's new political system, formally legitimized by the Constitution of the Kingdom of Nepal 1990, had the solid backing of the international community. Despite its structural inconsistencies and lack of an economic vision, the political system initiated through the 1990 constitution was hailed by all except some political parties, mainly by communist factions. It provided for a constitutional monarchy and multiparty parliamentary democracy, independent judiciary, a bicameral legislature, guaranteed the freedom of speech and the press and constitutional guarantee to the political parties and freedom in their functioning. Parliamentary elections were held in 1991, which returned the NC with G.P. Koirala as the Prime Minister in power with the CPN-UML, which had serious reservations on the constitution, emerging as a formidable opposition.

It was obvious from the very beginning that implementing a new constitution would be problematic, especially because of the conditional support of the communists to the democratic order and internal political bickering within the ruling NC. The dissolution of parliament by Prime Minister G.P. Koirala and going for mid-term elections in 1994 were hardly surprising. The second parliamentary elections in November 1994 returned CPN-UML as the largest party but short of a majority. It formed a minority government with Man Mohan Adhikari as Prime Minister, which, after nine months in office, dissolved the parliament and called for fresh elections in 1995. A Supreme Court verdict in 1995 put the last nail in the coffin of the

1990 constitution, when it rejected the power of the prime minister to dissolve the house.[2] While political parties failed to institutionalize democracy, the constitution came under direct challenge from the CPN-M determined to topple the parliamentary regime and 'seize' power through armed insurgency.[3]

The Royal Palace massacre in June 2001 turned out to be a boon in disguise for the Maoists to expand their organization, while bickering among political parties prevented institutionalization of multiparty parliamentary democracy under the 1990 constitution. King Gyanendra dissolved the parliament at the recommendation of Sher Bahadur Deuba, who was dismissed as an 'incompetent' prime minister in 2002. Gyanendra subsequently took over power in February 2005.

India, which was furious with the king for having backed China's participation in the SAARC (Jha, 2012), brought the Seven-Party Alliance (SPA), which was opposed to the king and his actions, and the Maoists, who were opposed to parliamentary democracy and was raising armed insurgency since 1996, together and got a 12-point 'understanding'—Delhi Agreement II—signed on 22 November 2005. Upon the signing of this agreement, India significantly increased its role and influence in Nepal's domestic politics and internal affairs.[4]

Protests followed in Kathmandu in April 2006 when the SPA and the Maoists joined hands to topple the King's regime (Muni, 2012 and Jha, 2012). Indian mediation followed, which resulted in surrendering of power by the king to political parties, the appointment of G.P. Koirala, a leader of the NC, as prime minister and the restoration of the dissolved HoR, which had been dissolved, as indicated above, by King Gyanendra on the recommendation of Prime Minister Deuba in 2002. The restored parliament adopted 25-point declarations, which drastically cut the king's power, abolished bicameral legislature and converted itself into a national assembly. In addition, it declared that those provisions of the Constitution of the Kingdom of Nepal 1990 which contravene the declarations will be null and void.

The size of the converted house was expanded to include the representatives of the Maoists without election, and it even discarded the existing constitution and promulgated an interim constitution in 2007, suspending the monarchy until elections were held to the CA to draft a new constitution (Dhungel, 2007). Koirala got the country declared a federal state through an amendment to the interim constitution on 14 March 2007. These actions raised serious questions on the due process of law and the way changes were orchestrated. Dissenting voices were nipped in the bud.

CA I was elected in April 2008 for a period of two years and its term was subsequently extended many times till November 2012. But, despite several extensions, it failed to deliver a new constitution mainly due to the tug of war among the major political players (NC, CPN-UML and CPN-M, and Tarai/Madhes-based political parties) on the forms of government, the basis of carving out provinces and their delineation and the nature of state from religious perspective. The only thing it did at its very first meeting, on 28 May 2008, was to abolish the monarchy.

As a result, a new government with the chief justice of the country as chairperson of the Council of Ministers was formed, and elections to the CA II were held on 19 November 2013. CA II was rushed through the Constitution of Nepal 2015 on the 'fast track' after the four main political players sealed a 16-point deal on 8 June 2015.[5] The constitution adopted and promulgated on 20 September 2015[6], has thirty-seven parts, 308 articles and nine annexes.

The Constitution of 2015 has made three key innovations. First, it legitimized the abolition of the Hindu monarchy and created a republic. Second, it ended the unitary system of government with three layers of government: federal, provincial, local governments, which would use state powers. The Constitution has divided the country into seven provinces (pending their names and delineation), districts (seventy-seven as per the Constitution of 2015, are to function as coordinator) and 753 village and town municipalities were created by the government as per the constitutional provision. In addition, special, protected and autonomous regions may be created by the government for socio-cultural protection and development according to federal law.[7] Third, it seeks to redefine the relationship between the people and the state in a democratic framework.

Furthermore, the constitution defines Nepal as 'an independent, indivisible, sovereign, secular, inclusive, democratic, socialism-oriented federal democratic republic' (Article 4). It provides for an independent integrated system of judiciary—district courts, provincial courts and Supreme Court—and a number of constitutional bodies. It guarantees a very exhaustive and long list of fundamental rights to the people (thirty altogether for whose implementation, the government is to frame laws within three years, i.e. 2018) and their duties (four) towards the state (Part 3, 2015 Constitution). Also, it has provided a long list of directive principles, policies and obligations of the State (three with sixteen subheadings; each sub-heading having a number of provisions) (Part 4, 2015 Constitution).

With regard to the form of government, the Constitution provides for 'multi-party, competitive, federal, democratic, republican, parliamentary form of government based on pluralism' (Article 74). It vests executive power in the Council of Ministers, which is responsible for issuing general directives and controlling and regulating governance of Nepal. The Council of Ministers is headed by the prime minister. It provides for a ceremonial president and a vice president. A chief minister, who heads the Council of Ministers in provinces, is elected by the provincial legislature from among its members. Governors were to be ceremonial heads of provinces. The 753 rural and urban municipalities are headed by elected chairpersons/mayors and they are assisted by the elected vice-chairpersons/deputy mayors and a number of other elected ward members.

Constitution Implementation Status

The first major step for the implementation of the Constitution was the successful and peaceful holding of local, provincial and parliamentary elections in 2017 with an enthusiastic participation of the people across the country. Local elections were held in three phases to elect 35,041 representatives. CPN-UML won majority of seats in almost all the 753 municipalities except in province number 2—comprising eight districts of the Tarai/Madhes bordering India, as shown in Table 1.

Table 1: Comparative election results of 2013 and 2017

Party	CA II Elections 2013	Local Elections 2017
NC	2,418,370 (26%)	2,982,240 (33%)
CPN-UML	2,239,609 (24%)	3,064,539 (34%)
CPN-MC	1,439,726 (15%)	1,602,450 (17%)
RPP RPP-Nepal	630,697 (7%) 260,234 (3%)	290,156 (3%) [unified]
Madhesi Forum Federal Socialist Forum	214,319 (2%) 121,274 (1%)	386,783 (4%) [FSF]
Nepal Loktantrik Forum	274,987 (3%)	124,654 (1%)
Rastriya Janata Party(RJP)	510,644 (5%)	251,615 (3%)
Others/Independents	1,374,002 (14%)	

Source: *Naya Patrika*, 12 October 2017.

Table 2 provides details on the position of political parties in the elections that were held for local positions. The voter turnout was as high as 71 per cent according to the Election Commission. The largest communist parties maintained a strong presence at the local level in all the provinces except in Province 2.

Table 2: Detailed party positions in 753 local government bodies

Party	Mayor/ Chairman	Deputy Mayor/ Vice Chairman	Ward Chairman	Ward Members
1. CPN-UML	294	331	2,559	10,915
2. NC	266	223	2,287	8,680
3. CPN-MC	106	111	1,103	4,121
4. Federal Socialist Forum, Nepal	34	32	262	1,111
5. Rastriya Janata Party	25	30	194	862
6. Madhesi Loktantrik Forum (Loktantrik) and Nepal Loktantrik Forum	9	8	88	356

7. RPP	5	7	59	214
8. Rastriya Janamorcha Party	3	4	33	146
9. Naya Shakti Party, Nepal	2	1	22	85
10. Nepal Janata Dal	2	0	7	30
11. Nepal Workers and Peasants Party	1	1	22	75
12. Independents	6	5	91	131
13. Bahujan Shakti Party	0	0	8	34
14. Rastriya Janamukti Party	0	0	3	17
15. Rastriya Prajatantra Party (Democratic)	0	0	2	6
16. Federal Democratic National Forum	0	0	1	6
17. CPN (Marxist-Leninist)	0	0	1	3
18. Nepal Pariwar Dal	000	0	0	1
Total	753	753	6,742	26,793

Source: Election Commission of Nepal

The second important step was the election of the provincial assemblies and federal parliament simultaneously in November and December 2017. The Constituency Delimitation Commission submitted its report on 30 August 2017, recommending 165 constituencies across the country for the election to the HoR and 330 constituencies for the election of the seven provincial assemblies[8].

The Communist Alliance of CPN-UML and CPN-MC secured most of the seats in the provincial assemblies (Table 3). Following the elections, CPN-UML has chief ministers in four provinces (Provinces 1, 3, 4 and 5) while CPN-MC has two Chief Ministers (Provinces 6 and 7). The Federal Socialist Forum has a Chief Minister in Province 2, as it secured majority in only this province.

Table 3: Results of provincial assembly elections 2017

Party	FPTP	PR
1. CPN-UML	168	75
2. NC	41	72
3. CPN-MC	73	35
4. FSFN	24	13
5. Rastriya Janata Party	16	12
6. RPP	0	3
7. Independent	3	0
8. Rastriya Janamorcha	2	2
9. Naya Shakti Party Nepal (NSPN)	2	1
10. Nepal Workers and Peasants Party	1	1
11. Bibeksheel Sajha	0	3
12. Nepal Sanghiya Samajbadi	0	1
13. Sanghiya Lokatantrik Rastriya Manch	0	1
14. Rastriya Prajatantra Party (Democratic)	0	1
Total	330	220

Source: Election Commission of Nepal

The biggest winner in the first past the post elections held for the HoR turned out to be CPN-UML, which won 80 seats followed by the CPN-MC with 36 seats, NC with 23 seats, Rastriya Janata Party (RJP) with 11 seats, and FSFN with 10 seats (Table 4). RPP, Naya Shakti Party, Nepal (NSPN) and Rastriya Janamorcha Party (RJP) got one seat each and an independent member was also elected.

The popular mandate was thus of CPN-UML Chairman K.P. Sharma Oli for the nationalist position he took during the Indian blockade following the promulgation of a new constitution in September 2015 and the opening he made with China, especially the transit transport agreement, to balance the Indo-centric foreign policy Nepal had been pursuing since 1990. Secondly, it was also a popular endorsement of the Communist Alliance's slogan of a strong government for providing political stability and propelling the country to economic prosperity.

Last but not the least is the strong party organization of CPN-UML. In contrast, NC focused on the threat of 'totalitarianism' with the rise of the Communist Alliance, even if the party's own leaders have highly authoritarian inclinations, and thus failed to inspire the Nepali voters.

Table 4: Results of HoR elections on 26 November and 7 December 2017

Parties	Votes	%	FPTP	PR
1. CPN-UML	3173494	33.25	80	41
2. NC	3128389	32.78	23	40
3. CPN (MC)	1303721	13.66	36	17
4. RJP	472254	4.95	11	6
5. FSFN	470201	4.93	10	6
6. RPP	196782	2.06	1	0
7. Independent	–	–	1	0
8. RPP (Democratic)	88377	0.93	0	0
9. NSPN	81837	0.86	1	0
10. Nepal Workers and Peasants Party	–	–	1	0
11. Rastriya Jan Morcha	62,133	–	1	0
12. Others	–	6.58	–	–
Total	9,544,779	100	165	110

Source: Election Commission of Nepal.

In both HoR and the 59-member Rastriya Sabha (National Assembly), the Communist Alliance commands a comfortable majority. The HoR Speaker Krishna Bahadur Mahara and his deputy Shiva Maya Tumbahamphe, and Rastriya Sabha Chairman Ganesh Timilsina and Deputy Chairperson Sashikala Dahal are also Communist Alliance nominees. Bidya Devi Bhandari and Nanda Bahadur Pun both are nominees of the Communist Alliance and have been endorsed for their second terms in office.

On 15 February 2018, President Bhandari appointed Oli as the new Prime Minister. He sought a vote of confidence in Parliament after being appointed and secured more than three-fourths of support, including of the RJP and FSFN, who during the elections were vowed opponents. There were initial delays in giving a complete shape to the new government and questions have been raised on the longevity of the Communist Alliance, given their acrimonious personal disputes in the past.

Principal Fractures

Just because the constitution has come into operation does not mean that it has been accepted by all sections of the society and that substantive issues that seriously divided the country during its drafting, have been resolved once and for all. The Tarai-based parties have not abandoned their demand for a major constitutional amendment. It has been the bargaining point for their participation in the current Communist Alliance government. If the constitutional amendment issue is revived again, other issues such as the secular nature of the state, form of government, the financial viability of federalism, abolition of monarchy and a host of other issues may come up for revision, since these innovations were neither made by the political leadership (that has been running the country since 2006-07) by seeking public opinion, nor have they put the draft constitution into national referendum. As such some of the issues which are still contested and might come up time and again for revision, are discussed below.

Form of government

During the drafting of the constitution in 2015, a number of proposals on the form of government were floated and the debate on the merit of these proposals continues to persist, irrespective of the promulgation. The debate was obviously dominated by the CPN-M's proposal for a directly elected president with full executive authority, a position which the party has not yet abandoned. The argument was that the Maoists had launched the so-called People's War to topple the Westminster model of democracy, which has failed to serve the interest of the people. It is difficult to say how genuinely the Maoists were committed to changing the political system. However, they met with counter-proposals from the mainstream political parties, mainly NC, who insisted on basically the Westminster model under the cover of a 'reformed' parliamentary system. CPN-UML proposed a directly elected prime minister, which some of its leaders continue to uphold.

Ultimately, the CA accepted the said type of Westminster model and got it included in the constitution. Such a system of government was accepted, despite the fact that, time and again, the Westminster model of democracy has failed to provide political stability in the country ever since the opening of the democratic order in 1951. The governments have tended to be short-lived, for example, there have been as many as twenty-six governments over a period of twenty-six years since the restoration of multiparty government in 1990, including ten governments in the period of ten years of post-2006 political change (Risal and Risal, 2004 and Thapa, 2012). Even after the recent 2017 elections and left alliance getting the mandate to rule the country, many people doubt as to whether or not the country would have a stable government for five years.

Election system

Nepal has had a long tradition of having the first-past-the-post (FPTP) system for parliamentary elections. This practice was introduced for the first time in 1959, during the election of the national legislature under the Panchayat system after the 1980 national referendum, and then three parliamentary elections held in 1991, 1994 and 1999 under the multiparty dispensation. After political developments in 2006, CA elections were held in 2008 and 2013 on the basis of a mixed system that combined the FPTP and the proportional representation (PR) systems. The idea of the PR system was to ensure broader participation of all regions, ethnic communities, gender and communities in the political decision-making process.

The mixed system, no doubt, saw improved representation of the intended communities and constituencies. But the PR system has come under criticism for reflecting the same political culture as the FPTP system primarily because the PR system was used against its very spirit for partisan gains. Serious questions have been raised on the intent of the political parties and the process they had pursued in preparing the closed list of candidates for the PR election. Comments in the media suggest that a large amount of money had changed hands during the selection of candidates.

The mixed electoral system has been so abused that politicians have especially used the PR system to either get their spouses or family members represented in parliament or sell tickets to the highest bidder. Bidding for a member to contest a parliamentary seat, as reported in the various media, is as high as NPR 50 million ($454,990). Nepotism and favouritism were the other key determinants. This has made a mockery of representation.

Despite the fact that people, during the 2017 general elections, gave a clear majority to the Communist Alliance in both the federal and provincial levels, based on the behaving pattern of the political parties, mainly those in power, there is every possibility that the PR system would remain as a hanging sword over the heads of the political parties from the point of view of gaining majority at the federal and provincial levels; meaning, the PR system could remain as an important factor for making the political system fragile.

In order to correct this flaw, the Legislature-Parliament, in September 2017, passed a law. According to the law, in order to qualify for the PR seats, political parties now have to secure at least 3 per cent of the popular votes in the HoR and 1.5 per cent in the provincial assembly elections. Despite such threshold, the mixed system only further expands the role of the syndicate in the political process—the main focus of which is to share power to influence the outcome of the vote in elections to capture as many seats as possible by taking advantage of the incumbency in office, money and muscle power. The continuation of the political syndicate even after elections prevents political parties from being accountable and promotes the culture of impunity. Pressure is building to review the mixed system and further reform the election system.

State restructuring and the Tarai/Madhes question

In order to address the concerns of the Tarai/Madhes-based parties, the government had submitted a constitution amendment bill in April

2017,[9] but failed during the voting in the Legislature Parliament (see Chapter 8). The RJP, formed after the alliance of Madhesi parties, said it accepted the results but would not give up its demands. It also decided to take part in the elections held for all three levels of government, despite the failure of the vote on the bill.

Will Tarai/Madhes parties—the RJP and FSFN—attempt to revive the creation of two, if not a single, province of all the plain areas in the Tarai bordering India? Will attempt be made to retain the current arrangement while carving another province in the west in the name of the Tharu community? These questions pose challenges to a successful implementation of the constitution of 2015. For example, the debate on the remaining five Tarai districts, i.e. Jhapa, Morang and Sunsari in the east and Kailali and Kanchanpur in the west remains unsettled. Still there is a significant section in the country which is opposed to the way seven provinces were created without taking into account the intrinsic and inalienable relationship that interlinks the three main ecological zones of the country—Himal, Hills and Tarai. The issue has already divided the Nepali society and is likely to continue to divide for a long time to come.

It may be mentioned that federalism was basically a Maoist agenda reluctantly accepted by the NC and CPN-UML for political expediency rather than genuine commitment. Despite public commitment, top leaders of the two parties admit privately that federalism is not going to work because so little is understood of the concept and paucity of resources to implement the highly ambitious structures.

The same is the case with the issue of citizenship—one of the issues raised by the Tarai/Madhesi parties that had found a place in the second amendment to the constitution, but had failed during voting. The issue is still there. One of the issues is on citizenship to foreign women married to a Nepali national. The 2015 Constitution provides that if a 'foreign woman who has a matrimonial relationship with a citizen of Nepal may, if she so wishes, acquire naturalized citizenship of Nepal as provided for in the federal law.' This provision is contested by a section of the Madhesi parties. They want 'acquisition of naturalized citizenship to be automatic on application' (*Indian*

Express, 24 September 2015).

Indeed, a foreign woman married to a Nepali citizen should get the Nepali citizenship if she wishes. It may also be added that a foreign woman married to a Nepali national instantly qualifies for Nepali citizenship while such women in other South Asian countries, including India, have to wait for several years before they even officially qualify to apply for citizenship[10]. Thus, the question that arises is how the provision of the constitution on granting naturalized citizenship to a foreign woman married to a Nepali citizen could be belittling to the Madhesi or, for that matter, any other community?

The other contested provision by the same section of the population is that of debarring naturalized citizens from occupying some important positions of the country, such as the president and vice president, etc. (Article 289). As to the dissatisfaction to the provision of Article 289, it may be mentioned that, in the USA—considered to be the most democratic country in the world—a naturalized citizen cannot run for the office of the President. Citing this fact, one could pose a question to those who are opposed to the provisions of Article 289: Why should Nepal allow its naturalized citizen to seek election to, and hold the post of, the president and some other crucial positions?

Religion

Religion became a political issue in Nepal when the nation was abruptly proclaimed a 'secular' republic in 2008. Political leaders involved in the process are now admitting that 'huge amounts' of money passed hands to turn Nepal into a 'secular' country. Since the Hindu nationalist BJP swept parliamentary elections in India in 2014, various forums have sprung to revive Nepal as a Hindu state. There was an overwhelmingly popular demand that the national referendum be held to determine whether Nepal should be revived as a Hindu country or stay secular, when opinions were collected on the draft of the 2015 constitution. But the opinions were rejected by the political syndicate reportedly under Western pressure. In any case, Nepal as a Hindu nation was not problematic at all and demand for secularism was never one of the demands of political movements. Yet, one wonders whether the popular demand for the revival of a Hindu nation would have been possible if the BJP had not won the Indian elections.

It is understood that the current BJP government of Narendra Modi, who once was a Pracharak of the Rastriya Swayamsevak Sangha (RSS)—a staunch Hindu religion-believing organization and popular base of the BJP—himself a Hindu, seems to be under pressure from the RSS to see that Nepal is revived as a Hindu state. The Indian establishment may also continue to put pressure on the political leadership, mainly the leadership of all the three major political parties to agree to amend the provision of the constitution on religion.

Likewise, funding, mainly from several external sources, may continue to play a crucial role in accelerating religious conversions, which are already happening at an alarming pace. A recent report in the *Guardian* says money was being used to promote Christianity in Nepal (*Guardian*, 15 August 2017). Such developments are appreciated neither by a majority of the Nepali people nor by external players such as India. Also there is fear among many people that undercurrent religious tensions could take a bad turn unless the issue is addressed properly taking in the opinion of a majority of the people.

Relationship among tiers of government

It may be reminded that during their random discussions on state restructuring with a cross-section of people living in different parts of the country, Mueller-Boeker and Dhungel (2015) had found that there was a consensus among the people on the need for fully empowered local bodies that are area-based and subject matter-based user groups or committees. They had told frankly that the elections to the local bodies should be held as soon as possible so that they could contact their locally elected representatives for getting their day to day needs addressed, and also had indicated that the idea of federalism was an externally imposed notion.[11]

Since the local elections and taking over the running of local government bodies by people's representatives, differences of opinions were noticed between these representatives and the attitude of the Nepal government ministries and departments regarding the actual roles of the local government bodies, which are recognized as the third layer of government by the Constitution of Nepal, 2015. Nevertheless, it was observed during field trips to some districts that people have high expectations from the newly elected local representatives, especially in the field of service delivery. The sooner an understanding is reached between the government ministries and departments and local government bodies, the better it would be for both and for the improvement of the service delivery system in the country.

In addition, it is most likely that conflicts between the provincial governments and local government bodies might arise since both are constitutionally guaranteed levels of government and independent from each other. Also, there is a possibility that the provincial governments would turn out to be weaker in relation to the local government bodies as they have a long history in the country and are directly responsible for service delivery at the local level.

Cost of managing federal structure

The most important issue related to federalism that has come out recently is that seven provincial legislatures are going to be costlier than the federal parliament from the perspective of running and managing them (*Nagarik*, 17 October 2017). Thus serious questions have been raised on the viability of the costly federal structures and whether Nepal's sluggish economy could actually sustain them without major economic reforms and overhaul. Economists and experts are already suggesting seeking loans and external financial support to sustain the federal structures. Some provinces have started complaining that the federal government has not been extending the necessary cooperation. In a letter to Prime Minister Oli, Chief Minister of Province 2 has asked not to obstruct the working of the provincial governments, and has threated to go on strike at the Janaki Temple in Janakpur if the federal government continued to obstruct the workings of the provincial governments.

In course of time, the government may be able to address the issues of the financial resource constraints through internal borrowing, which is already high and external support. Thus, the management of the conflict between the three-levels—central, provincial and local level governments—on the political control over the resources is likely to be most challenging in implementing the federal structure. Because of these reasons, the national level political leaders, although not in public, have already started raising doubts on the utility of three levels of government, especially that of the provincial level.

Why These Fractures and Reactions to the Constitution of Nepal?

One of the major reasons of the fractures is the tendency of political parties, mainly the three major political parties, whose leaders had formed a syndicate to hijack the decision-making power of the people's representative body (legislative parliament) in the name of sahamati (consensus) or sahakarya (cohabitation). The syndicate had abused the state authority or power to serve their vested partisan interests at the cost of others. This tendency reminds one of the term sarbasammati (consensus), characterized by the then 'party-less' Panchayat regime.

Under the concept, a decision is taken on an issue or issues through debate and consultation, mainly by core decision-makers (political and administrative elite) in Kathmandu and passed on to others to be accepted. The concept began to be challenged subsequently by the Western value system of majoritarian rule, which was experimented during the multiparty democracy and constitutional monarchy following the changes in 1990.

Since 2006, the emphasis of Nepal's political culture has reverted to the days of Panchayat and the syndicate has hijacked people's power. This was clearly seen in the making and adoption process of the 2015 constitution, resulting in the emergence of a number of fractures in the national political scene. As a result, a large section of the Nepali society had felt alienated from the country's governance system and political process.

No doubt the left alliance commands the majority at the federal and six of the seven provincial governments along with the capture of almost all the local governments. But the question could still be asked whether left alliance leaders, mainly PM Oli, the chairperson (as of March 2018) and main leader of the CPN-UML and Prachanda—the supremo within the CPN-MC—would allow the legislatures to be the real decision-making bodies or form a syndicate, take the decisions and pass on to the legislatures just to adopt and approve. From all indications, the syndicate system may continue to remain in the Nepalese governance system. Although the NC is in opposition, it might demand its share in the decision-making process as well by making a plea that it was one of the major players that brought federalism, republican order and secularism in the country.

The factures also have external dimensions. In many of the political changes in Nepal since 1950, external factors have often played a decisive role. The end of the Rana oligarchy and the 'democratic opening' in 1951 was just a byproduct of the collapse of the British Empire and India's independence and the mediating role played by Indian Prime Minister Jawaharlal Nehru. It was through Nehru's mediating role that a political agreement was reached between King Tribhuvan and the NC, which had launched an armed rebellion against the Rana oligarchy. The agreement was also known as the Delhi Compromise (Delhi Agreement I), which ended the armed insurrection.

Thus, in 1951, the king promised elections to the CA, which would draft a new constitution. It never happened. Rather, Nepal adopted, under King Mahendra, the Westminster parliamentary democracy under the constitution of 1959, drafted by a Nepali team with the advice of British constitutional expert Sir Ivor Jennings. This constitution also became a victim of a military buildup in India and China and a war between these countries in 1962. King Mahendra promulgated a new constitution, inspired largely by Indonesia's Guided Democracy and Pakistan's Basic Democracy. The 1962 constitution placed the Hindu monarchy at the centre stage of the Nepalese political process. It was the only constitution in Nepal that lasted for twenty-eight years. And Nepal was dramatically transformed politically, socially and economically during the rule.

There was a tremendous increase in political awareness in the country under the 1962 constitution. It led to a growing demand for political and economic reforms that were happening elsewhere in the world. The communist regimes in the Soviet Union and Eastern Europe began to collapse in the 1990s, and pressure mounted on King Birendra to lift the ban on political parties. Multiparty parliamentary democracy was 'revived' in 1990 partly because of the 'popular aspirations of democracy', but decisive was the external force, especially India's backing to punish the monarchy for having imported arms, including anti-aircraft guns, from China in 1988. India's refusal to renew the trade treaty and its backing of the 'popular movement' compelled King Birendra to revive the multiparty parliamentary democracy under the Constitution of the Kingdom of Nepal 1990.

The CPN-M, which was largely perceived as being used by India to launch a proxy war in Nepal, got an upper hand after the Royal Palace massacre of June 2001 and, by 2005, it had received India's backing to overthrow the monarchy (Muni, 2012). It was India that set the atmosphere for the SPA and the CPN-M to sign the 12-point Agreement. It was this agreement that played a crucial role in the election to CA I, abolition of monarchy and federal restructuring, in addition to turning the kingdom into a secular republic. The consequence of all this was that the 1990 constitution was discarded and Nepal got an interim constitution in 2007 and finally a new constitution in 2015.

It may be mentioned that India's reaction on the finalization and adoption of the constitution of 2015 was swift and harsh. On 18 September 2015, New Delhi rushed its Foreign Secretary Subramanyam Jaishankar as Modi's special envoy to persuade Nepali leaders to defer the promulgation. When he returned on 19 September, 'India...expressed hope that Nepal's political leaders will display flexibility and maturity to ensure a durable and resilient constitution.'[12]

On 20 September, India 'noted' the promulgation of a constitution and said, '[a]ll outstanding issues and differences should be resolved through dialogue in an ambience free from violence and intimidation.' On 22 September, India's External Affairs Ministry expressed 'serious concern' over the removal of the provisions of delineation of electoral constituencies on the basis of population from the Interim Constitution. Two days later, it enforced an unofficial economic blockade to stop essential supplies to make Kathmandu kneel down, which lasted till it was lifted to allow Nepal's prime minister to visit India in February 2016.

China—which is, at present, one of the major external players in Nepal's affairs—and some other countries welcomed the polity established by the 2015 constitution. Chinese Foreign Ministry spokesman Hong Lei in Beijing, 'noted with pleasure', the assembly's endorsement of the constitution, adding: 'The Chinese side supports and respects Nepal's independent choice of social system and development path and wishes for political stability and economic development of Nepal' (Statement at regular press briefing in Beijing, 17 September 2015). When asked about the dissatisfaction among a minority, Lei said, 'China sincerely hopes that all political parties in Nepal can bear in mind the fundamental interests of their country and the people, address the differences through dialogue and consultation, and bring happiness to the people' (Statement in Beijing, 21 September 2015).

The United States took a different and somewhat balanced position on the issue. Department of State Spokesman John Kirby described the promulgation as 'an important milestone in Nepal's democratic journey' and urged the government to 'continue efforts to accommodate views of all Nepalese and ensure that the constitution embraces measures consistent with globally accepted norms and principles, including gender equality, religious freedom, and the right to citizenship' (Statement in Washington, 22 September 2015).

In Conclusion

There was a high expectation that a constitution drafted, adopted and promulgated by the people's elected assembly (CA) would satisfy people's expectations and put an end to the political transition that had started with the abrogation of the Constitution of the Kingdom of Nepal 1990 and adoption of the Interim Constitution 2007. But, during its adoption phase, and immediately after the promulgation of the 2015 constitution, the country faced unrest in some Tarai areas and India's unofficial economic blockade, and even those political parties that had voted for the constitution, instead of joining hands in its implementation, are now wrangling on the amendment to the constitution. The NC, CPN-UML and CPN-M (now CPN-MC), which should have worked together and owned the constitution, are now politically at loggerheads on these issues. As a result, Nepal's tryst with democracy and political stability, still looks elusive.

The demand for revival of monarchy is growing, which is visible from the crowd former king, Gyanendra, is attracting wherever he goes and the tacit recognition given to him by both India and China. Likewise, the demand for the revival of the Hindu state is steadily on the increase. All these developments mean not only challenges or contestations to all the major innovations of the 2015 Constitution, but also an indication of continuation of the political transition in the country. There are indications that the constitution may turn into an ineffective document and the country may face another round of conflict.

The prolonged political transition, which, on face value, looks to be over after general and local elections, has already made the economy stagnate and miss the opportunity to be benefitted from the huge markets of her two fast-developing neighbours[13]. Also the country is facing serious issues, such as the continuation of social tension, mass exodus of the youth (both brain and muscle) to foreign countries in search of employment, impunity and serious governance situation, weak state machinery, total lack of accountability feeling among political decision-makers towards the Nepali people, gradual loss of credibility of political leaders of all political parties and increased foreign influence in the decision-making process of the country (Shrestha and Dhungel, 2016). Above all, the image of the country is declining day-by-day.

Due to these very reasons, public frustration is on the rise. As a result, some have even talked of the military to take over for some years, cleaning the mess and handing over the politicians by organizing fresh elections. This institution remains the least politicized and least corrupt of the state institutions and leadership, to take over the duty of running the country and get rid of the prolonged political transition, while also addressing the contested issues through discussions with the stakeholders concerned, both internal and external.

However, a military takeover could only be a temporary solution because this option has its own inherent limitations, i.e. the least politicized institution will get politicized, which would give rise to military officers craving for political ambitions. It will be a major setback to democracy-building. Nepal's military is virtually and solely dependent on foreign countries for supplies of arms, which means external powers will use the military to control the country indiscreetly, thus preparing a coffin for democracy.

There is a sizeable section in society which thinks that the 1990 constitution was a democratic constitution, best tailored to the country and had the ability to deliver if allowed to function properly. No leader has explained the need why it was abandoned, and most importantly, without following a due process of law. So, they feel that it should be revived. But its revival, although not impossible, looks slim, given the deep perception of the current political leadership responsible for its abrogation, which may not like to be seen as the defeated player in Nepalese politics.

Observing the situation of Nepal, Professor Imtiaz Ahmed, a well-known South Asian political scientist, who teaches at the Dhaka University and was the former Executive Director of Colombo-based Regional Strategy Security Studies Center (RSCS), during a meeting with one of the contributors of this chapter at an international conference, suggested, 'Why cannot Nepal work through the system of parliamentary enactments if its political leaders cannot agree on the basic political issues? There is no written constitution in the United Kingdom where affairs of the state are managed through parliamentary enactments. So, for you as well, there is no need for a written constitution, if political leaders cannot agree on the basic issues and thereby letting the country in a perpetual political uncertainty'.

One can hardly challenge this argument or suggestion of an eminent political scientist from the region, but the fact remains that, ever since the overthrow of the Rana oligarchic rule in 1951, Nepal has always been governed and managed on the basis of a written constitution, and the idea of running and managing the country's affairs through parliamentary enactments may not be realistic.

Thus, to save the country possibly falling into another round of conflict and putting an end to all the political issues and also meeting the challenges the 2015 constitution faces, it would be desirable on the part of the political leadership to look into the contested issues from a broader nationalistic perspective not in a piecemeal manner just to satisfy a section of the society. In other words, it would be a pragmatic option for Nepal and its political leadership to seek the opinion of the people in addressing the demands of the various sections of the society and seeking the solution to contentious issues. In this regard, it may be mentioned that the Constitution of Nepal 2015 has provided a system holding national referendum (Article 275) to address the matters of national concern.

∽

***Dwarika Nath Dhungel** is currently a senior researcher of Social Sciences. He is Former Executive Director, Institute for Integrated Development Studies (IIDS), Kathmandu, and Former Secretary, Government of Nepal.*

***Jan Sharma** is senior research fellow at the Center for South Asian Studies, Nepal.*

Bibliography

Government and Allied Publications

Law Book Management Committee (LBMC), Ministry of Law, Justice,

Constituently Assembly and Parliamentary Affairs. *Constitution of Nepal 2015*. Kathmandu: Law Book Management Committee.

Government of Nepal (GoN). 2016. *Joint Statement on the State Visit of Prime Minister of Nepal, Rt. Hon'ble Mr. Pushpa Kamal Dahal 'Prachanda' to India,* (15-18 September 2016), Ministry of Foreign Affairs, Kathmandu.

His Majesty's Government/Nepal (HMG/Nepal). Shree 5 Maharajadhiraj Bata Bakseka Ghoshana, Bhashanra Sandeshharu (Royal proclamations, Speeches, and Messages), His Majesty's Government, Panchayat Ministry, Publicity Department, Kathmandu, 11 June 1965.

Other Publications

Mueller-Boeker, U. and Dhungel, D.N. 2015. Field notes of the visits to some Tarai districts of Mid and Far Western Development Regions and Sindhupalchowk districts in Central Development Region, February and May 2014.

Dhungel, D.N. 2007. *Inside Out: Political Parties of Nepal*, Kathmandu: Institute for Integrated Development Studies (IIDS) and International IDEA.

Eissiedel, von S., Malone, D.M. and Pradhan, S. 2012. *Nepal in Transition: From People's War to Fragile Peace.* New Delhi: Center on International Cooperation, Cambridge University Press.

Devkota, G.B. 1960. *Nepalko Rajnitik Darpan (Nepal's Political Mirror).*

Gyawali, S.P. 1998/1999. *Byakti ra Bichar: Ek Wakilko Sansmaranra Chintan (Person and Thoughts: Remembrance of a Lawyer and His Thoughts).* Kathmandu: Jagadamba Prakashan.

Jha, P. 2012. 'A Nepali Perspective on International Involvement in Nepal.' In: Eissiedel, von S., Malone, D.M. and Pradhan, S. (Eds.) *Nepal in Transition: From People's War to Fragile Peace.* New Delhi: Center on International Cooperation, Cambridge University Press.

Muni, S.D. 2012. 'Bringing the Maoists down from the Hills: India's Role.' In Eissiedel, von S., Malone, D.M. and Pradhan, S. (Eds.) *Nepal in Transition: From People's War to Fragile Peace.* New Delhi: Center on International Cooperation, Cambridge University Press.

Oli, K.P.S. 2016. *Sanghiyata Nui Aphuharule Nachaheko (We did not want Federalism),* http://www.khabardabali.com/ and http://ktv.ekantipur.com/programs/fireside.html

Risal, B. and Risal, R.M. 2004. *Nepalka Mantriharu (Ministers of Nepal).* Kathmandu: Capital Printer's Inc.

Sharma, J. 1990. 'Kathmandu Spring Tests Monarchy', *Wall Street Journal*, 3 April 1990.

Sharma, J. 1998. *Democracy Without Roots*. New Delhi: Book Faith India.

Shrestha, A.M. and Dhungel, D.N. 'Emerging Consensus', *My Republica*, 28 September 2016.

Sever, A. 1993. *Nepal Under the Ranas*. New Delhi: Oxford & IBH Publishing Co. Pvt. Ltd.

Thapa, D. 2012. 'The Making of Maoist Insurgency'. In Eissiedel, von S., D.M. Malone and Pradhan, S. (Eds.) *Nepal in Transition: From People's War to Fragile Peace*. New Delhi: Center on International Cooperation, Cambridge University Press.

Press Briefings/Statements

Beijing, 17 September 2015.

Beijing, 21 September 2015.

Washington, 22 September 2015.

Joint Statement on the State visit of Prime Minister of Nepal, Rt. Hon'ble Mr Pushpa Kamal Dahal 'Prachanda' to India (15–18 September 2016)

Newspaper and Websites

The *Guardian*, 15 August 2017; https://www.theguardian.com/global-development/2017/aug/15/they-use-money-to-promote-christianity-nepal-battle-for-souls

Rai, O.A. 'Constitution deal inked', http://www.nepalitimes.com/blogs/thebrief/2015/06/08/constitution-deal-inked/

Shrestha, A.M. and Dhungel, D.N. 2016. *Annapurna Post*. http://www.annapurnapost.com/annanote/news/905/Nepal

Nagarik, 29 November; 2, 3, 5, 6 December 2016; 17 October 2017

My Republica, 14 March 2016

Khabar Dabali, 2016

The Himalayan Times, 25 September and 8 October 2016; and 11 April, 14, 26 May 2017

Kantipur, 30 November 2016

The Kathmandu Post, 16 March and 5 December 2016 and 29 May 2017

Kantipur TV, 5 December 2016

Ekantipur, 6 March and 30 April 2017

Naya Patrika, 6 March 2017 and 12 October 2017

http://annapurnapost.com/annanote/news/4704/Hold-all-three-tier-elections-by-Jan-2018,-says-Supreme-Court

http://economictimes.indiatimes.com/articleshow/49024413.cms?from=mobile&utm_source=contentofinterest&utm_medium=text&utm_campaign=cppst

http://kathmandupost.ekantipur.com/printedition/news/2017-03-06/number-of-local-units-reaches-744.html

https://www.theguardian.com/global-development/2017/aug/15/they-use-money-to-promote-christianity-nepal-battle-for-souls].

http://www.annapurnapost.com/news/59722

http://www.southasia.com.au/2016/12/04/

http://www.worldbank.org/en/news/press-release/2018/04/17/world-bank-maintains-fy2018-growth-projection-at-46-percent

www.lawcommission.gov.np

www.llrc.gov.np

www.mofa.gov.np/jointstatement

Endnotes

1 http://www.worldbank.org/en/news/press-release/2018/04/17/world-bank-maintains-fy2018-growth-projection-at-46-percent

2 This was in sharp contrast to the Supreme Court decision in 1994 when the NC had dissolved parliament and called for fresh elections. What followed were a series of unholy and corrupt political alliances, rise and fall of coalition governments in quick succession, emergence of the Pajero culture, bribes and sex scandals that played roles in forming coalitions.

3 The Samyukta Jana Morcha (United People's Front [UPF]), had emerged as the third largest party in the 1991 election. It was the political front of CPN (Unity Center), which broke up that led to the emergence of the CPN-M, which was subsequently rechristened as the Unified CPN-M and now CPN MC.

4 The alliance consisted of the NC, NC (Democratic), CPN-UML, Nepal Worker and Peasants, Party, Sadbhavana Party (Anandi Devi), United Left Front, and UPF. One of the key understandings was that 'autocratic monarchy is the main hurdle' in realizing the wish of the Nepali people for democracy and that 'peace, progress and prosperity in the country are

not possible until full democracy is established by bringing an absolute monarchy to an end.'

5 A devastating earthquake hit Nepal on 25 April 2015 when main parties were negotiating but had not agreed on many issues including the form of government. As a consequence, the NC, CPN-UML, UCPN-M and Madhesi parties were facing the wrath of the people against their failure to deliver a constitution. Despite opposition from fringe parties, 'the four major political parties inked a 16-point deal... paving the way for the Constituent Assembly (CA) to write Nepal's new constitution. The elements of the deal were the agreement for having eight provinces, names and boundaries of provinces to be decided by future provincial councils, a 275-member lower house with 60 per cent of them elected directly, a 45-member upper house, to have a 3 per cent threshold, among others.' (http://www.nepalitimes.com/blogs/thebrief/2015/06/08/constitution-deal-inked/).

6 During the adoption of the constitution, a majority had voted (in other words, 507 out of the effective strength of 598 members) but only 532 who were present during the vote had voted. Only 25 members voted against the constitution.

7 The seventy-five districts have been restructured into seventy-seven in seven provinces. Province 1 consists of fourteen districts, Province 2, eight districts, Province 3, thirteen districts, Province 4, eleven districts (Nawalparasi district, east of Bardaghat Susta), Province 5, twelve districts (Rukum eastern part and Nawalparasi, west of Bardaghat Susta), Province 6, ten districts (Rukum western part), and Province 7, nine districts [Constitution of Nepal, 2015, Article 56 (3) and Schedule 4].

8 The delimitation commission gave 90 per cent weightage to population distribution and 10 per cent to geography while considering a number of other factors such as social diversity and laws governing electoral constituencies.

9 The bill sought to have: (i) an electoral college comprised of the members of the provincial legislatures for the election of a fifty-six-member upper house of parliament of which twenty-one members (at least one woman, one Dalit and one disabled or marginalized person from each of the seven provinces and remaining thirty-five members to be elected on the basis of the population ratio of the said provinces; (ii) provide naturalized citizenship to a foreign woman married to a Nepali citizen provided she had initiated the process to relinquish the citizenship of the country at the time of her marriage on the basis of the law passed

by the federal parliament; (iii) form a federal commission to review the number and boundary of provinces and make suggestion for changes as per the terms of reference and working procedure decided by the government; (iv) provide federal parliament power of approving the bill submitted by the government in relation to the change in the number and boundary of the provinces on the basis of a recommendation of the federal commission; and (v) include all mother languages in the annex of the constitution on the basis of the recommendation of a language commission and also include a list of approved languages by the government of Nepal on the recommendation of the language commission as official working languages in the annex of the constitution (Source: Legislative-parliament secretariat and *Ekantipur*, 30 April 2017)

10 Such a wait is for seven years in case of India and Sri Lanka, five years in Pakistan and Afghanistan, twelve years in the Maldives provided she is a Muslim and two years in Bangladesh after marriage. In Bhutan, only after a child is born out of marriage does the woman qualify to apply for citizenship. Nepal is the only country that does not set such time limit.

11 During the field visits to the districts of Banke, Bardiya and Kailali, Kanchapur in February 2014 and Sindhupalchowk district in May 2014, Ulrike Müller-Böker, a professor of Human Geography, University of Zurich and Dwarika Nath Dhungel, Senior Researcher, Social Sciences, it had come out clearly that for the local people, it was the local government units that were the most important public institutions for their daily life. Regarding the state restructuring, it was clear that members of the different ethnic groups were living together; they had not faced any problem and wanted to live together and wanted state restructuring not on the basis of the ethnic line. These findings had been included in the draft paper by Mueller-Boeker and Dhungel. During a visit by Dhungel, Santa Bahadur Pun, former Managing Director, Nepal Electricity Authority and Officer on Special Duty, Ministry of Water Resources, and Gauri Man Kadaria, Director in Chief, Nepal Electricity Authority, to the eastern part of the country—Dhankuta, Terathum, Sankhuwasabha and Bhojpur—between 28 March and 2 April 2014, they had randomly interacted about the state restructuring with different sections of the society. During discussions, they found that the local people considered local government units important and opposed state restructuring on ethnic line.

12 http://economictimes.indiatimes.com/articleshow/49024413.cms?from=mobile&utm_source=contentofinterest&utm_

medium=text&utm_campaign=cppst

13 Professor Jeffrey D. Sachs during his Nepal visit in November 2016 said, 'I don't think Nepal has done all that it should have done or could have done, given that the two giant neighbours have been among the fastest growing countries in the world.' (*The Kathmandu Post*, 5 December 2016). Professor Sachs in his statement had also expressed dissatisfaction with Nepal's political situation, which the media did not report but one of the contributors, Dwarika Nath Dhungel, had also attended.

6

FOREIGN POLICY: CHALLENGES AND OPPORTUNITIES

Mohan Prasad Lohani
Nishchal Nath Pandey

The significance of Nepal's geostrategic location cannot be overemphasized. This situation within and without has 'both permanent and challenging political implications for Nepal' (Khanal, 2000). In addition, 'Its central location on the southern slope of the imposing mountain system that separates the Tibetan plateau from the plains of India has always strongly conditioned the country's... foreign policy' (Rose, 1971). The basic determining features of Nepal's foreign policy such as geopolitics, underdevelopment, land-lockedness, national and external security and, above all, Nepal vis-à-vis its immediate neighbours, India and China, have been articulated by many scholars and experts in their analytical papers and discourses. Thus, these factors have made Nepal's foreign policy a 'difficult, serious and sensitive subject'.

Foreign Policy and Its Evolution in a Historical Perspective

Historians claim that, though Prithvi Narayan Shah's military campaign started as an act of expansion of Gorkha, it ended in the unification of Nepal (Manandhar, 2016). Because of Prithvi Narayan Shah's farsightedness, the kingdom was saved from being divided into pieces and could maintain its independence throughout its history (Vaidya, 1993).

Fully aware as Prithvi Narayan Shah was of the geostrategic location of the country, the imagery he used to describe his kingdom as a 'yam between two boulders' is as valid today as it was when the founder of modern Nepal realized the importance and necessity of adopting a 'delicate and cautious' foreign policy towards two big powers as its next door neighbours.

> This country is like a gourd between two rocks. Maintain a treaty of friendship with the emperor of China. Keep also a treaty of friendship with the emperor of the southern sea (the Company). He has taken the plains. He will realize that if Hindustan unites, it will be difficult, and so he will come seeking places for forts. Prepare forts, without burdening the people. Set traps in the trails. One day that force will come. Do not go down to the plains to fight. Withdraw to the hills to fight. Chure Pass will be much used. Store arms and ammunition there for five to seven generations. The Ganga is also a line of defence. If this does not suffice in war, regardless of trickery or schemes, the strength of Nepal lies in her forts. If he takes these, the four emperors will come. God has given us the places for these forts. There is no need to ask where.
>
> —Divya Upadesh of Prithvi Narayan Shah

Jang Bahadur, a highly charismatic figure in the history of Nepal, pursued the policy of unreserved friendship with the British power in India. Such friendship, in fact, became the cornerstone of Nepal's foreign policy without deviating from its traditional policy of isolation and exclusion of foreigners with whom only minimal contact was maintained at the official level. Jang Bahadur's visit to Europe set the pattern for this policy, which was rigidly and conscientiously followed by his successors for a century with real success in achieving the desired object—the maintenance of the independence and territorial integrity of Nepal in the face of the fierce wind of change that was blowing strongly across the entire region and that had brought the Indian subcontinent as a whole under foreign domination (Shaha, 1983).

Opening Up: Diversification of External Relations

In the late forties of the last century, Nepal, together with India and China, witnessed changes of historic significance. While India gained independence in 1947, China declared itself the People's Republic by installing a communist government in 1949. The century-old family rule was overthrown in Nepal as a result of the people's movement of 1951. A dramatic shift in the traditional policy of isolation took place and Nepal moved fast towards diversification of its external relations.

Nepal, which had till then diplomatic relations with only four countries, namely India, France, the UK and USA, was able to diversify its external relations after King Mahendra's accession to the throne in 1955. The year 1955 was, in fact, a milestone for Nepal in opening up to the world outside. The country attended the Afro Asian Bandung Conference in April, established diplomatic relations with the People's Republic of China (PRC) in August and got admitted to the United Nations in December.

Guided by the motto 'Friendship with all and Enmity towards none', Nepal has established, during the last sixty years, diplomatic relations with more than 140 countries and, apart from membership of the UN and its specialized agencies, has joined international and regional organizations like the World Bank, IMF, WTO, ADB and Economic and Social Commission for Asia and the Pacific (ESCAP).

Nepal and the United Nations

As stated earlier, Nepal joined the United Nations on 14 December 1955. With its faith in the principles and purposes enshrined in the UN Charter irrevocable, it continues to attach considerable significance to the crucial and positive role of the UN in debating and finding solutions to issues of global concern, such as general and complete disarmament, including nuclear disarmament under UN supervision, Universal Declaration of Human Rights (1948), international terrorism as well as security and development of smaller member states like Nepal. In fact, Nepal's foreign policy, as stated earlier, is based on its abiding faith in the UN Charter.

LDCs and LLDCs

As one of the landlocked developing countries (LLDCs) categorized by the UN, Nepal has continued to champion the cause of LDCs in several UN forums, including four international conferences on LDCs (Paris 1981 and 1991, Brussels 2001 and Istanbul 2011). It successfully discharged its responsibility as chair of the Global Coordination Bureau of LDCs for a three-year period (2009–12). It played a coordinating role, on behalf of all LDCs, in facilitating the adoption of the Istanbul Program of Action. Nepal, as an LDC, has consistently urged the developed industrialized countries to fulfil their commitments of 0.15–0.20 per cent of GNP as official development assistance (ODA) to LDCs and provide duty-free and quota-free access to the markets of developed countries for LDC exports. Nepal hopes to graduate from LDC status by 2022. It is a challenging task requiring not only massive investments to attain 8 to 9 per cent annual growth rate but also good governance, efficiency and time-bound implementation of nationally and internationally set goals and targets.

Nepal, a landlocked country which consistently insisted, as a matter of principle, on international recognition and guarantee of all landlocked states' right of access to and from the sea, actively participated in the Third UN Conference on the Law of the Sea (1972–82) and ensured the provision in the Law of the Sea Convention for right of access to and from the sea and other rights for landlocked countries.

Involvement in UN peacekeeping operations

Nepal's peacekeeping role as the sixth largest troop contributor has been widely acclaimed. So far, 110,779 army, police and armed police personnel, including senior officers, have participated in UN peace missions. Nepal has shown its readiness to provide up to 5,000 military peacekeepers at the request of the UN. A standby arrangement with the UN for 2,000 troops for peacekeeping purposes bears testimony to its firm commitment to the UN peace mission.

Nepal's faith in the world body is further corroborated by the UN involvement, known as the UN Mission in Nepal (UNMIN), in monitoring the peace process in the country after the decade-long insurgency (1996–2006). UNMIN accomplished the task as mandated by the world body when the former Maoist combatants were integrated into the NA and returned to the UN Headquarters after successfully supervising the CA elections in 2008.

While peacekeepers from NA and the armed police force have earned accolades for their credible and creditable performance in peace missions to several countries, a few black spots, such as the outbreak of cholera allegedly caused by a Nepali contingent in Haiti, a corruption scandal arising from low-quality logistics-related purchases for the Sudan peace mission and withdrawal of some Nepalese peacekeepers on charges of violation of human rights cannot be dismissed as stray incidents, for such incidents are likely to damage the reputation of Nepalese peacekeepers as well as the country itself.

Several army generals from Nepal have served as Force Commanders in various peace missions in the past. Nepal's foreign minister, in a meeting with UN Secretary General, called for increased quota of top positions to senior army and police officers in peace missions in view of its sizeable contribution as the most reliable peacekeeper, admired by the world body and its member states.

Such international reputation militates against the Gurkha recruitment policy under the 1947 Tripartite Agreement. Under this agreement, both Britain and India inducted the then British–India Gorkhali battalion in their respective armies. Nepal agreed to recruitment under certain conditions. The then prime minister of Nepal categorically stated that the Gorkha regiment in the British and Indian armies could not be treated like mercenaries and the terms and conditions of their service should be in keeping with national pride, dignity and self-respect (Shrestha, 2016). Critics of the Tripartite Agreement have forcefully argued that it is time for Nepal to review its Gorkha recruitment policy and adopt a new approach befitting the country's independent foreign policy based on Panchsheel, the UN Charter, Nonalignment and commitment to international law and world peace.

Nonalignment, SAARC, BBIN and BIMSTEC

Nepal became a founding member of the Non-Aligned Movement (NAM) in the early sixties of the last century and has participated in all summits at the highest political level. NAM was born to become an independent political and moral force representing the voice of the developing world, including newly independent countries that opted for nonalignment by keeping away from two military alliances—NATO and Warsaw Pact—led by the USA and the former Soviet Union.

The relevance of NAM came to be increasingly questioned after the end of the Cold War, which coincided with the disintegration of the Soviet Union and dissolution of the Warsaw Pact. NAM, with its membership exceeding hundred, meets every three years at the summit level and approves the political and economic agenda of global interest and concern. Its record on implementation of its own decisions, resolutions and programmes of action has been, however, far from satisfactory and even disappointing.

Nepal is also a founding member of SAARC, which was founded in 1985 with a view to enhance the well-being of the people in the region and promote regional peace and stability through concerted efforts on the basis of unanimity. It has completed three decades of its existence and, like NAM, has few achievements to its credit. Its impact, precisely speaking, has been more of symbolic in nature than substantive.

The BBIN initiative is a logical extension of the South Asia Growth Quadrangle (SAGQ) founded twenty years ago. A subregional grouping designed to focus on areas such as water resources management, connectivity of power, transport and infrastructure meets with participation of official representatives of the four countries. The Bay of Bengal Initiative for Multi-Sectoral Technical and Economic Cooperation (BIMSTEC) comprises seven countries from South and South East Asia, namely Bangladesh, Bhutan, India, Myanmar, Nepal, Sri Lanka and Thailand. Nepal joined this subregional grouping, founded in June 1997, in February 2004. BIMSTEC aims at promoting technological and economic cooperation by focusing on areas such as commerce, investment, technology, tourism, human resource development, agriculture, fisheries, transport and communication, textiles and leather. There are fourteen priority sectors of cooperation and Nepal is in charge of poverty alleviation. Nepal is also the current chairperson of the organization and is expected to host the 4th BIMSTEC summit Free Trade Area Framework Agreement (FTAFA) to which Nepal is also a signatory. It holds importance for Nepal in the sense that it will encourage foreign investors to trade with and invest in BIMSTEC member countries. As an LDC, Nepal hopes to benefit from ongoing trade negotiations covering goods and services, investment, economic cooperation, trade facilitation and technical assistance.

Promoting Economic Diplomacy

Economic diplomacy has become a new and critical component of Nepal's foreign policy, and the country has been justifiably striving in recent years, to promote it as effectively and efficiently as possible to eradicate poverty and achieve the Sustainable Development Goals (SDGs, 2015–30). Quite obviously, economic elements need to be incorporated into foreign policy and diplomatic activities. The efficient conduct of economic diplomacy depends, to a large extent, on the deployment of trained personnel and expertise in all diplomatic missions. These missions should be provided with minimum resources to undertake promotional activities. In the day-to-day schedule of missions, priority needs to be accorded to the task of promoting and strengthening economic ties with the countries to which missions are assigned. It is important to remember that successful diplomacy seeks to bridge differences and widens the common ground to realize or achieve the shared interests. Diplomats should be evaluated on the basis of their performance, that is, the efforts they have put in and their achievements. In the light of the foregoing, the government of the day will draw a set of foreign policy guidelines and articulate the new focus on economic relations (Dahal, et al., 2008).

Nepal and Neighbouring Countries

Both history and geography are critical components of a country's foreign policy. While history is a useful guide to the present and future road map to reach the desired destination, geography is a determining factor in shaping the country's foreign policy with due consideration to geopolitical compulsions under which a country like Nepal, situated between the two most populous neighbours and fast-rising economic powers, has to chart a course suited to its national interest while taking full cognizance of their legitimate concerns.

Nepal and India

The history of Nepal–India relations has been simultaneously chequered and complex. Chequered, because cultural affinities between the two countries go beyond the British colonial rule in India to the days of the Ramayana and the Mahabharata. These are complex in the sense that religion, culture, social interactions, Nepal's excessive dependence on India for economic development, including trade and transit, and, above all, an open border with security implications for both Nepal and India are important variables of multi-dimensional nature that can, by no means, be overlooked.

Open border is a unique feature of Nepal–India relations. It has certainly made life easier for people on both sides. However, in recent years, the misuse of the border by smugglers, drug traffickers, terrorists, criminals and other anti-social elements has caused immense concern to both Nepal and India at the official level. Sealing the border is an extreme view unacceptable to the people of both nations, particularly those who have lived in border areas for centuries and have enjoyed the benefits of unrestricted cross-border movement of goods and people. Experts in both countries have realized the urgency of adopting some concrete measures such as record-keeping and registration of visitors at entry–exit points and provision for ID cards for effective border regulation and also to meet the security concerns of both Nepal and India.

India's cooperation in overthrowing the Rana regime is inseparable from the people's movement of 1951. While India played a significant role in assisting the democratic forces of this country to usher in democratic rule in 1951, restore parliamentary democracy in 1990 and facilitate understanding and agreement between the SPA and the Maoist insurgents in 2005, it has been pointed out by several critics that India has tried to meddle in Nepal's internal politics, including micromanagement of its administrative and security agencies to the chagrin of its own well-wishers.

India did not welcome the new constitution of 2015 and its resentment expressed itself in the form of a five-month long so-called 'undeclared blockade' (September 2015–February 2016) that was imposed with a view to strangulating Nepal economically, causing much pain and suffering to the common people. It was an unfriendly act bordering on hostility which no Nepali could condone. The following observation is pertinent in this context: 'Unless Nepal is assured of economic blockade not imposed any more in the future, it would be difficult for them to forget the hardship they had to face for almost five months notwithstanding the visits Nepalese leaders pay, like the current PM K.P. Sharma Oli's visit, to New Delhi to improve and strengthen the bilateral relationship' (Dhungel, 2016).

The people of Nepal feel utterly disturbed when they come across unconfirmed reports that India would like the Nepalese peacekeepers in UN missions to come under the command of the Indian Army before they are deployed in various countries. Such reports have, however, been refuted by the NA and the Ministry of Foreign Affairs.

Likewise, Nepal as a sovereign independent country which is keen to maintain balanced relations with its neighbours, is annoyed at press reports about the concern of Indian MPs in parliament over the growing influence of China in Nepal and India's failure to curb the decline of its own influence. China's overtures to Nepal to build roads and railways extending to its southern border adjacent to India have caused concern to Indian MPs and politicians. India's Minister of State for External Affairs is reported to have assuaged the MPs' outrage with the following statement: 'Because of open border, common culture, geography, history, people-to-people relations and close economic ties, we have special relations with Nepal. Nepal's trade with India is two-thirds of its total trade with the rest of the world. India serves as transit for 90 per cent of Nepal's export–import trade with third countries. Therefore, Nepal–India relations have become by no means weak' (Akbar, 2016).

While the Koshi (1954), Gandak (1959) agreements and Mahakali Treaty (1996) signed between Nepal and India have not been received well, mention should be made of some positive developments in Nepal–India relations. In the late seventies of the last century, the Morarji Desai-led government of India complied with Nepal's longstanding demand for two separate treaties of trade and transit. In the mid-90s, because of an amazingly hassle-free cooperation between the private sectors of Nepal and India, the volume of bilateral trade considerably went up, reducing trade deficit suffered by the country to a low level. Unfortunately, this positive attitude was not maintained by our southern neighbour, and trade deficit with India has alarmingly gone up in recent years. Late I.K. Gujral, the Prime Minister of India who is credited with having sought to improve friendly relations with all neighbouring countries under a non-reciprocity formula known as the 'Gujral Doctrine', visited Nepal in 1997 and as a gesture of cooperation, agreed to open the land route between Nepal and Bangladesh through Indian territory. Because of lack of infrastructure, the land route has, however, not become fully functional.

In the opinion of a well-known diplomat and foreign policy expert of Nepal, 'Indo–Nepal relations are so old, deep-rooted and widespread that they go long back in history and cut across all aspects of state-to-state and people-to-people interactions—politics, economics, security, culture and religion. Sadly, official policy often obfuscates the true nature of this relationship. Some recent events give both sides not only pain but also reason to reflect, why and how such a relationship has reached this point' (Simkhada, 2014).

As Nepal has adopted a new constitution which is already in the process of being implemented, a new Treaty of Peace and Friendship based on Panchsheel and other internationally accepted principles would go a long way in redefining and reorienting Nepal–India relations in the changed context. The group of eminent persons (EPG) constituted separately by Nepal and India has already started its work to examine and review the entire gamut of Nepal–India relations. Its report is being keenly awaited by all.

Nepal and China

It has been sixty years since Nepal and China, bound by age-old ties of exemplary friendship, established diplomatic relations on 1 August 1955. Over the years, bilateral relations between the two countries have remained close, cordial, cooperative and problem-free.

China has assisted Nepal in development endeavours and activities ranging from infrastructure building such as roads, bridges, power projects and communications, so vital to the process of industrialization, to water resources development, health, education, sports, construction such as the National Trading Complex, City Hall in Kathmandu, International Convention Centre and other support activities, such as training, commodity assistance and food assistance.

Peace and development are the priority concerns of both Nepal and China. Both countries share identical views on major global and regional issues. It is heartening to note that there are no outstanding issues awaiting resolution between the two. The recent signing of a trade and transit treaty between Nepal and China has become a milestone in bilateral relations. China under the leadership of President Xi Jinping, has accorded high importance and priority to Trans-Himalayan Connectivity, which is linked, in a broader context, to the One Belt One Road (OBOR) initiative of the Chinese leader. In the opinion of a former Minister for Foreign Affairs: 'The idea of revitalizing the Silk Road to which the present Chinese leadership has attached considerable importance is more than sentimental attachment to the past; it reflects also the economic need of the present which is gradually emerging as the felt need of all countries in the region' (Lohani, 2016).

Nepal is greatly enthused by the neighbourhood policy of President Xi Jinping who represents the fifth generation leadership preceded by four other illustrious leaders—Chairman Mao, Paramount Leader Deng Xiaoping, President Jiang Zemin and President Hu Jintao. Nepal admires the remarkable progress made by China during the last three and a half decades in all sectors of national life. Ever since the establishment of diplomatic relations, Nepal has immensely benefitted from Chinese grants, interest-free and concessional loans made available in response to the priorities and actual requirements of this country. After President Jiang Zemin's state visit to Nepal nearly twenty years ago, no high-level Head of State visit from China has taken place. President Xi's visit to Nepal is being eagerly awaited by the people of this country.

Nepal regards China as a reliable development partner. China is fully aware of its LDC status. Nepal hopes to graduate from this status by 2022, but this hope can become a reality only when the country achieves 8 to 9 per cent growth rate by attracting massive investment flows.

When the disastrous earthquake struck Nepal on 25 April 2015, China not only expressed sorrow over the massive loss of lives and property but it also promptly sent disaster response teams and offered to help in reconstruction and rehabilitation. President Xi Jinping, in a message to former President Ram Baran Yadav on the eighth Republic Day, reiterated his commitment to help Nepal and described Nepal's crisis as 'our own crisis'. Precisely speaking, China's comprehensive assistance to the quake-hit Nepal drew worldwide applause.

China and India are Nepal's close neighbours and development partners. They have generously assisted in its development endeavours in various sectors ranging from infrastructure building to tourism promotion, water resources development and industrialization. Nepal has noted with appreciation the 'Neighbourhood Policy' being pursued by both China and India. The Nepalese admire the tremendous progress made by the two nations and aspire to benefit by being land-linked with, and serving as a vibrant bridge between, them (Bhattarai, 2016).

It is in the interest of Nepal to maintain balanced relations between both its immediate neighbours and benefit from their high growth rate by attracting investment capital and technology on favourable terms and conditions. Trilateral cooperation between China, India and Nepal has received priority attention recently and needs to be augmented on the basis of in-depth discussion, homework, dialogue and mutually beneficial agreements.

Border Infrastructure and Connectivity

Nepal is the oldest nation state in South Asia. It was independent even at a time when the entire region was under British colonial rule. The country established diplomatic relations with the UK before India, Pakistan and Bangladesh became independent countries. Diplomatic relations were established with the USA, even before with our own two immediate neighbours, perhaps depicting our innate sense of anxiety about threats to our territorial integrity, emanating from one of the two. Therefore, Nepal's international relations exercise is as old as the nation. Nepal has been twice elected to the UN Security Council; it is one of the largest troops contributing nations to the UN peacekeeping missions; it is the founding member of SAARC; an ardent believer in NAM and believes in peaceful coexistence for one and all. Yet, Nepal is lagging behind not only in economic development but also on the diplomatic front, an area that had always been its pride. While Nepal trumpeted with glee the support for its ZoP proposal from 116 countries, the same support was not forthcoming from India. In the late eighties, Nepal had to bear pain and suffering from an Indian trade embargo for fifteen months due to the alleged import of Chinese arms by Nepal in defiance of consultations with India. These are two glaring instances of the country's diplomatic failure. Nepal's diplomacy continued to become a casualty after the 1990 political change. Why so?

The answer to this question is twofold. First, it is embedded in the grim reality of its perpetual political instability after 1996. There have been nineteen prime ministers, on average, one per year, undermining the national prestige so necessary to plan, execute and consolidate relations with friendly countries and project Nepal as a nation of the future in multilateral and international forums.

In fact, not only the foreign policy, but issues such as resurrecting the economy, strengthening trade competitiveness, harnessing the tourism and water resources potential, safeguarding cultural and religious ethos, maintaining social cohesion, etc. have also been on the backburner in Nepal. With fissures seen in the religious, ethnic and linguistic mosaic of the country, some even fear disintegration of the Nepali state along ethnic lines if the current political transition is not handled properly. There are 'glaring gaps [that] exist between the de jure sovereignty that the international system affords such states and their de facto capabilities to serve their population and act as a responsible member of the international community. The ground reality is that many states have collapsed and are unable to provide even the most basic services to their citizens' (Ghani and Lockhart, 2008). Seen in this perspective, a balanced foreign policy that is able to position Nepal with pride in the community of nations is the need of the hour.

India and China have risen many times in their history. And each time Nepal has benefitted. As an entrepôt nation, Nepal has historically reaped the advantage of trading between these two. During the prosperous Yuan and Ming dynasties and during the Mughal era, Nepal also went through its golden period. Therefore, in view of the historical legacy behind us, there is a general feeling that the rising India and rising China phenomenon is going to be critical again for Nepal. Its political leadership has not been able to utilize this prospect for the overall benefit of the people. Although there is tall talk about being a vibrant bridge or a viable transit state, no concrete foundation has been laid even as the two countries open up more trade links and border points on their own. With India and China rising again, can Nepal reinvigorate its economy, reconnect the damaged trade ties and build itself once again as a vibrant economy?

So, when we talk about economic cooperation, we need to focus on rising India and rising China as well as on how we can benefit from their economic progress. First, the subregional aspect of north India, Nepal and Tibetan Autonomous Region (TAR) or north India, Nepal and southwest Tibet must be understood. This is the political geography Nepal has to realize. And it is high time for India and China also to start concentrating on infrastructural development, connectivity, roads and railways, better health sector, better education in their own bordering districts, not only along the Nepal border but also the borders along other countries. Therefore, without the development of bordering areas, this marvel of rising India and rising China will not be felt in the smaller countries of the neighbourhood.

There is a greater need for India and China to cooperate in the neighbourhood, be it in Southeast Asia or South Asia. Since both are vulnerable in certain areas, there is a dire need to cooperate and stabilize the neighbourhood. Cooperation will not, however, happen unless the Nepalese are willing to understand the gravity of the issues at hand, that of providing stability, policy coherence, reconstruction of earthquake-ravaged infrastructure and implementing projects without corruption, nepotism, delay and political interference.

Nepal cannot overlook security-related vulnerabilities when it concerns issues of connectivity and border infrastructure in this part of the region. India has been touchy, especially on the possibility of the train coming from China connecting the Nepal border in a few years. This train from Golmud in central China has already become operational, connecting Lhasa followed by Shigatse. It is being extended to the Nepal border. China itself is sensitive to Tibet's security. But the Nepalese public do feel that there is some positive change with the Modi government in India and his historic visits to Nepal and China. The Prime Minister of India 'Modi-fied Indo-Nepal relations' when he brought optimism among the Nepalese while addressing the CA during his visit to Nepal in August 2014.

China–Nepal–India Trilateral Cooperation

If border infrastructures and connectivity are strengthened, as discussed above, trilateral cooperation involving China, India and Nepal will get off the ground from the conceptual stage and move forward significantly to make China–Nepal–India Economic Corridor (CNIEC) a reality. Experts believe that both New Delhi and Beijing should cooperate and work together to build connectivity across Nepal so that the 'resulting connectivity infrastructure operates on common platforms for the benefit of all'. By jointly working on Nepali infrastructure projects, New Delhi and Beijing can reduce the distance between them, both physically and politically. Nepal could, thus, serve as a 'bridge between India and China'. China has already expressed its commitment to build Nepal's railways. While Indian response is equally positive, there are contradictory statements issued, from time to time, by Indian authorities and the intellectual community on the Chinese assistance in building connectivity across Nepal. In the opinion of an Indian writer, 'If both the Asian giants are allowed to do this, Nepal will not only get a huge infrastructure boost but also emerge as a key link country for India and China, facilitating trilateral trade and exchanges' (Ghosh, 2016).

Chinese Foreign Ministry spokesperson Hua Chunxing, describing Nepal and India as China's friendly neighbours, stated at a Goa meeting in October 2016 that his country was keen to promote trilateral cooperation 'with Nepal and India'. Such cooperation, China believed, would contribute to stability and development in the region. Nepal welcomes the recent Chinese statement to 'deepen practical cooperation in various fields and forge a community for shared future with Nepal'.

Nepal and Other Countries in Asia and the Pacific, Europe, North America and Gulf Region

In addition to relations with its immediate neighbours discussed above, Nepal's bilateral relations with other SAARC member states like Afghanistan, Bangladesh, Bhutan, Maldives, Pakistan and Sri Lanka have remained friendly, cordial and are based on goodwill, mutual understanding and cooperation. There are potential areas for cooperation like trade, investment and tourism that need to be further explored and intensified. All its South Asian neighbours are not only committed to improving the quality of life of their people but have also realized the importance of promoting peace and stability in the region and accelerating the pace of economic growth.

While Nepal attaches importance to its relations with all countries of Asia and the Pacific, mention should be made of deepening cooperation with Australia, Japan, Malaysia and the Republic of Korea. Nepal and Australia established diplomatic relations in February 1960. Australian cooperation in Nepal covers areas such as forestry, civil aviation, communications, health, education and human resource development. Japan has remained a major donor country and has continued to provide valuable economic assistance, in the form of grants and loans that has improved basic infrastructure such as power generation, e.g. Kulekhani I and II and Kaligandaki 'A' hydropower projects, roads, airports, bridges, water supply facilities and telecommunications. Nepal has appreciated the involvement of Japanese volunteers in relief and rehabilitation operations and efforts following the earthquake of April 2015. Both Nepal and Japan celebrated in 2016 the Diamond Jubilee of the establishment of diplomatic relations.

Malaysia and the Republic of Korea (South Korea) have been generous in providing employment to Nepalese migrant workers. Both have recognized Nepal as one of the source countries of foreign workers and have also realized the necessity of a labour agreement to ensure the rights of and facilities for such workers, including their security and protection. The number of such workers seeking employment in Malaysia and the Republic of Korea has increased over the years. Both Malaysia and South Korea are also involved in bilateral economic projects in Nepal.

Likewise, a large number of Nepalese workers are working in Gulf countries like Kuwait, Qatar, Saudi Arabia, UAE, Bahrain and Oman. This Nepalese manpower has helped the economy at home through remittance amounting to billions of rupees. The government of Nepal has established diplomatic missions in all the Gulf countries to look into and respond to the grievances of the Nepalese workers there.

Although the number of tourists visiting Nepal from the Gulf nations is still small, it is expected to increase because of greater access to more information about the country.

Turning now to the major countries of Europe and America, only recently Nepal and the UK celebrated the bicentennial relations amidst various programmes and activities. The British Gurkhas, who have been serving the British Army since 1815 after the treaty of Sugauli, have remained a 'strong connecting link' between Nepal and the UK. The British Government has been extending its assistance to Nepal in different socio-economic fields like agriculture, transport, local development, communication, education, administration, health, water supply, forestry and defence. Such assistance has been mostly on a grant basis. The exchange of high-level visits, from time to time, has significantly contributed to further strengthening the existing cordial relations between the two.

While UK decided to quit the European Union (EU) following a referendum last year, Nepal's relations with Germany and France, two influential members of the EU, have remained friendly over the years. Nepal has noted with appreciation the German willingness to cooperate, particularly in combating poverty, protection of environment, healthcare and harnessing its abundant water resources. Both Germany and France have further supported Nepal in promoting human rights, institutionalizing democracy, alleviating poverty and strengthening good governance in this country. It may be noted that Nepal and France established diplomatic relations in 1949 even before the overthrow of the Rana regime in 1951.

As a member of Nepal Aid Group, France has assisted Nepal in its development endeavours through multilateral agencies like the UN and Organisation for Economic Co-operation and Development (OECD). France hosted two UN conferences on the LDCs in 1981 and 1991, testifying to its goodwill towards these countries. Late King Birendra addressed the First UN Conference on the LDCs on behalf of the nine LDCs of Asia and the Pacific region. The EU, one of the principal trading partners of Nepal, has provided entry- and quota-free facilities to Nepalese export under its Everything But Arms (EBA) policy for the LDCs.

Exactly sixty years ago, diplomatic relations between Nepal and the erstwhile Soviet Union were established in 1956. Soon after the disintegration of the Soviet Union, Nepal lost no time in extending full and formal diplomatic recognition to the Russian Federation as a sovereign and independent state with the status of a permanent member of UN Security Council in December 1991. There are enormous possibilities for promoting trade, investment, tourism, as well as economic and cultural cooperation between Nepal and Russia. More than five thousand Nepalese students have already received training and obtained higher degrees from Russian universities in technical fields and other branches of learning. These Russia returnees have been serving the country in different capacities.

Nepal has maintained extremely cordial and friendly relations with Scandinavian countries like Norway, Denmark, Sweden and Finland, which have not only cooperated with Nepal in building its economy through several development projects, particularly under Nordic Development Fund but have also shown readiness to strengthen democratic institutions by facilitating the peace process. They have supported Nepal's aspirations for peace, security and development under an inclusive, progressive and democratic framework.

As regards Nepal–Canada relations, Canadian Aid programme in Nepal began in 1958, seven years before the establishment of formal diplomatic relations in 1965. Two years ago, Nepal–Canada Friendship Association celebrated the golden jubilee of diplomatic relations by highlighting cordial bilateral relations based on mutual trust, understanding and cooperation. Nepal and Canada share identical views on many international issues. In the UN, Nepal and Canada worked together way back in 1978 to set up UN Interim Force in Lebanon (UNIFIL) to prevent conflict and monitor a ceasefire in the Israel-Lebanon border. In recent years, many Nepalese nationals have been granted permanent residency status by the Canadian government to settle and work in Canada as skilled workers. Canada has also given asylum to some Bhutanese refugees under Third Country Resettlement.

Finally, Nepal–USA relations have remained close, friendly, cordial and cooperative ever since the establishment of diplomatic relations between these countries in 1947. In the opinion of a well-known diplomat, 'Nepal–US friendship is independent, it can thrive only within a political climate, of which our friendly relations with India and China are very important factors' (Khanal, 2000). The American administration has, however, categorically stated through its diplomats that it continues to look at the Nepal–USA relations independent of any third country's perception of Nepal. The USA is a major trading partner of Nepal and the latter's export of woolen carpets and readymade garments has received tremendous boost in the past under Generalized System of Preferences (GSP) facilities provided by the USA. It has always given priority to the strengthening of democratic institutions in Nepal, as well as speeding up economic growth through good governance and rule of law.

Perspective

Unfortunately, with the border blockade a year later and the promulgation of the constitution without taking India into confidence, Delhi was even reluctant to welcome the new constitution drafted for the first time by an elected assembly of Nepal. India's external affairs minister, speaking in parliament on the Nepal situation, said that there were pledges and assurances given by top Nepali political party leaders on how they would guarantee an inclusive constitution, but they failed in their promise. None of the leaders named by the Indian minister even cared to clarify. This proves that Nepali politicians visit New Delhi, talk about domestic political issues, come back with assurances but fail to implement them after returning to Kathmandu. The unreliable and double-speaking attitude of our politicians has resulted in the erosion of national credibility. As a result, the country's diplomatic acumen and maturity has been questioned.

India, on the other hand, has its own timidity in having a larger heart in dealing with smaller neighbours, primarily Nepal, Bangladesh, Sri Lanka and the Maldives, giving rise to an anti-Indian feeling among the people in the neighbourhood. As the young people of these nations start settling abroad, they, too, have become active on social networking sites, pouring occasional venom against Indian high-handedness. While New Delhi remains assertive and influential among politicians and bureaucrats of these smaller countries, it is its image among the youth of the region that it has to really work upon and repair. 'The past 5 decades of India–Nepal relations have witnessed many lost opportunities, costly misjudgements and avoidable misunderstandings. It is remarkable that successive governments in both countries have so comprehensively failed to establish a stable, mature relationship based on mutual trust and a long-term vision of cooperation' (Rajan, 2002).

A large part of the blame also lies with Nepalese leaders who visit Delhi to curry favours for themselves or for their kith and kin but fail to implement the assurances that they give in Delhi, resulting in frequent misunderstandings. India also has not resisted the temptation to deal directly with individuals rather than institutions of Nepal and even indicate their preferences explicitly for higher political offices, consequently angering other rivals and opponents.

The Nepalese have had eight prime ministers in ten years following the end of insurgency in 2006 and five constitutions in six decades. No country can build a stable polity and strengthen democracy without a workable constitution and without strengthening its vital democratic institutions. So, we will be neither a vibrant economy nor a stable democracy if we do not focus on strengthening vital institutions of the state and providing good governance. Nepal's current focus is stabilizing our polity, building a healthy political culture, adopting and implementing a constitution which is inclusive in nature. Only then can we really pay attention to reconstruction, attracting FDI and reinvigorating our ailing tourism industry. Despite labour disputes, power shortage, incessant bandhs and strikes, Indian FDI has been forthcoming, mainly in the hydropower sector. This is a healthy trend. In all this, a leadership that has the vision and integrity to take Nepal forward is the dire need of the hour. Everyone feels this is what Nepal is lacking. Since there is such acute political instability, it is affecting all aspects of national life, including the international domain. Our foreign policy priorities have shrunk, attention diverted to managing day-to-day internal problems often related to constitutional issues and the never-ending transition. We contested the UNSC elections and were defeated in a humiliating manner by rival Indonesia. We did not take stock of the lessons learned and lacunae faced by our campaign. Instead, we fought another election, this time for UN Presidency. There too, we were defeated.

Our neighbours well recognize that Nepal is going through a period of prolonged transition and have started to seek guarantee of security and sustainability of projects that they undertake inside Nepal. Talking about our northern neighbour, Chinese investment in Nepal has also been growing. In fact, it is on an upward scale all over South Asia. It also seems impatient with the agreements being stalled, despite years spent on their signing with Nepal.

Analysing how India–China relations are improving, we need to comprehend that their bilateral trade now stands at $75 billion and this is expected to reach $100 billion by 2020. As Chinese economy is showing signs of a slowdown, it would obviously seek the vast South Asian market for its goods. Uttar Pradesh and Bihar, which are landlocked states of India, have an open border with Nepal. When the Chinese railway from Golmud–Lhasa–Shigatse comes to the Nepal border at Rasuagadhi–Syafrubesi in 2020, it will open up a new vista of cooperation between the three countries.

It is for India to adjust to China's rising influence in South Asia just for the same reason that the Chinese have to adjust themselves to the rising Indian influence in Southeast Asia. India's expanding relations with Japan, Vietnam, the Philippines, Singapore and its involvement in ASEAN cannot be divorced from China's deepening relations with Bangladesh, Sri Lanka, the Maldives, Afghanistan and Nepal. China's observer status in SAARC has opened up a new vista of opportunity for it. One of the several major events held each year is the Kunming South Asia Expo wherein South Asian products are showcased for Chinese buyers, which is helping to generate awareness of and interest in South Asia in the huge Chinese market. In 2010, a total of 46,360

Chinese tourists visited Nepal. This figure doubled in 2013. There is a possibility that very soon the Chinese will be the largest segment of tourists visiting Nepal. Today, more Chinese cities are directly connected by flights to Kathmandu than Indian cities.

Recently, a Chinese civil aviation construction company bagged the deal to upgrade the Gautam Buddha International Airport in Bhairahawa. The company was the lowest bidder. The second lowest bidder was also a Chinese company. This is an airport at the Indo–Nepal border and just in the vicinity of that airport there is an Indian Air Force base at Nandanagar in Gorakhpur. If this had happened fifteen years ago, it wouldn't have been possible to implement the project. But there seems to be a realization in Delhi that, as far as airports, roads and overall infrastructure development are concerned, Chinese investment is acceptable in the neighbourhood. So, the nature of geopolitics is changing. Therefore, whether we want to call it a trilateral alliance, the bridge state or a transit state, Nepal is emerging as a viable gateway of north India to Tibet and vice versa. Diplomacy cannot lag behind such developments.

One major foreign policy endeavour that Nepal is very close to is SAARC, whose headquarters is based in Kathmandu. It is, therefore, a foreign policy priority for Nepal to make sure that SAARC is not dead. The organization offers a platform for the leaders and people of South Asia to work together in a spirit of amity, goodwill and understanding. It aims to promote the welfare of the people and improve their quality of life through accelerated socioeconomic growth and political development in the region.

If one is to analyse the eighteen summits in the last three decades, all have some significant hallmark even though most of the time summits have failed to achieve the declared goal(s). From the first summit's 14-point Dhaka declaration to the 18th summit's 36-point Kathmandu declaration, SAARC has made 765-point declarations so far in the last thirty years. Various issues of common interest of the region, such as poverty alleviation, eradicating terrorism, promoting energy trade, ensuring food security, climate change adaptations, etc. have been identified. However, since there still exists a wide gap between promise and performance; SAARC's achievement is disappointing.

'It is estimated that 53.1 per cent of the total population in South Asia live below the poverty line, 28.2 per cent below nationally defined poverty line and about 40 per cent below the internationally defined poverty line of US$1.25 PPP per day. The proportion of vulnerable population is highest in Bangladesh followed by Bhutan and India' (SAARC Secretariat, 2010).

SAARC, as the common regional body, has not been able to make a dent in poverty and hunger prevalent in our societies. 'South Asia is a region ripe for change. Democracy is thriving and so are the expectations of its people. There are more people below 24 years across SAARC than those above it. They are connected as never before with their country and with the world. They are thirsting for change and aspire today for all that is available elsewhere in the world' (Banerjee, 2015). They are getting impatient with their governments' collective inaction as regards the common problems that South Asia faces today. South Asians are getting better connected in Europe, America and Australia than within their own region.

Even after thirty years of its establishment, the regional association is recognized only for its survival and giving continuity to a dialogue for cooperation among member states. So much so that at the 14th summit held in New Delhi, the leaders declared that 'there was an urgent need to move SAARC from declaratory to implementation phase'. But very little has been achieved to this end. It must make sure that the SAARC Secretariat does what it is envisaged to do and also to see that all pledges made at the 18th summit, held in Kathmandu, are met before it hands over the chair.

Another crucial area that needs focus is energy security, which is nowadays becoming an important component of international relations exercise. Nepal has never given adequate priority to its energy and food security and never viewed these issues from the perspective of national security even though crisis overtook the country in the past because of its inability to provide both facilities to its citizens. The Nepalese have already faced three blockades in the '70s, late '80s and in 2015. A workable plan of action is yet to be devised to mitigate difficulties for the people and ensure smooth supply of petroleum, gas and other daily essentials. Crippling load-shedding continues to hinder economic progress of the country.

'Nepal as a land-locked and least developed country has remained more vulnerable to the vagaries of interruption in physical supply and price variability of fossil fuel. The country lacks a comprehensive energy security plan that is supportive and harmonious to the development of various sectors of economy including agriculture, manufacturing, and services industries' (Ojha, 2015). Not only from the point of view of over-reliance on the already clogged Kolkata port, but also from the overall perspective of better connectivity with TAR of China, opening up of alternative supply lines for oil, gas and daily essentials cannot be divorced away from the foreign policy debate of Nepal. For this also, the highest political leadership has not been consistent in its approach. Leaders publicly stress the need for diversifying Nepal's over-reliance on the Kolkata port, but step back the moment Indo–Nepal relations normalize, as evident from the experiences of the post-1989 phase and the post-2015 fiasco. As a result, the capital city of Kathmandu does not have a reservoir for oil capable of holding on for even a week if disruptions occur at the border in Birgunj.

'Multi-faceted challenges that Nepal is facing today have never been greater and more serious in nature. The situation is likely to get more complex in years to come. This is because, in the fast moving world, Nepal is lagging very much behind. The internal politics of Nepal is in disarray and there are indications that both India and China may enter into a new phase of tension for greater influence in the neighbourhood. Nepal has a bigger challenge than many other countries to ready itself for the newly fast evolving situation but it is worst prepared for it' (Subedi, 2010). In all aspects of foreign policy, be it SAARC or UN, and be it bilateral engagements or energy security, it is the top political leadership that has to evince keen interest and direct the concerned officials to take necessary steps. For this, a more serious approach or even deeper commitment of the political leadership, particularly the prime minister and foreign minister of the day, is a prerequisite.

In Conclusion

Nepal, a country never subjugated by any colonial power unlike others in the region, is proud of its national independence. It liberated itself from a 104-year-old oligarchic rule and isolationist mindset and diversified its external relations. Despite several feathers in its cap, such as membership of UN (1955) and its specialized agencies, membership of NAM (1960) and SAARC (1985), as well as active participation in UN peace missions since 1958, Nepal's lacklustre diplomacy over the years has become a matter of deep concern. It calls for serious soul-searching and concerted efforts to upgrade the country's diplomatic profile.

Situated geostrategically between India and China, Nepal can benefit from its neighbours' economic growth and prosperity provided it is able to put its house in order to ensure political stability and coherence in policy prescriptions within a democratic framework and give priority to foreign service and diplomacy as the best available tools or instruments for promoting the country's national interests by safeguarding its national independence, sovereignty and territorial integrity, which is the primary objective of a country's foreign policy.

In the opinion of a former foreign minister, 'The pace at which the two neighbours' economic potential and international image are moving forward or going up has not only begun to change the regional and global dynamics and equation but has also presented to Nepal a new situation, besides challenges and opportunities... Nepal needs political stability to benefit from the world's two big markets at our own door step as well as centres attracting global investment' (Pandey, 2016).

In a rapidly globalizing and interdependent world, no country can develop all by itself in isolation from the rest of the world. A country like Nepal, which has yet to free itself from the stigma of being the least developed among developing countries, must gear its foreign policy, cautiously and prudently, to optimize benefits from cooperation at all levels—bilateral, regional and multilateral—by securing national consensus among all sections of the population, including political parties on issues of vital national interest.

Because of its geostrategic location, Nepal remains a country of strategic importance not only to its neighbours but also to other powers in the region and beyond. Madhukar Rana, a strategic analyst, is of the opinion that, 'The significance of Nepal's geostrategic location will grow in the 21st century as compared to the previous... In the emergent world order which will be full of uncertainty and foreign policy risks, it is vital that Nepal gets its bilateral relations in order first and foremost. This, it needs underscoring, is far more vital than being in UN and joining regional and sub-regional associations.'

The country's avowed policy has been to prevent any attempt to misuse its territory for hostile operations against its neighbours. This policy needs to be pursued seriously and scrupulously without letting the neighbours question its credible stance. Friendship is based on mutual trust, goodwill and understanding. Trust deficit has given rise to bilateral tensions, particularly in Nepal's relations with India. Nepal should play a proactive role in removing such distrust that has resulted, more often than not, in repeated impositions of blockades from its neighbour. All outstanding disputes can and should be amicably resolved through dialogue, negotiations and mutual consultations. While Nepal should be prepared to accommodate the legitimate concerns of its neighbours, the latter are expected to become sensitive to the legitimate aspirations of this country for peace, freedom, security and development.

The foreign policy of a country is regarded as an extension of its domestic policy. It is for Nepal to sort out and settle its internal problems to the satisfaction of all concerned. In the absence of political stability, the economy is bound to be retarded. Only after a stable government has been installed, economic diplomacy becomes effective. Nepal should conduct such diplomacy by appointing well-trained and competent officials and experts to various positions in diplomatic missions abroad. It should continue to enjoy the goodwill of the international community by respecting and implementing all international conventions and treaties it has signed and ratified in the past. There are challenges no doubt, but opportunities and prospects are equally available and forthcoming if Nepal exhibits maturity, exercises prudence and learns from past experiences in foreign policy formulation and execution.

∽

Mohan Prasad Lohani *has been Nepal's ambassador to Bangladesh, Sri Lanka and Maldives. He has also taught English at Tribhuvan University.*

Nishchal Nath Pandey *is a well-known academic and is currently Director of Centre for South Asian Studies (CSAS), Kathmandu.*

Bibliography

Banerjee, D. 2015. 'Deeper SAARC Integration: A Time for Action.' In: N.N. Pandey (Ed.) *Deeper Integration for Peace and Prosperity in South Asia*. Kathmandu: KAS-COSATT.

Bhattarai, S.N. 2016. 'Welcome Remarks.' In: *Report on Workshop on 'China–Nepal–India: Economic Corridor (CNIEC)': Feasibility and Approaches.* Kathmandu: China Study Center.

Dahal, M.K., et al. 2008. *Nepal: A Generic Guideline for Development through Economic Diplomacy.* Kathmandu: Institute of Foreign Affairs.

Dhungel, D.N. 2016. 'Nepal–India Relations: Unexplained Sufferings.' *New Spotlight,* 4 March 2016, Vol. 9, No. 16.

Ghani, A. and Lockhart, C. 2008. *Fixing Failed States*. New York: Oxford University Press.

Khanal, Y.N. 2000. *Nepal's Non-Isolationist Foreign Policy.* Kathmandu: Satyal Publication.

Khanal, Y.N. 2000. *Nepal's Non-Isolationist Foreign Policy.* Kathmandu: Satyal Publication.

Lohani, M.P. 2016. 'Nepal–China Relations: Six Decades of Friendship, Partnership and Cooperation.' In: *Friendship Journal of Nepal-China Studies*. Kathmandu: China Study Center.

Lohani, P.C. 2016. 'Road to Prosperity: The South Western Silk Road.' In: *First Year of China's Diplomacy Under the New Leadership, 2013-14.* Kathmandu: China Study Center.

Manandhar, T.R. 2016. 'Historical Background'. Unpublished paper.

Ojha, P. 2015. 'Macro-Economics: A Radical Re-thinking in Growth, Inequality and Inclusiveness in Nepal'. In: Pyakuryal, B. (Ed.) *Energy Security and Oil Sector Reform.*

Rajan, K.V. 2002. 'External Affairs: Cross Border Relations'. In J.N. Dixit (Ed.) *Nepal.* New Delhi: Lotus Books.

Rose, L.E. 1971. *Nepal: Strategy for Survival.* Berkeley: University of California Press.

Shaha, R. 1983. 'Introduction'. In: John Whelpton. *Jang Bahadur in Europe.* Kathmandu: Sahayogi Press.

Shrestha, H.L. 2016. *Nepali/Gorkhali in Peace Mission (UN) and Foreign Armies.* Baglung: Deep-Amrit Prakashan.

Simkhada, S.R. 2014. 'Indo–Nepal Relations on A New Even Keel'. In: Mandal, M. (Ed.) *Indo–Nepal Relations.* New Delhi: Maulana Abul Kalam Azad Academy Institute of Asian Studies.

Subedi, S. 2010. 'Emerging Security Challenges of Nepal'. In: Bhattarai, R. and Wagle, G.S. (Eds.). *The Challenges of National Security of Nepal and the Role of International Law and Foreign Policy.* Kathmandu: NIPS.

Vaidya, T.R. 1993. *Prithvinarayan Shah: The Founder of Modern Nepal.* New Delhi: Anmol Publications.

Journals and Newspapers

Regional Poverty Profile 2009–10 (2010), Kathmandu: SAARC Secretariat.

Akbar, M.J. *Nagarik,* 31 December 2016.

Ghosh, R. 'Trilateral Cooperation: Nepal can be a bridge between India and China'. *Times of India,* 13 October 2016.

Pandey, R.N. 'Constitution in the street and history in risky slope'. *Kantipur* Daily, 13 December 2016.

7

NATIONAL SECURITY: CHALLENGES AND PERSPECTIVES

Rabi Raj Thapa
Chiran Jung Thapa

Nepal remains precariously perched in a formidable geopolitical region. Its perpetual vulnerability is that it remains squeezed between India that surrounds it on the east, west and south, and borders China in the north. The asymmetry in size and capacity of its neighbours illustrate its vulnerabilities. India and China have two of the largest standing militaries in the world; both possess nuclear weapons; both are the largest carbon-emitting countries, making the environment one of the most polluted in the world; and both have two of the largest populations in the world. The two countries have revving economies and have an insatiable appetite for resources. The colliding interests of both countries in Nepal pose a significant threat to it. The fact that these two neighbours have gone to war in the past and still have outstanding border disputes, which intermittently stoke tensions along their borders, also adds to Nepal's vulnerability. China's so-called liberation of Tibet through a takeover and India's annexation of Sikkim on 26 April 1975 serve as sobering reminders to Nepal of the challenges to its sovereignty, territorial integrity and independence.

First and foremost, Nepal's threat perception needs to be taken into account. Even since its birth as a modern nation state following the unification process initiated by Nepal's founder, King Prithvi

Narayan Shah in 1744, the threat perception has always centred on the two large neighbours of Nepal. Even in his *Divya Upadesh*, King Prithvi Narayan Shah has projected Nepal as a fragile yam between two boulders. This strategic fragility reckoned by Shah still persists in the psyche of Nepali strategic thinkers and security personnel.

The perpetual strategic vulnerability emanating from Nepal's two giant neighbours, however, is a bit skewed because its threat perception considers India more of an existential threat to its sovereign existence than China. Security thought and doctrines in Nepal have mainly been shaped to counter India's multiple machinations and manoeuvrings and possible incursions. Ever since the Indian Independence in 1947, Nepal has always felt that India consistently pursues a policy of destabilizing it.[1] In that pursuit, it has repeatedly harboured anti-establishment elements.[2]

To the Nepali strategic thought, India poses an existential threat to Nepal's sovereignty and territorial integrity. The annexation of Sikkim, the dismemberment of Pakistan and creation of Bangladesh in 1971 remain sobering reminders for the entire region regarding the threat India poses to the region. Bhutan, a quasi-sovereign kingdom remains subservient to India. The fact that India did not recognize Nepal's aspiration to be declared a ZoP announced by Late King Birendra in 1976, the fact that it imposed three crippling blockades on Nepal and that it has continually harboured and incubated anti-establishment groups, have left most in the country deeming India as the greatest external threat.

The country is also prone to natural disasters such as earthquakes, floods and landslides. The massive earthquake in April 2015 revealed Nepal's fragility. Aside from the geopolitical challenges, as a member of a globalized and interconnected world, Nepal is also susceptible to the same transnational security challenges that are afflicting other countries. The impacts of climate change are being felt across Nepal through the melting of its glaciers and erratic weather patterns.

Transnational crimes such as human trafficking, organ trafficking, drug trafficking, trafficking of animal parts and other banned substances and counterfeit currency trading have also affected Nepal.

The spread of Internet across Nepal has also resulted in a steep spike in cyber-related crimes, according to the Nepal Police. The scourge of international terrorism hit Nepal when recently, several Nepalese nationals working as security guards in Afghanistan were killed in a suicide bomb attack. Given the improved air connectivity with the rest of the world, communicable diseases can easily enter and spread across Nepal.

Notion of Security Perspective

The phenomenal change in global political order and the nature of emerging asymmetric threats has warranted a rethink of the notion of security. With the end of the Cold War, the prospects of a major intra-state war between the two superpowers, the USA and the Soviet Union, has diminished. As a result, the traditionalist way of viewing security through the military lens is also decreasing. Now, the concept of security has broadened significantly as it has come to encompass a wide array of social, economic and even psychological dimensions. Mainly due to globalization, inter-state relations have improved as there has been a rise in economic, social and security interconnectedness.

While the interconnectedness and interdependency have enhanced cooperation than confrontation, threats, like resource depletion, global warming, health endemics, terrorism, that are more transnational and asymmetric in nature, have dominated the security perspective of thinkers and practitioners. Increasingly, the notion of security is becoming more focused on the security of the individual. This is best illustrated by the evolution of the concept of human security, which posits that all humans should be free from fear and want. Although the concept of human security is increasingly being embraced in the security realm, its all-encompassing position and the ambiguity in its limitations alongside the vast amounts required to attain it, has served as a great inhibitor.

Security Apparatus

National Security Council

As per the 2015 constitution, Nepal has a National Security Council (NSC). The members of the NSC include the prime minister; the heads of defence, home, foreign and finance ministries; the chief secretary and the chief of army staff (CoAS). The constitution stipulates that the NSC would serve to safeguard Nepal's national interest, enact security and defence policies and control and deploy the NA. Initially, CoAS was not included in the NSC. However, after the NA's objection, CoAS got included in the NSC.

Perhaps the most conspicuous feature about the NSC is the value and priority accorded to it by parliamentarians. This is reflected through its limited scope mentioned in the constitution. The NSC, which should have been the preeminent body of the government, is featured only in the middle of the constitution after all other state-related provisions. Even the security agencies that send their personnel to work for the NSC accord least priority to the body.

According to many security officials, NSC has become a dumping ground for security agencies. All four security agencies are represented in the secretariat, but NSC is the least preferred posting. This is mainly because the body is mostly defunct. Reportedly, since the constitution was promulgated, the NSC has hardly convened and no substantive deliberations regarding national security issues have taken place among its members.

The NSC's defunct status is also due to the lack of a coherent and nationally owned National Security Policy (NSP). Although the former government led by K.P. Oli drafted and passed the NSP, it barely saw the light of day because the government fell before it could enact the policy. The government (2016–17) led by Pushpa Kamal Dahal completely disowned the document drafted by the previous government and failed to replace it. The political divergence between the ruling parties has greatly hampered the realization of national security as it is being viewed from a partisan lens.

Nepal Army

Two institutions are attributed to the birth of modern Nepal—monarchy (Shah dynasty started by King Prithvi Narayan Shah) and the Gorkhali Army. The history of the modern NA dates back to the famed army of Gorkha (currently one of the districts located 140 kms west of Kathmandu) that has acquired worldwide acclaim for it gallantry. Led by King of Gorkha, Prithvi Narayan Shah, the Gorkhali Army unified Nepal by winning over all scattered and separate principalities. The foundation of modern Nepal, therefore, has a history intertwined with today's NA.

Structurally, the 94,000 strong NA is headed by a four-star General—Chief of Army Staff (CoAS). Under him are two three-star Lieutenant Generals—Chief of General Staff (CGS) and Chief of Staff (CoS). The CGS handles operations, training and intelligence, while the CoS oversees UN peacekeeping operations, nature conservation and wildlife preservation, National Cadet Corps (NCC) and various welfare schemes. The NA is divided into six divisions: Far Western, Mid-Western, Western, Central, Eastern and Valley. Each division is headed by a two-star Major General. It also has separate aviation, artillery, engineers, signals, air defence and Special Forces brigades.

Until the abolition of the monarchy in 2008, there was a widespread public perception that worked against the NA's professional image and saw it as a feudal king's private army. This mainly stemmed from the fact that monarchs of modern times—King Mahendra, King Birendra and King Gyanendra—until 2006, were the supreme commander of the military and had the final decision regarding the promotions and postings. A military body called the Principal Military Secretariat (PMS) was housed within the royal palace, headed by a senior General. This perception was further reinforced by the fact that the king and other male members of the royal family frequently donned military attire. The king also attended most army functions as the chief guest and conferred medals, insignias and other awards to the army's ranks. Furthermore, the slogan, 'in the service of the monarch lay our strength', was instilled in the army's ranks and file.

Following the abolition of the monarchy, the conjugal relationship that had persisted between the king and the army has been completely severed and a new chapter in its history is under way. In contrast to the popular belief that the army would step in to safeguard the monarchy, it accepted the verdict of the CA to abolish it. By doing so, it managed to boost its public image. First, it has been able to dispel the notion that it was the king's private army. Also, the absence of bloodshed during such a colossal political transformation was credited to the restraint and the professionalism of the NA, giving a boost to its public image. Even the Maoists—the party whose two leaders, Pushpa Kamal Dahal 'Prachanda' and Baburam Bhattarai have been the executive head of the country after 2006 and had previously publicly maligned NA—have publicly applauded its role in the transition process. All political forces and the general public are aware that had the NA or disgruntled factions in the organization opted against the political transformation, the circumstances would have most certainly been bloody.

Since the political transformation of 2006, the primary challenge confronted by the NA is its adjustment to the new political realities and democratic dispensation. First, it had to build its democratic credentials by coming under civilian control. Although it effectively managed to dispel the allegation that it was the king's private army by not siding with the monarch, there were continued suspicions held by the political forces it had to surmount. Several sources in the NA asserted that even G.P. Koirala, the NC leader who became prime minister after the 2006 uprising, distrusted the NA to the extent that he urged the Maoists to maintain their combatants and arms as a bulwark against NA's possible interventions in the political landscape.[3]

Second, despite the recognition of the necessity to come under civilian control, NA still remains wary of the civilian authorities. Having witnessed the structural politicization and decay of the Nepal Police, the APF, and the entire bureaucratic apparatus, the NA is still struggling to fully embrace the new civilians at the helm. Similarly, the civilian side is yet to fully comprehend NA's role, operations and other matters of military affairs. More importantly, the Ministry of Defence (MoD) critically lacks knowledgeable and competent staff.

Furthermore, in the legislature, there is a lack of understanding of the role and functions of a national army.

On the logistical front, one of the critical deficiencies of the NA is its inadequate aviation assets. This was mostly felt during its counter-insurgency operations. The only effective edge NA actually had over the Maoist insurgents was air power. Many senior generals, along with ground commanders, have admitted that the lack of proper aviation assets became NA's Achilles heel. Had the NA been endowed with a handsome fleet of aviation assets, it could have been deployed rapidly upon receiving distress signals. They could then have been able to resupply and provide suppressive firepower in support, which would have greatly increased the likelihood of inflicting a heavy casualty on the insurgents and could have possibly turned the tide in its favour.

The lack of aviation assets became more pronounced after the mega earthquake that struck Nepal in April 2015. NA has the primary role in disaster rescue and relief operations. There was a critical need to supply relief materials to victims, and rescue and ferry them to safer locations. As many roads were blocked due to landslides and there were continuous aftershocks, in such circumstances, operating with only a handful of aircraft, the NA was overstretched.

Another challenge currently afflicting the NA stems from the introduction of the fast track promotion system. The system, introduced in February 2013, was aimed at providing better performing officers promotion based on merit (Dahal, 2013). It was welcomed by the ranks as earlier capable officers were unable to climb up the hierarchy due to a clog in the system. One could not get promoted unless there was a vacant slot at the top. After the system was introduced, however, it was indiscriminately executed to bump up those within the CoAS Gaurav Shumsher Rana's (2012 to 2015) coterie and expunge the disliked ones. Such nepotism not only distorted the essence of the system but also ended up critically dampening the morale of the officers. By totally discounting the highest medal of honour, Nepal Tara, as a meritorious achievement, the newly introduced system sent home some of the most valiant officers. Aside from a handful from his coterie, even the most deserving candidates are actually suffering due to an early bump up. There were eight lieutenant colonels who were sent home as a result of the fast track system. These eight later jointly filed a case in the Supreme Court against the NA's decision to retire them and promote others based on the fast track system; that case, however, is still pending (Dahal, 2013).

One of the alarming aspects vis-à-vis NA is that its apolitical nature in recent times has been encroached upon due to external political influences. The tussle between the NA's CoAS, General Rukmangad Katwal, and the Maoist Prime Minister, Pushpa Kamal Dahal, in 2008–09 was a defining moment in its institutional history. Essentially, when PM Dahal sought to sack General Katwal, the latter refused to comply and it was equated as NA's unwillingness to withstand political influences in its apolitical and professional domain. Ultimately, Dahal was compelled to resign after other political forces and external foreign powers backed General Katwal. The then President, Ram Baran Yadav (with the support of the Indian establishment) as the supreme commander of the NA, acted against the government's decision. The President supported the CoAS by sending him an official letter instructing him to stay put and not relinquish his position as demanded by the prime minister.[4]

During General Gaurav Rana's tenure as CoAS, too, there was a clear attempt to politicize the NA by allowing political influence to reign supreme. According to several reports and sources in the NA, Lt General Pawan Pande—who was second-in-command and General Rana's in-law—was provided an unrestricted leeway to lobby for the CoAS post.[5] While Pande was in a dogged pursuit to become CoAS by amending the Army Act, Rana did nothing to arrest his brazen actions. Any other soldier or officer would have been immediately court-martialled for this deed. Pande, however, was allowed to walk scot-free.

Nepal Police

The origin of Nepal Police begins with the 'Police Sawal' (Police Directives) issued by Prime Minister Chandra Sumsher in 1914. He had formed police units in Birgunj (mid-south adjoining Indian border of Nepal) and later Kathmandu with the inspector as the head of the unit. It was just a localized police unit under the command of Bada Hakim or chief of the district. However, the history of the present-day police begins after the enactment of the Police Act 2012 (1955), which has survived and served seven constitutions and various forms of government. Most of the fundamental features of Nepal Police are similar to the traditional colonial police system of India, which was passed on to them by the British colonial police system called the Police Act 1822.

Nepal Police is led by the Inspector General (IG) and eight Additional Inspector Generals (AIGs) along with 1,362 senior officers. According to Nepal Police, the strength of the force currently stands at 72,729[6]. The organization is divided into major administration bodies, from headquarters to zonal, district and local police administrative units. Besides, there are some specialized wings and units like the Metropolitan Police in the valley, Nepal Police Academy, Nepal Police Hospital, Crime Investigation Bureau (CIB), Narcotic Control Bureau (NCB), Traffic Police. Within the police headquarters, under the direct supervision and direction of the chief of Nepal Police are some important departments like Research & Planning, Women & Child (Protection) Directorate, Interpol, Human Rights Unit, Police Schools and Tourist Police.

The 2015 constitution has already stipulated a federal model of Nepal Police into central, provincial or state, local and metropolitan levels. A taskforce formed under the chair of a former IG has already submitted the proposal of federalizing Nepal Police to the government, but it is yet to be put into practice.

The police force has the primary responsibility of enforcing the law and, thereby, ensuring public security and safety. The organization's institutional effectiveness, however, has not been in tandem with the people's aspirations and international professional standards. This is mainly due to the Maoist conflict, endemic corruption, rampant politicization and deficiency of adequate resources. These four variables have adversely affected the responsiveness and professionalism of the Nepal Police and have resulted in diminished public trust in the organization.

One of the primary factors that have inhibited responsiveness of the Nepal Police is the decade-long Maoist conflict (1996–2006). No other organization bore the brunt of the insurgency more than the Nepal Police. Its personnel were the prime targets of the Maoist insurgents because they embodied the state. According to the Nepal Police Headquarters, some 1,479 police personnel lost their lives and thousands were wounded. Hundreds of police posts across the country were destroyed. As the police strategically abandoned the destroyed posts, public faith in the organization dwindled and in turn hit at its morale. What further pummelled its morale was that the public and human rights organizations held it responsible for extrajudicial killings and unlawful or excessive use of force during the conflict.

Before the NA was deployed to neutralize the Maoists in 2001, the Nepal Police was the only organization fighting the insurgents. There was a sense of abandonment amongst the Nepal Police personnel because when Maoists mounted massive attacks on their posts, no support came from the NA despite being in close proximity. The subsequent governments also did not provide the needed wherewithal such as modern weaponry and air assets to the Nepal Police.

During the Maoist insurgency, when the government saw that the Nepal Police was ill-equipped to neutralize the insurgents, instead of equipping and providing it with better resources, it created a new security agency in 2001—the Armed Police Force (APF). The establishment of APF had an enormous impact on the Nepal Police. Most of their units in the Maoist-dominated areas were placed within APF battalions in the mid and far west regions. It was only after the Comprehensive Peace Agreement (CPA) of 2006 and cessation of hostility, that the animosity between the two forces surfaced on rights, responsibilities and jurisdiction. Before the formation of APF, the security situation was precarious and Nepal Police was fully dependent on APF.

After the cessation, the government failed to manage the two in a balanced and harmonized way. There are numerous security organizations in India, Pakistan and Bangladesh, but they have less interagency cooperation and coordination problems as compared to Nepal. Currently, the government policy of deploying all security forces in all duties is resulting in duplication of effort, and thereby leading to confusion and conflict between the security organizations of Nepal. For example, in any VVIP security duties, all four security organizations are deployed, despite their different mandate, roles and responsibilities.

Another major affliction in the Nepal Police is corruption. A total of thirteen IGs have taken charge of Nepal Police since 1990. Of the thirteen, six have been officially charged with corruption as part of the Commission for Investigation of Abuse of Authority (CIAA) investigations between 1990 and 2011. They have allegedly amassed wealth that is disproportionate to their earnings. Corruption is not just endemic at the top level but has permeated across the chain of command all the way to the lowest level. Scores of senior and junior officers have been charged and indicted for corruption (Sharma and Kharel, 2011).

Many officers attribute corruption to compulsion. They assert that it is simply unfeasible to subsist on the meagre pay scale. Several senior police officers have admitted that corruption has become systemic in the organization because the amount earned through corruption is needed to pay off powerful politicians for career advancement.[7]

In the course of interviews, several police officers asserted that the scale of corruption in other government institutions such as immigration and customs, land revenue office and ministries is much higher than in Nepal Police. They further claimed that since Nepal Police is the front-line agency, its actions are always put under the scanner.

Another deficiency that afflicts the organization is the dissonance between the scope of work and the resources provided to it. Nepal Police is the most overstretched and overworked security agency in Nepal. According to AIG, Bigyan Raj Sharma, Nepal Police had over one thousand different ordained tasks.[8] Not only are its numbers insufficient to meet current public demands, but the organization critically lacks resources to carry out the designated tasks.

A senior AIG lamented that the government only provides one-third amount of the petitioned budget for the organization. The challenge is self-evident from the incongruity in the budget allocation and the rising demand of police services. While the budget is always limited, the its still has to function and provide all the mandated services. This is most conspicuous in the allocation of fuel for the Nepal Police vehicles. Policing work frequently demands response, which in turn necessitates their personnel to visit incident sites. The visit usually requires vehicles and fuel. And, according to the Nepal Police sources, the fuel apportioned to each unit is so meagre that it is abysmally insufficient to meet even a quarter of the demand.

Politicization of Nepal Police and/or interference in police work by politicians is perhaps the biggest challenge faced by the force today. Almost all the senior police officers interviewed, admitted that politicization of the Nepal Police ensued after the democratic political dispensation in 1990. For example, in February 2017, the GoN decided to promote DIG Jaya Bahadur Chand instead of Nawaraj Silwal, who was the seniormost among the four contenders to the post. Silwal filed a case in the Supreme Court against the government and the court issued a stay order on the implementation of the government decision till the court gives its verdict. The government had to give the command of the police force to a medical doctor, AIG Dr Dinesh Chandra Pokhrel, as officiating IGP after amending the police regulations.[9]

According to a study undertaken by the United States Institute of Peace (USIP), 63 per cent of Nepal Police respondents reported of 'enduring political interference within the working of the institution of the Nepal Police or while Nepal Police officers were carrying out their duties' (Budhathoki, 2011). Senior police officers disclosed that 'the culture of Hamro Manchey (favouritism) rather than Ramro Manchey (meritocracy) has taken root in the Nepal Police after politicians began to appoint, transfer and promote police personnel based on political preference, acquaintance and affiliation.

This reportedly has given rise to a culture of favouritism,

nepotism and cronyism within the organization, resulting in Nepal Police personnel relying more on political patronage than on personal performance to advance their career. Essentially, in the absence of an impartial and impervious Police Service Commission (PSC) in place to calibrate the aptitude and performance of police officers, politicians, particularly those at the helm of Ministry of Home Affairs (MoHA), have more control over the careers of police officers. A senior retired police officer lamented that the careers of police personnel are at the mercy of politicians. Thus, the psyche of police officers is being adversely impacted by politicization, whereby officers are more inclined towards serving the interest of political actors than law enforcement.

Another challenge is the growing number of bright officers leaving the organization. This growing trend is mainly attributed to the delay in promotion, politicization in promotion and posting and the prospects of better job opportunities in other private and/or non-governmental sectors. On the lower and other ranks, the prospect of other security jobs abroad and within Nepal has tempted them to resign on pension immediately after they become entitled for it. The interference of oversight bodies, mainly the MoHA in micro-management of policing, has left all able officers either to appease political stalwarts, to be left frustrated and humiliated or to resign and look for better alternatives outside the organization.

There is a rising tendency amongst the public to attack police officials and police outposts (Basnet, 2016). In the last two years alone, there have been five major incidents where mobs have mounted attacks on police posts and personnel. These attacks are attributed to public dissatisfaction with Nepal Police's performance and rising level of impunity in society. Not only have police personnel been attacked but even their weapons have been looted in several cases. This alarming trend not only exhibits contempt for authority but also demonstrates the volatile operating environment for the force.

Since 1990, one of the major encroachments on the Nepal Police's authority has been exercised by the government itself, through the formation of various investigative commissions of inquiry (CoI).

Every time there is a major criminal case, instead of allowing the Nepal Police to investigate, the government sets up CoIs, which are led by civilians. Although the commissions are extraordinary, ad hoc mechanisms established parallel to a regular criminal justice system and are not empowered to prosecute crimes, nor do they have the power to determine the guilt or innocence of the person. The role that CoIs play is complementary to the criminal processes and can never be a substitute for normal criminal investigations and prosecution. Essentially, the rule of law is being compromised by the manipulation of the politicians in power who decide which criminal act goes through the criminal justice system. According to a study conducted by the International Commission of Jurists in 2012, entitled 'Commissions of Inquiry in Nepal: Denying remedies, entrenching impunity', most of the CoI reports appear not to have been made public nor have their recommendations been implemented.

Armed Police Force

The government led by Krishna Prasad Bhattarai (May 1999–March 2000) felt an urgent need to establish a better equipped and better trained force to combat the growing Maoist insurgency and decided to create a separate paramilitary unit in the year 2000. This stemmed from the conviction that the beleaguered Nepal Police was ill-prepared and ill-equipped to combat the Maoist insurgents. To make matters worse, constitutional impediments barred the government from mobilizing a better trained and equipped NA. Therefore, the establishment of a separate force had become imperative to quell the raging insurgency. Hence, on 13 January 2000, a seven-member task force, Sashatra Prahari Sewa Gathan Sujhav Aayog (Consultative Taskforce on the Formation of Armed Police Service 2000), was formed with the objective of developing a framework for the establishment of a paramilitary force under the chairpersonship of former home secretary, Khemraj Regmi. The commission presented its report within six weeks and the decision to erect APF was underway immediately after that.

The task force came up with a recommendation of developing an armed police force of paramilitary nature of 25,000 personnel in two phases. In the first phase, it was mandated to have transferred personnel—6,000 from NA and 9,000 from Nepal Police—on a voluntary basis. But in practice, only 120 high ranking officers from NA joined this new organization and the 9,000 police personnel who joined the force either gradually resigned or deserted. Then, in the second phase, it was mandated to raise the remaining numbers from direct recruitment, and the Public Service Commission (PSC) was given the authority to administer the intake exams. Between 2001 to 2006, APF went through a very crucial and challenging phase, in which it lost its first chief, IG Krishna Mohan Shrestha, who was assassinated by the Maoists, and around three hundred personnel.

Although the initial size of the force was limited to 11,000 during its formative years, following the 2006 peace accord, the number has quadrupled to more than 40,000. Its mandates too have increased. It now sends its personnel to UN peacekeeping missions like the Nepal Police and NA do, has its own disaster management school and recently even started its own staff college course. The APF also appears to have better political leverage than the other security agencies. This is manifested through the VIP security it provides to the entire spectrum of high-level political actors. An APF guard unit is attached to all senior leaders in the country. From the former monarch on the right to all senior leftist leaders and the NC leaders at the centre, the APF has the entire spectrum covered. Not only that, it has even taken up perimeter security of several key embassies in Kathmandu. It currently guards the US embassy and its other affiliate properties.

Similar to the Nepal Police, one of the major challenges faced by the APF is corruption. Until now, there have been seven IGs in the APF. Of the seven, four have been charged with corruption by the CIAA. On the recommendation of the CIAA, the government had even suspended a sitting IG in December 2015 on charges of embezzlement. Beside IG Kishore Lama, who was only in office for two weeks, the fact that all other former IGs who are alive have been charged with corruption is telling of how endemic corruption is within the organization.

The most serious challenge that has shaken the APF is the disgruntled personnel within its ranks. Within its sixteen-year history, this force has also endured some incidents of mutiny by its ranks. The first such incident happened at Chandika Battalion, located in Parbat district, on 18 June 2008. Those involved in the revolt had accused senior officers of mistreatment of lower ranks, which included demeaning behaviour, frequent thrashing and also commissioning poor quality rations. Only a few days after that incident, another similar incident took place at Bageshwari Barracks, located in Samsherganj in Banke district, on 21 June 2008. In a similar manner, lower ranks accused senior officers of abuse and mistreatment and feeding them poor quality rations.

These incidents highlighted some of the systemic shortcomings of a fledgling organization. Unlike the other two agencies, the APF was still in its infancy and was learning to evolve as a tightly knit and disciplined uniformed agency. Several APF officers attributed the insubordination in these incidents to the disorientation of the agency itself. APF had officers coming from police as well as army backgrounds; so, the merger of two different sets of institutional ethos could have come into friction and resulted in that outburst.

The disorientation that could have sparked the mutinies, however, afflicts the agency even now. Till date, there are murmurs within the force about whether it is a police force or a military force or is somewhere in the middle. To illustrate further, IGP Sanat Basnet and IGP Shailendra Shrestha joined the APF from the NA. So, many officers within the organization claim that these two chiefs tried to mould the force in accordance with the military standards. The IGPs prior to them and after them came from the Nepal Police; so, they tried to steer the organization in line with the police standards.

Since the inception of the APF, there have been some conflicts and confusion between Nepal Police and APF, whether it is on the matter of allocation of resources, functional jurisdiction or the seniority of organization. These issues were dormant during the conflict period, which surfaced visibly after 2006. The government oversight bodies and the successive organization heads are well aware of the threats and risks involved in it. But, despite all these dilemmas, the government, the successive prime ministers and the home ministers were more occupied with manipulating and playing in between the organizations and further their personal and political party interest in sharing in termination, promotion and transfer of police personnel of both organizations indiscriminately.

Some of the issues of conflict and confrontation stem from the personality clashes of the organizational heads rather than major policy issues. The conflict and controversy between the heads of Nepal Police and the Armed Police on the issue of arrest by the APF was aggravated out of proportion to bring division among the two complementary forces. This issue was aggravated by top brasses of the two organizations and neglected by the oversight bodies, i.e. the MoHA, Office of the Prime Minister and Secretariat of the Council of Ministers, who could have resolved it amicably.

National Investigation Department

Just like the enterprise should be, very little is known about Nepal's intelligence and counter-intelligence capabilities. In Nepal, there are several entities that have been ordained with intelligence functions. The primary agency conferred the task of intelligence is the National Investigation Department (NID), under the MoFA. Alongside NID, each of the aforementioned security agencies—NA, Nepal Police and APF—has its own intelligence wings. NA has its own intelligence wing in the form of Directorate General of Military Intelligence (DGMI), headed by a Major General. Likewise, the Nepal Police's intelligence wing is called the Central Intelligence Bureau (CIB). APF also has its own intelligence wing, headed by a Senior Superintendent of Police (SSP). The National Security Council Secretariat also reportedly has some intelligence functions given that there are members representing all four security agencies working at the secretariat. There is, however, no existing mechanism to coordinate these various intelligence capabilities.

Intelligence is supposed to be a product, process and profession. In the true sense, none of these three is truly applicable in Nepal's case. The primary reason the intelligence capability is so weak and ignored is that there is no proper consumer of intelligence in Nepal. Generally, the need for intelligence arises from three considerations. First, to avoid strategic surprises because the intelligence community is constantly keeping track of all threats, challenges and incidents that have the potential to inflict harm to national interest and national security. Second, given that policymakers are transient, the presence of an intelligence mechanism is to provide long-term expertise. Third is to support the policymaking process. None of these considerations seem to have been realized and/or understood by those in the policymaking realm.

The nation is so caught up in the whirlwind of intractable political wrangling that the issue of intelligence has not been a priority for the consumers of intelligence. In the absence of demand and specified target coming from the rightful consumer, alongside proper guidance and support, NID remains in a state of dormancy and decay.

Every intelligence process comprises seven distinct phases: identifying requirements, collection, processing, exploitation, analysis, production, dissemination and feedback. Juxtaposing these phases with Nepal's intelligence process will show that, currently, only a sporadic collection process is under way. According to several NID officials and Department of Military Intelligence (DMI) officials who were interviewed, Nepal only undertakes collection. Even the collection is done more at a tactical level rather than on a long-term strategic basis. Within the NA, there is some level of identifying requirements, collection and dissemination process because the institution itself is the consumer of the product. There is, however, no rigorous system in place to undertake thorough processing, exploitation and analysis. The feedback loop is also absent.

There are several intelligence collection methods: Imagery intelligence (IMINT), Signals intelligence (SIGINT), Measures and signatures intelligence (MASINT), Human Intelligence (HUMINT)—also known as espionage—and Open Source Intelligence (OSINT). Of these, Nepal mostly employs HUMINT and OSINT. Although NID does conduct HUMINT, the agents it employs apparently lack the skills to conduct intelligence work. According to a former head of NID, the agency has been heavily politicized following the 2006 political transformation. Reportedly, due to the ease of hiring individuals as informers, several Home Ministers have inducted large numbers of untrained political party cadres into the NID.

Another shortcoming that afflicts the organization is lack of a system to attract highly capable individuals to join the organization. The recruitment drive for the NID has become so politicized that it is akin to an opportunity for the incumbent Home Minister to dole out government jobs to his people.

NID, headed by a chief officer with a total strength of approximately 1,000 personnel, is also on other fronts of intelligence. There are four broad activities which are integral to intelligence: collection, analysis, covert action and counter-intelligence. NID faces severe constraints in respect to the latter three activities. The organization has never been endowed with an analysis capability. It mostly relies on unprocessed information. It also does not have covert action capabilities. The Special Forces unit in the NA is the only unit in the country that has some covert action capability.

Similar to other security agencies, another limitation that afflicts the NID is the budgetary constraints. Intelligence is a costly affair and requires significant investment. For example, obtaining information through SIGINT intelligence requires a number of high-end listening gadgets and highly paid proficient operators and interpreters. Unfortunately, given that there are always budgetary limitations, very little priority is accorded to NID. It is the agency that receives the least amount of funding from the government. The organization has fallen under a vicious trap because, in the absence of proper identification of requirements, it cannot provide relevant intelligence to lawmakers, thus remaining distant, aloof and ignored. This, in turn, has curtailed its ability to influence lawmakers as well as demand a larger share of the budgetary pie.

Challenges

Criminalization of politics and politicization of crime

One of the most unsettling trends taking root in the Nepalese society is the criminalization of politics and politicization of crime. Following the peace accord of 2006, political parties have established youth-led outfits and have frequently condoned and defended the unlawful activities of these groups. News reports of politicians using undue influence to extricate these criminals from the clasp of the law are also common. Flouting the rule of law, these political actors have brazenly challenged the authority of the state and continue to interfere in the jurisdiction of law enforcement agencies. More alarmingly, criminal activities are being given a political hue and protection. Criminals are increasingly becoming affiliated to political parties to secure protection against law enforcement agencies.

The link between politicians and criminal groups is validated by the withdrawal of criminal cases. In October 2008, the Maoist-led government withdrew 349 criminal cases, including cases of serious human rights violations committed by the UCPN-M cadres. Likewise, the CPN-UML-led government has withdrawn cases against 282 persons, including two hundred charged with murder and eighty-two with arson (Gautam, 2009).

The slayings of notorious criminals—Dinesh Adhikari (aka Chari), affiliated to the UML and Kumar Shrestha (aka Ghaite), affiliated to the NC—by the police in encounters, adequately demonstrate the criminal–politician nexus. Prominent politicians came out in support of the dead criminals and lambasted the police, labelling the encounters as fake and extrajudicial. Claiming that these two aforementioned criminals were members of their respective parties, and providing political colour to the crime committed, political parties are playing a role in exonerating these criminals.

The case of the murder of several police officers in Tikapur where one Senior Superintendent, two Inspectors and four other officers were brutally lynched and killed in broad daylight by a mob is also telling.

In clear violation of rule of law, former Home Minister Bimalendra Nidhi had admitted that the government was preparing to withdraw cases against those accused of the gruesome murders in Tikapur.[10] To add credence to the intersection between political and criminal realms, pictures of Prime Minister Pushpa Kamal Dahal meeting the mastermind and most wanted person accused of Tikapur murders in New Delhi surfaced recently (Ghimire, 2016).

Similarly, there are plenty of cases of Nepalese lawmakers who have criminal history, and many of them have been found to be indulging in criminal acts. According to Nepal Police records, many of the lawmakers in the parliament have criminal records. A lawmaker from the UCPN-M and controversial ex-minister Lharkyal Lama, was arrested in March 2016 after the CIAA found fourteen unused bullets and some shrapnel in his bank locker.[11] Similarly, parliamentarians of the same party were found to be involved in human trafficking.[12] Political heavyweights such as government ministers and senior party leaders allegedly make calls to secure their release. If they are not released, pressure tactics such as vehicular obstructions (chakka jams) are frequently employed by political parties to secure their release.

Migration menace

The World Bank's Nepal Migration Survey of 2009 indicates that nearly half of all households in Nepal have, or had, at least one member abroad (World Bank, 2011). According to the National Population and Housing Census of 2011, of the 5.4 million households in Nepal, 1.3 million have someone in the family living outside the country. This meant that a quarter of the total households had someone abroad. Similarly, the Nepal Living Standards Survey (NLSS) 2010/11 states that 56 per cent of the Nepalese households receive remittances. As a result, the topic of migration in Nepal today has almost become synonymous to the remittance that is reportedly keeping its economy afloat.

One of the most ignored vulnerability regarding Nepal's growing migration trend is its over-reliance on remittance. One-third of the

GDP relies on an external variable which is susceptible to abrupt fluctuations. From a security standpoint, reliability is often equated as vulnerability. Likewise, by over-relying on remittance, Nepal's economy is putting itself on a precarious edge. Any incident and change in policy in the countries the migrants are in, could result in large-scale repatriation of migrants, which would have a detrimental impact on the economy.

The current vulnerability narrative vis-à-vis migration predominantly focuses on the adversities of the migrants, but the adverse impact it has on the local communities is also coming to fore. Indications of rising security challenges due to migration relate to issues which are socio-cultural (including at the family level), health, economic and/or criminal in nature. Today, the rise in alcoholism, domestic violence, crime, illicit affairs and divorce rates is being increasingly attributed to migration. Cases of spouses in Nepal misusing the money sent by spouses working abroad are rampant as are stories of spouses in Nepal who are abandoned by their husbands or wives working abroad. This is leading to increased conflicts within families.

Assessments carried out by Saferworld in several (mainly Tarai) districts in the east, centre, midwest and far west of Nepal observed the negative implications for community safety, particularly for vulnerable groups, such as women and children (Saferworld, International Alert, et al., 2013). These assessments noted increasing levels of sexual and gender-based violence, including rape, trafficking, polygamy and domestic violence, which were partially attributed to the absence of male household members to provide security and protection. With mostly male members of the family abroad for work, the women have been found to be more vulnerable to domestic violence, and sexual and gender-based violence (SGBV) from family members and other community members. Likewise, drug abuse amongst children of migrant workers was found to be high according to Nepal Police sources.

Even after return, there are other challenges faced by migrants and their families. Cases of migrant spouses transmitting sexually transmitted diseases such as HIV to their spouses are reportedly on the rise. Also, those families whose men do not return either because they have died or because they have started a new family where they have migrated to, are at great risk. Women without birth or citizen certificates whose husbands are away from home are unable to access state health and educational benefits or to seek formal employment. While some migrants return with handsome dividends, there are many who return empty-handed and heavily in debt. Migrants often return traumatized and frustrated and psychological problems make it harder for them to function and reintegrate into their communities and families. Cases of trauma and frustration leading to alcoholism and display of aggressive and violent behaviour, often resulting in domestic violence, and SGBV is reportedly increasing according to Nepal Police sources. In addition, disillusioned returnees are often more vulnerable to being mobilized for radical causes or crime, leading to a rise in criminal activities and radicalized elements in communities.

International terrorism

Today, every country in the world is susceptible to the scourge of international terrorism. There are several ways in which a country can be directly or indirectly affected by terrorism. First, it could be hit by a terrorist attack. Second, citizens of a country could be involved in terrorist activities. There is also a risk of citizens of one country being attacked by terrorists in a different country. Similarly, it is likely for a country to be used as a safe haven or a transit point by terrorists to plan its activities.

Nepal, as a country that has open border with India and increasing air connectivity with the rest of the world is vulnerable to international terrorism. According to a report[13] released by the US State department in 2015, Nepal could potentially be used by terrorist groups as a transit point owing to the lax security along its borders with India and at its only international airport in Kathmandu.

The lax security at Nepal's international airport has already resulted in a major terrorist incident in the past. An Indian airliner bound to India from Nepal's airport was hijacked in December 1999. The hijacking had grave implications for Nepal, resulting in the erosion of national sovereignty and integrity. After that incident, citing insufficient security provisions at the international airport, India demanded to station its own security officials. Although Indian security officials were not allowed the airport citing sovereignty issues, every passenger bound towards India from Nepal's airport has to undergo an additional security vetting conducted by Indian airline officials on an elevated platform right before boarding the aircraft.

More importantly, the prospects of Kashmiri and/or Pakistani terrorists exploiting the open border to perpetrate acts of terrorism against India have always remained perilously high. For that reason, India always cites the open border as a great vulnerability to its security and demands that Nepal be extra vigilant along the borders to curb nefarious activities.

The prospects of Nepalese nationals falling victim to terrorist incidents has also risen exponentially with increased outbound migration. There are hundreds of thousands of Nepalese nationals in different parts of the globe today. The vulnerability and likelihood of falling victim to terrorist incidents automatically increases with this surge of travelling Nepalese citizens. This has been reflected twice in recent times. In 2004, twelve Nepali nationals were killed by terrorists in Iraq. Similarly, in June 2016, fourteen Nepali nationals were killed in a suicide bomb attack in Afghanistan.[14]

Another potential that has worried the security officials in Nepal is the involvement of Nepalese nationals in terrorist activities. Almost a month after the 9/11 terrorist attack in the USA, a Nepali national was apprehended at Chicago O'Hare International Airport after he tried to board an aircraft with nine knives, a mace and a stun gun. Although no clear links between this man and terrorist networks were established, the incident greatly imperilled Nepal's national repute. It was such a sensitive time in the USA and all over the world that had a Nepalese been implicated, it would have had grave implications for the entire nation as it would have subjected every Nepalese national to greater suspicion and scrutiny.

Nepal was again in the limelight right after the Boston Marathon bombings in April 2013. This was mainly because the attackers had used pressure cooker bombs, which was widely known to be the signature bombing method of the Nepali Maoist groups. With only that device as the clue for the investigators, Nepal naturally became a suspect. Most recently, a Nepalese man was deported from Malaysia in charge of being involved in facilitating operations of terrorist groups, including Islamic State of Iraq and Syria (ISIS).

Some Perspectives

Security is the primary function of any state. The social contract between the government and the governed is derived from the government's responsibility of providing security to its citizens. In Nepal's context, no government since 1990 has actually governed with the security function as the main priority in mind. Strategic thought regarding security has been critically missing amongst those at the helm. This was reflected by the fact that no government deemed it necessary to have a National Security Policy. Also telling is the fact that no government since 1990 has accorded value to strengthening Nepal's national intelligence architecture, which is primarily a requisite to making the nation secure. Instead, according to several officials from the NID, most of the Home Ministers who have taken office in the last twenty years have recruited their political cadres into NID. Such politicization and degradation of the most crucial national body blaringly speaks of the acute strategic myopia that afflicts Nepal.

One of the major impediments to the formulation of a coherent National Security Policy was the absence of clearly defined national interest. National interest is the inherent centripetal ingredient in statecraft that provides direction to national policies. Essentially, the concept of national security is rooted in the perpetual pursuit of protection, preservation and promotion of national interest. Therefore, all policies are derived by taking the national interest into consideration and all policies combined together constitute a comprehensive national security policy. According to several government officials who have served at the highest positions, there is reportedly no clarity in national interest amongst government officials and each government agency operates by employing its personal intuition and insights as to what best serves the interest of Nepal (Adhikari, 2014).

Another dimension that hampers Nepal's national security architects is the prevailing thought that national security remains the sole domain of the security apparatus. According to sources in the NA, there have been two attempts to draft a National Security Policy by the NA. The first attempt was during General Dharmapal Bar Singh Thapa's (1995–1999) tenure and the second during General Rukmangad Katwal's tenure (2006–2009). Recognizing the absence of a national security policy, the NA took the initiative and consulted various experts and professionals, drafted a policy and submitted it to the government for further deliberation. However, it was not endorsed by the government.

Another telling example is the fact that the National Security Council Secretariat is led by a Major General of the NA and there are representatives of all other security agencies in the Secretariat. Although it is officially under the Ministry of Defence, civilian authorities still reckon national security to be an enterprise of the security agencies and have displayed no dispensation to change that status quo. The National Security Council is the least preferred venue for any government official because it is a toothless entity whose function is merely to exist as another office and serves little or no purpose in informing or bolstering Nepal's statecraft. Another indicator was the fact that most of attendees of the recently organized National Security Conference were security professionals.

Similarly, there is no unity of purpose amongst the various agencies that play a vital role in realizing national security. Policies such as economic, environmental, social, agricultural, educational, health, information and technology, foreign and defence are integral parts of the national security policy. There is, however, no alignment between the line agencies that are responsible for formulating each of these various policies. There has, till now, been no instance when these line agencies have congregated to discuss national security and their respective roles in realizing national security. Other government agencies have yet to internalize the fact that they, too, have a vital function in the national security architecture and it is a collective effort of various agencies that serves to guarantee national security.

In Conclusion

Nepal's geopolitical vulnerabilities will remain for a foreseeable future. The challenges that emerge from an interconnected and globalized world will also remain. The highly politicized and polarized nature of the society is adversely affecting the entire security apparatus. The security agencies are actually quite capable of delivering the services as mandated by law. It is the structural politicization and its subsequent corruption in the security agencies that distort and impede its ability to perform. Therefore, uprooting these afflictions will require a great deal of political will at the top. Whether it is external or internal security challenge, only long-term political stability in the country can enhance Nepal's prospects of realizing a secure environment. Political instability will not only affect security agencies, but also adversely impact the country's ability to realize national security.

***Rabi Raj Thapa** is former Additional Inspector General of Armed Police Force-Nepal, and is currently Chief Academic Coordinator of Armed Police Force Command and Staff College, Nepal.*

***Chiran Jung Thapa** is an independent security and defence analyst.*

Bibliography

Adhikari, A. 2014. *The Bullet and the Ballot Box: The Story of Nepal's Maoist Revolution*, New Delhi: Aleph Book Company.

Adhikari, I. 2015. *Military and Democracy in Nepal*. New Delhi: Routledge.

Adhikari, R.R. 'Defending National Interest in the Emerging Internal,

Regional and International Challenges'. One Day National Seminar, 9 September 2014. Kathmandu: Institute of Foreign Affairs (IFA) and Friedrich-Ebert-Stiftung (FES).

Bhattarai, R. and Wagle, G.S. 2010. *Emerging Security Challenges of Nepal.* Kathmandu: Nepal Institute of Policy Studies.

Budhathoki, C.K. 2011. *Nepalma Surakchya ra Nayaka lagi Ahwan-Kanooni Sasahn tatha Nepal Prahariko Bhumika Sambandhama Nagarik ko Dristikona (Call for Security and Justice in Nepal: Citizens' Perception of Rule of Law and Role of Nepal Police).* Washington, D.C.: United States Institute for Peace.

Collins, A. 2013. *Contemporary Security Studies.* United Kingdom: Oxford University Press.

Crozier, R. and Candan, Z. 2010. *Participation and obstruction: Justice and security sector reform in Nepal.* Brussels: International Alert.

Dhungel, D.N. and Shrestha, A.M. 2006, 'National Security'. In: Dhungel, D.N. and Shrestha, A.M. (Eds.). *Nepal, Conflict Resolution and Sustainable Peace.* Kathmandu: Institute for Integrated Development Studies.

Directorate of Public Relations/ Nepalese Army (DPR/NA). 2008. *The Nepalese Army: a force with history, ready for tomorrow.*

Gurung, C.M.S. 2016. *Janatako Chhoro: An autobiography by General Chattra Man Singh Gurung.* Kathmandu: Kamala Gurung.

Surendra, K.C. 2014. *Byathamerokathadeshko.* Kathmandu: Ratna Sagar Prakashan.

Khanal, R. and Adhikari, P. 2009. *National Security of Nepal.* Kathmandu: Sangam Institute.

Lowenthal, M. 2003. *Intelligence from Secrets to Policy.* Washington, D.C.: CQ Press.

Nepal, K. 2013. *Kasauti ma Nepal Prahari.* Kathmandu: Center for Security and Justice Studies.

Saferworld, International Alert, et al. 2013. *Snapshot of Local Security and Justice Perceptions in Selected Districts of Nepal. District assessment findings.*

Sapkota, B. (Ed.). 2009. *The Nepali Security Sector: An Almanac.* Hungary: Brambauer Publishers.

Sharma, S. 2014. *Prayogshala.* Kathmandu: FinePrint.

Sharma, S.P., Vaidya, T. and Manandhar, T.M. 1992. *Nepalko Sainik Itihas.* Kathmandu: Royal Nepalese Army Headquarters.

Sharma, S., Rourke, S. and Poudel, U. 2010. *Nepal State of the State.* Kathmandu: Janasewa Printers.

World Bank. 2011a. 'Large-Scale Migration and Remittance in Nepal: Issues,

Challenges and Opportunities'. Kathmandu: Poverty Reduction and Economic Management Sector Unit, South Asia Region, World Bank

Articles

Basnet, M.B. 'Karan, Prahari Vyavahar'. 21 December 2016, http://nepal.ekantipur.com/news/2016-12-21/20161221140824.html

Gautam, B. 'Government withdraws some 300 murder, arson cases'. *My Republica*, 17 November 2009, <http://www.myrepublica.com/portal/index.php?action=news_details&news_id=11876>

Ghimire, Y. 'A "chance" meeting in Delhi, may stall political settlement of Madhesi issue in Kathmandu'. 2016, http://indianexpress.com/article/opinion/web-edits/beyond-the-news-nepal-a-chance-meeting-in-delhi-may-stall-political-settlement-of-madhesi-issue-in-kathmandu/

Sharma B. and Kharel, P. 'A culture of collusions'. *The Kathmandu Post*, 25 June 2011, <http://www.ekantipur.com/the-kathmandu-post/2011/06/24/features/a-culture-of-collusions/223254.html>

Dahal, P. 'New regulations change Nepal Army promotion criteria'. *The Kathmandu Post*, 15 February 2013, http://kathmandupost.ekantipur.com/printedition/news/2013-02-14/new-regulations-change-nepal-army-promotion-criteria.html

Dahal, P. '8 officers move SC against NA'. *The Kathmandu Post*, 18 March 2013, http://kathmandupost.ekantipur.com/printedition/news/2013-03-17/8-officers-move-sc-against-na.html)

Websites

http://thehimalayantimes.com/nepal/malaysia-deports-nepali-charged-links-isis/

http://thehimalayantimes.com/nepal/several-nepalis-killed-kabul-suicide-attack/

http://www.pahilopost.com/content/-321.html

https://www.state.gov/j/ct/rls/crt/2014/239408.htm

www.academia.edu/.../Leadership_Adaptation_and_Traits_in_Nepalese_Police_Force...

http://kathmandupost.ekantipur.com/news/2016-10-05/nidhi-process-initiated-to-withdraw-tikapur-cases.html

http://kathmandupost.ekantipur.com/news/2017-02-13/aig-dinesh-chandra-pokhrel-named-officiating-igp.html

http://edition.cnn.com/2001/US/11/04/inv.ohare.arrest/index.html

http://www.myrepublica.com/news/4556)

http://admin.myrepublica.com/politics/story/38641/disputed-ucpn-m-lawmaker-lharkyal-lama-held-with-bullets.html

http://www.asianews.it/news-en/Riyadh-expels-Nepalese-migrants--28082.html)

http://www.thestar.com.my/news/nation/2016/07/10/nepali-workers-decline/)

http://therisingnepal.org.np/index/news/12802

http://kathmandupost.ekantipur.com/news/2014-05-25/committee-formed-to-probe-ssp-kharel.html

www.nepalpolice.gov.np/image/statistics/webpage/index/html

Endnotes

1 The revelations by R.K. Yadav, a former Indian spy, in his book *Mission Raw* validate India's motive vis-à-vis Nepal.

2 The NC was an anti-establishment group harboured by India in the late '40s and early '50s. Later, other political parties that opposed the Panchayat rule were supported by India. Chandra Shekhar, who later became prime minister, came to Kathmandu to give a fiery speech against the Panchayat regime. Similarly, the Maoists, who wanted to topple the democratically elected government and the monarchy, were found to be incubated by India as most of the leaders lay comfortably sheltered in various parts of India through most of the insurgency years.

3 Several senior NA officials have publicly spoken about this issue and even a Maoist leader has affirmed G.P. Koirala's position regarding the NA.

4 This was affirmed by Lalit Basnet to the writer during a meeting with him.

5 http://www.pahilopost.com/content/-321.html

6 Of the total police personnel, 3 per cent are senior officers (Inspector of Police and above), 16 per cent are junior officers (Assistant Sub-Inspectors and Sub-inspectors) and the rest 81 per cent are head constables, constables and followers (www.nepalpolice.gov.np/image/statistics/webpage/index/html)

7 http://kathmandupost.ekantipur.com/news/2014-05-25/committee-formed-to-probe-ssp-kharel.html

8 AIGP Bigyan Raj Sharma was a former spokesperson of Nepal Police and had spoken about Nepal Police's innumerable number of duties to the contributors of this chapter.
www.nepalpolice.gov.np/image/statistics/webpage/index/html

9 http://kathmandupost.ekantipur.com/news/2017-02-13/aig-dinesh-chandra-pokhrel-named-officiating-igp.html
10 http://kathmandupost.ekantipur.com/news/2016-10-05/nidhi-process-initiated-to-withdraw-tikapur-cases.html
11 http://admin.myrepublica.com/politics/story/38641/disputed-ucpn-m-lawmaker-lharkyal-lama-held-with-bullets.html
12 http://therisingnepal.org.np/index/news/12802
13 https://www.state.gov/j/ct/rls/crt/2014/239408.htm
14 http://thehimalayantimes.com/nepal/several-nepalis-killed-kabul-suicide-attack/

8

CONFLICT TRAUMA: MAOIST INSURGENCY AND TARAI AGITATIONS*

Aditya Man Shrestha
Chiranjibi Bhandari
Rajib Timalsina

Nepal has a history of violence and armed struggle for capture of state power and political rule. But, never in this history has an event as earth-shaking and massive as the one that the CPN-M unleashed in 1996 that kept the whole country captive for a decade, taken place before. It resulted in the loss of thousands of lives and serious damage to the national economy. After the insurgents joined the mainstream politics in 2006, the 1990 constitution was jettisoned, a new interim constitution (2007) was proclaimed—under which elections to the CA were held—monarchy was abolished and the political system of the country was changed from a monarchical parliamentary system to a Federal Democratic Republic.

A new constitution, Constitution of Nepal 2015, was drafted and adopted by the people's elected CA. But immediately after its promulgation in September 2015, it faced challenges and violent agitations, mainly from the Tarai/Madhes-based political parties, and the country faced an undeclared economic blockade by India. The Madhesis are still not satisfied with the provisions of the new

---

*Several sections of this chapter are heavily based on the background paper prepared, and inputs provided, by Madan Kumar Dahal, Dwarika Nath Dhungel, Rajesh Jha 'Ahiraj' and Anil Shrestha.

constitution and its implementation is still uncertain. As such, despite the expectation of the people that, with the coming into end of the armed insurgency and framing of a new constitution, the country's political transition will be over, Nepal is still in transition. People are still suffering from the trauma of the CPN-M-led armed conflict. In addition, the country experienced another trauma caused by a movement launched by the Tarai/Madhes-based political parties.

Maoist Insurgency

The radical communists, self-styled as Maoists (CPN-M), launched their insurgency from remote mountains in the western part of Nepal, which was under distant control of the government. It was a paradox that arms were raised at a time when a full-fledged democracy was functioning in the country, with popularly elected representatives running the administration. It was the time when people were enjoying unrestrained freedom of speech, thought and expression. It was all the more astonishing that those who had once raised arms to destroy the whole citadel of state had themselves participated in the process.

Inception and agenda of the conflict

The process to restore democracy began in 1990, after a lapse of thirty years of the king's direct rule under Panchayat, and raised high hopes for transformation. A parliamentary system of government was promulgated as a result of what went down in the history of Nepal as the first people's movement. There were three main forces: the NC, CPN-UML and the king. However, the process of drafting the constitution gave ample room for the radical left to grumble, especially against the institution of monarchy, which, they alleged, did not fully reconcile itself to its limited constitutional role. Many communist leaders from the Samyukta Bam Morcha (United Left Front) were not satisfied. However, they accepted the constitution with reservation and participated in the subsequent political processes. The Samyukta

Janamorcha–Nepal (United People's Front–Nepal), a radical group, participated in the 1991 general elections, and emerged as the third largest party in parliament with nine out of 205 seats in the HoR. The party, however, failed to secure even a single seat in 1994 due to a split.

The hardliner group was led by Pushpa Kamal Dahal and Baburam Bhattarai and the soft-liner faction by Niranjan Govinda Baidhya and Nirmal Lama. The hardliner communists organized the CPN-M, and Baburam Bhattarai, on its behalf, submitted 40-point demands to Prime Minister Sher Bahadur Deuba on 4 February 1996 (Annexure 1). They were divided into three broad headings pertaining to nationality, people's democracy and livelihood. The government was given two weeks' time to respond—by 17 February 1996. If not, they claimed that they would be 'forced to adopt the path of armed struggle against the existing state power'. But the government did not take their demands seriously and Prime Minister Deuba left for India on an official visit.

The Maoists, however, launched an armed attack on 13 February and made simultaneous assaults on three police posts—one each in Rolpa and Rukum districts in western Nepal and one in Sindhuli in eastern Nepal and also on the office of the Small Farmers' Development Programme (SFDP) in Chyangdi village in the Gorkha district. The same night, thousands of leaflets and posters were distributed in major cities and thirty-six district headquarters.

The government dealt with it as a law and order problem and, accordingly, initially mobilized its police force and, as fights escalated, the NA. A separate force (APF) was later established to respond to the Maoist insurgency. The government refused to recognize the Maoist war as a political problem and, therefore, stressed military solution and suppression of insurgents. The more coercive methods the government used to counter the rebels, the stronger and widespread the Maoists emerged. For several years, the encounter was limited between the rebels and the police force. But after 2001, it dragged the NA in the fray and the scale of bloodshed went up. When the first ceasefire was declared on 21 July 2001, only six districts, viz. Rolpa, Rukum, Jajarkot, Salyan, Pyuthan and Kalikot, were seriously affected by the Maoist insurgency (Dhungel, 2004). By the end of the conflict, the Maoist presence was visible in as many as seventy-three of the seventy-five districts.

There is no doubt that the majority of the readings related to the armed conflict of Nepal refer to the 40-point demands as the point of departure to start the Maoist armed conflict. It is true that the post-1990 political developments frustrated the people with their instability, inter- and intra-party wrangling resulting in bad governance, misuse of national treasury and neglect of people's needs. The frequent change in government led the Maoists to argue that parliamentary democracy was a sham that could not work for the benefit of the people (Thapa and Sijapati, 2004). However, Deepak Thapa (2010) states that it is possible that, demands or no demands, the Maoists would have begun the uprising since they had already opted for the use of violence for achieving their political ends because they wanted to destroy the political system, particularly the abolition of the monarchy. As a tactical strategy, the Maoists proposed a round-table conference with the parliamentary parties and monarchy; an interim government; and a CA. They put these proposals forward during the negotiations held in August–November 2001 and April–August 2003.

The Maoists had adopted a multi-pronged strategy before and during the war. They had launched what is known as the 'Ideological Correction Campaign' (Ibid.) for the communist parties of Nepal. Right after the first people's movement in 1990, polarization between the communists led to emergence of more than a dozen parties. Each party sought to establish a separate identity by distinguishing itself from the others by claiming correctness in its ideology and practice in line with the world communist movement. The conditions required each faction to show distinct character. Most of the factions tried their best to appear distinct from the others. One strong faction of the UPF-N—one of the communist parties led by Pushpa Kamal Dahal and Baburam Bhattarai—transformed itself into the CPN-M by merging a few factions.

The Maoists were heavily favoured by many foreign countries which were unhappy with the political and social conditions of Nepal. India was not happy with the monarchy as it considered the Nepalese monarchs as obstructionists to its policy of hegemony on Nepal. European countries, especially the Scandinavian ones, abundantly financed ethnic communities to destroy the social and cultural fabric of Nepal. The USA was discontented with the Nepalese policy of proximity with China and discouragement of Free Tibet activities from within Nepal. Thanks to the sympathies of these countries, the Maoist struggle received wide and favourable publicity all over the world. The Nepalese authorities had no resources to match this publicity offensive. The Maoists could sustain their armed activities in Nepal with a free cadre movement in India and free flow of arms and ammunition from there.

India played a double game by declaring the Maoists as terrorists on the one hand, and facilitating guerrilla training for them on the other (Mishra, 2004; Shah and Adhikari, 2010). China was traditionally friendly to Nepal, especially with the monarchy. It considered monarchy as a stable force, but refrained from interfering in its internal affairs. China did not like the way the Maoists had used the name of Chairman Mao Tse Tung in indulging in political violence and hence did not help the rebels either in moral or in material terms. In fact, it discouraged the Maoists by arresting their workers who visited Tibet for purchasing arms. But when the second people's movement started in 2006 and picked momentum, China made its displeasure with the king's role known, which paved the way for India to press for the abolition of monarchy. The abolition was accomplished in 2008 when the first meeting of the first CA was held.

It was evident that the Maoists drew popular support from ethnic and rural communities due to some reformist activities like ban on alcohol consumption and polygamy in villages. Jana Adalats (people's courts), dubbed as 'Kangaroo courts', were formed, which carried out summary trials. The speedy trials and verdicts left a positive impact on villagers who had been denied justice or had seen justice been denied to others by the government's judicial system for years. Prohibiting the sale of alcohol and punishing people for playing cards also drew support from many village women who were suffering from domestic violence and discrimination (Upadhya, 2010).

The 2001 palace massacre further strengthened the Maoist insurgency by creating uncertainty in the state of affairs of Nepal. In the midst of the tragedy, the Maoist leader, Baburam Bhattarai, came out with a statement that the palace incident virtually brought the institution of monarchy to an end, which the Maoists were advocating for. Meanwhile, the elected government failed to hold election to the local bodies, Village Development Committees (VDCs), municipalities and District Development Committees (DDCs), which was scheduled in 2001–02 because of Maoist objection.

Meanwhile, King Gyanendra, crowned on 4 June 2001 following the royal massacre, had grown ambitious, and began asserting his position amid political wrangling among the political parties. He first took a bold step of dissolving the government of Sher Bahadur Deuba in 2002 and then took over all powers of the state unto himself in 2005. This led to a tripartite power struggle between the monarchy, the mainstream political parties and the Maoists. Finally, the rebels led by Pushpa Kamal Dahal, a.k.a. Prachanda, and the SPA headed by G.P. Koirala entered into a 12-point agreement in New Delhi under the patronage of the Indian government to abolish monarchy and restore democratic rule in Nepal. After entering into this agreement, the Maoists and the SPA formed a joint front to launch the movement against King Gyanendra with the support of external forces, especially India.

Cost of the Maoist conflict

The impact of the conflict was multi-dimensional as not only it was limited to human casualties, but it also caused destruction of considerable physical infrastructure. An estimated 17,000 lives were lost and 1,500 buildings were partially or completely destroyed. Similarly, a number of telecommunication towers, roads, air strips, bridges, government buildings, banks, police stations, school buildings and power plants were damaged during the conflict. During the conflict period, thousands of people were rendered homeless and property worth billions of rupees was damaged. In the period between

1996 and 2006, more than 17,828 people were estimated killed by either the rebel or the state forces (Jha, 2013). Jha also claims that this directly affected the lives of 450,000 families. In all, 5,800 people were disabled, 25,000 children orphaned, 9,000 women widowed and 14,852 people disappeared. The social life of the people during the conflict was disturbed and disrupted on account of frequent strikes, security checks, blockades, shutdowns, kidnappings, tortures, threats, humiliation, social isolation, rape and sexual harassment. Extrajudicial killings, extortions and abductions were rampant (Annexure 2).

As a result of the conflict, the GDP of the country declined from 4.8 per cent to 2.8 per cent between 2001 and 2005 (Jha, 2013). Between 1996 and 2004, private sector investment declined from 15.4 to 12.6 per cent. The government expenditure in the same year declined from 9 per cent to 6 per cent. The expenditure of the state on security sector almost doubled from 1.6 per cent of GDP to 3 per cent between 2001 and 2004 (Ibid). The conflict resulted in closure of industries under the Maoist threat, decrease in remittances from abroad and mass migration from conflict areas to relatively safer, parts (Annexure 2.1).

Maoists in mainstream politics

Following the 12-point understanding between the SPA and the CPN-M, a nationwide political movement was launched in April 2006. The country came to a halt as people came out on the streets on a massive scale and the king had no choice but to bow down to the people's power. It was a great milestone for the nation as not only the monarchy lost power but also the CPN M transformed from a violent rebel group to a mainstream political party[1].

Subsequent to the virtual downfall of the king, mainly due to the Indian establishment led by its foreign secretary Shyam Sharan (Muni, 2012 and Jha, 2012), many important political developments took place. To begin with, the dissolved HoR was reinstated on 24 April and election to the CA was declared. Monarchy was temporarily suspended. A new government was formed on 27 April 2006 with

G.P. Koirala as prime minister. Formal negotiations between the CPN-M and government started on 26 May and a series of summit meetings between the SPA and CPN-M resulted in important decisions, including the signing of the Comprehensive Peace Agreement (CPA) on 21 November and the promulgation of the interim constitution on 15 January 2007. In January 2007, the Maoists entered the reinstated parliament with eighty-three nominated members—about a quarter of the parliament's 330 seats.

A new election to the CA was held in 2008, in which the Maoist party emerged as the single largest party in the assembly. Ram Baran Yadav, proposed by the NC as its candidate, was elected as the first president of the country. The Maoists formed a coalition government the same year. Party chairperson, Pushpa Kamal Dahal, became the prime minister. But he resigned in 2009 following disagreement with the president over the dismissal of the army chief, General Rukmangad Katwal. In 2011, the party returned to power with the appointment of party vice chairperson, Baburam Bhattarai, as prime minister, but he also could not get the constitution declared by the CA (which was initially elected for two years and had its term extended for another two years. It was finally dissolved on 28 May 2012), and he also resigned from the post on 13 March 2013 (Annexure 3). As a result of their poor performance, the Maoists emerged as the third largest party in the second CA elections held in 2013 by a council of ministers headed by a seating Chief Justice and comprised of former bureaucrats as the ministers. After long and painstaking negotiations, the NC, CPN-UML and the Maoists agreed and declared the new constitution on 20 September 2015.

The declaration of new constitution with the concerted agreement of the three leading parties, including the Maoists, invited strong backlash from internal as well as external sources. The Tarai/Madhes-oriented parties launched protests, which lasted for more than four months and resulted in about fifty casualties and an undeclared economic blockade by India. They caused untold hardship in the daily life of the people. Although the Maoists were only a coalition partner in the K.P. Sharma Oli-headed government (October 2015–August

2016), Maoist chief Prachanda had to bear the brunt of the attack from both Madhesis and India. While he was charged of letting down the Tarai/Madhes-based parties by not fulfilling his commitment to adhere to ethnic federation, he was also accused of breaking his commitment to Indian leaders to shun from declaring Nepal secular and address the Madhesi grievances in the new constitution.

Furthermore, Prachanda was charged by the CPN-UML of backing out from the coalition government headed by Oli, on India's pressure. But the same Prachanda decided to form an alliance with Oli's CNP-UML and went to the general elections in 2017. Now they form the left alliance with CPN-UML and have a majority in the federal parliament and all the provinces except in Province no 2 (Annexure 4).

Changing character of the Maoist party

Between 1996 and 2016 (Annexure 3), the basic characteristic of the Maoist party underwent a big change. The initial guiding principle of the CPN-M was that it is the party that represents the Nepalese proletariat in the political arena and believes in Marxism-Leninism and Maoism. Several times, the Maoist leaders stated that the ultimate goal of their party was to achieve socialism and communism. In reality, the Maoist political agenda suffered from chronic contradictions between the rhetoric and the reality. The political agenda attracted popular participation in rural areas. After the much-hyped changes of 2006, the political character of the Maoist party revealed stark disparities between rhetoric and reality. It kept on declaring inconsistent promises. Although the Maoists entered the parliamentary system sharing power with other political parties through the CPA 2006, there was a lingering suspicion regarding their intention. Until they emerged as the largest party in the first CA in 2008, the Maoist leadership had hardly made their open commitment to parliamentary democracy.

Many ethnic and minority groups in Nepal, who had been feeling marginalized for a long time, started to organize themselves into various identity-based groups and raise their voices for inclusion in mainstream politics. The identity movement for social and cultural rights was dominant after the 1990 changeover, which gained new heights during the Maoist conflict. Many Tarai/Madhes-based regional parties and other hill-based ethnic groups made their presence felt by raising similar issues and tried to give a hard time to the established political leadership.

Revisiting the same 40-point demands after two decades, it appears that most of the points are relevant even today. However, the Maoists are less willing to talk about their relevance after they were caught in the whirlpool of mainstream politics. As many new actors such as ethnic and regional organizations emerged with muscles to flex in the national political scene, the Maoists are trying to revive the old agenda. It is a paradox that the Madhesi, Tharu and ethnic communities are demanding their rights at a time when the government is being headed by a Maoist party.

As a result of this alleged bungling, the Maoist party was divided into five groups between 2009 and 2016. In September 2009, the faction under Matrika Yadav left the party and named his group as the original CPN-M. In June 2012, another dissident group led by vice-chairperson, Mohan Baidya (Kiran), declared formation of a new party called Unified Communist Party of Nepal (Maoist). Then, in November 2014, Secretary of the Baidya faction, Netra Bikram Chand, quit the party and announced formation of a new party named CPN-M. And most recently, in January 2016, Baburam Bhattarai declared a new political party named 'Naya Shakti' (New Force). These frequent splits incurred a heavy toll of its workers' loyalty and faith in the leadership, not to speak of the negative image in the Nepali society.

When the Truth and Reconciliation Commission and the Commission on Disappeared Persons were activated, all the Maoist leaders faced a state of jeopardy of getting penalized for human rights violations. They all came together to fight against the potential punishment. Some of them rejoined the parent body, which changed its name to the CPN-Maoist Centre (CPN-MC). On 19 May 2016, eight Maoist parties were merged under Dahal. Despite the unification, four more offshoots of the former rebel forces remain in mainstream politics, led separately by Baidya, Bhattarai, Chand and Hemanta Prakash Oli.

On the whole, following the changeover in 2006, the Maoist leadership has headed the government thrice, including the Dahal-led government of 2016. It could not, however, deliver the results it had promised to the people, may be because being in a coalition government, it had many constraints on decision-making according to its priorities and choices. With the passage of time, its performance rating declined, intra-party conflicts surfaced and the high hopes the people had pinned on it were dashed. It suffered great setbacks with the onslaught of the opposition on its performance in administration, corruption charges and disruption of established customs and traditions in the government.

The Tarai/Madhes Agitation

The antecedents

The southern part of the country having 34,019 sq kms of landmass and stretching from Jhapa to Kanchanpur is popularly called as Tarai/Madhes. Of the seventy-five districts (as of February 2017), twenty are in this part. As per the population census of 2011, 13,319 million people, or about 50.3 per cent, live in this area. In 2011, only 69.9 per cent hill communities were living in the hills and 22.3 per cent in the Tarai. The Tarai harboured 32 per cent and 27.3 per cent of hill caste and Dalit populations, respectively. The overall picture is a process of population dispersal from the highlands to the lowlands, in which all hill caste and ethnic groups are increasingly involved (Sharma, 2014).

The Tarai/Madhes movement has its origins in the founding of Nepal Tarai Congress by Vedanand Jha, who quit NC in 1951. The party's objectives were the establishment of an autonomous Tarai state, recognition of Hindi as a separate language and adequate employment of Tarai people in the Nepal civil service. Since 1956, several parties have been established to oppose and end discrimination and exploitation of Tarai residents, including the Madhesi Mukti

Aandolan and Western Tarai Liberation Front.

In 1985, Ram Raja Prasad Singh, a leader of Tarai origin, orchestrated to bombard the Singha Durbar, the premises of the Central Secretariat, the Narayanhiti Royal Palace, a five-star hotel and other important locations in the vicinity of Kathmandu. The major objective of the movement was to overthrow kingship from Nepal through armed insurrection. Singh later contested as a CPN-M-supported candidate in the July 2008 presidential election. He was, however, defeated by Ram Baran Yadav, an NC candidate.

Gajendra Narayan Singh, who was once with NC, established the Sadbhavana Parishad in 1984, which was later converted into a party, Nepal Sadbhavana Party (NSP), in 1991. Singh's party took part in all the elections held after 1990 and he also became minister several times.

Upendra Yadav, another political activist with Maoist communist background and training, formed Madhesi Janadhikar Forum (MJF) as an NGO in 1998 and later converted it into a party in 2006 to work for the rights of Madhesi people and Madhes. He led an agitation for federalism and even set on fire the interim constitution (2007) at Maitighar Mandala, Kathmandu, on the plea that federalism and inclusiveness were deliberately neglected in it (Khanal, 2017). Yadav accused the Maoists of deviating from the original proposal of ten to fourteen federal states, thereby undermining the importance of federalism in Nepal. Furthermore, he campaigned for the 'One Madhes-One Pradesh' demand, but later compromised on the proposal for Madhes as an autonomous region as envisaged in the 22-point agreement signed between the G.P. Koirala-led government and Tarai/Madhes-based parties in August 2007 (Annexures 4 and 4.1).

Even before the formation of the MJF, NSP had come into existence and had been participating in the national political process. In the meantime, another Tarai/Madhes-based party came into existence under the chairmanship of Mahanta Thakur, who had quit the NC to propagate the Tarai/Madhes issues. Afterwards, several Tarai/Madhes-based parties were formed following splits in the MJF.

On 28 February 2008, the then Prime Minister G.P. Koirala signed a deal with the United Democratic Madhesi Front (comprising NSP, MJF and Tarai/Madhes Loktantrik Front or TMLP), which reiterated that Nepal shall become a Federal Democratic Republic by accepting people's aspiration of a federal structure with autonomous regions, including the Madhesi people's aspiration for an autonomous Madhes state.

The Tarai/Madhes-based leaders later compromised on their 'One Madhes-One Pradesh' demand, with two provinces in the Tarai/Madhes, viz. Madhes and Tharuhat. Furthermore, they demanded inclusion of Jhapa, Morang and Sunsari in eastern Tarai into Madhes Pradesh, and inclusion of Kailali and Kanchanpur in the western Tarai into Tharuhat Pradesh. This proposal was, however, vehemently opposed by the people of these districts and those supporting Akhanda Sudur Paschhim (Annexure 4 and 4.1).

In November 2013, election to CA took place, in which more than twenty Tarai/Madhes-based political parties participated; however, only nine, excluding Tharuhat-related parties (Tharus do not consider themselves as Madhesis), got elected. As such, in the Legislature-Parliament, they had a total strength of fifty in a house of 601 members (Annexure 4.2). Whereas, in the CA I election held in 2008, four Tarai/Madhes-based parties (MJF, TMLP, NSP, NSP-Anandi Devi) had taken part and they had secured eighty-seven seats in the house of 601 (Annexure 4.3).

Agitation launched after 2015 constitution

Immediately after the promulgation of the constitution in 2015, the Tarai/Madhes-based leaders launched agitations, including violent ones on the plea that it was not inclusive. The major dissatisfaction of the Madhes-based parties pertain to citizenship, language and the composition of the electoral college for election to the Upper House, and the demand for two provinces. They held dharnas at 'no man's land' on the Nepal–India border, starting September 2015, which lasted for about five months. As support to the dissatisfaction of the Madhesi leaders, India 'unofficially' imposed an economic blockade against Nepal, which lasted for 135 days and totally disrupted the flow of goods and services, resulting in great misery and sufferings to the people of Nepal.

In addition, C.K. Raut, a Tarai-based political activist, spearheaded the 'Swatantra Madhes', a campaign for securing independence of Tarai/Madhes from the country. He has organized military training for unemployed youth in the Tarai to raise arms against the establishment.

To satisfy the demands of Tarai/Madhes political parties, the 2015 constitution had provided one Madhes Pradesh and Province 2 (with eight Tarai/Madhes districts, viz. Saptari to Parsa in central Tarai) but without the three districts of Jhapa, Morang and Sunsari. But their demand for Tharuhat was not met, which was one of the reasons for the Tarai/Madhes-based parties to oppose the constitution.

In order to entertain their demand for another Madhes Pradesh in the western part of the country, the Dahal-led government submitted a constitution amendment bill to the Legislature-Parliament in November 2016 (*Kantipur*, 30 November 2016)[2]. But, the Tarai/Madhes-based parties, also indicated above, expressed their reservation on the proposed amendments and, in order to bring the various political parties to agree to the amendments, President Bhandari convened an all-party meeting at her official residence. At that meeting, one of the leaders of the UDMF, Mahanta Thakur, warned that Madhes will secede from Nepal if discrimination against Madhesi people continued (My Republica, 5 December 2016). Similarly Sanghiya Samajbadi Party Nepal (Federal Socialist Forum Nepal) Chairperson Upendra Yadab expressed dissatisfaction, saying that the second constitution amendment bill is incomplete and demanded alteration in the amendment bill (Ibid.). On 11 April 2017, the government decided to withdraw the bill and revised and submitted it to the parliament on 30 April 2017 for endorsement[3]. On 21 August 2017, the amendment bill was put to vote, where it failed to pass after 206 lawmakers voted against it (*The Himalayan Times*, 21 August 2017). In the meantime, some Tarai based parties merged and formed Rastriya Janata Party Nepal (RJPN)[4]. As such, at present there are three major Tarai based parties—Rastriya Janata Party, Federal Socialist Forum-

Nepal (Sanghiya Samajwadi Party-Nepal) and Nepal Democratic Forum (Nepal Loktantrik Forum)—which also participated in the 2017 elections (Annexures 5, 5.1., 5.2 and 5.2.B).

External factor

It is a fact that India is a major factor in relation to the Tarai/Madhes agitation. It may be reminded that it was Indian intelligence's strategy to separate Madhes from Nepal during the premiership of Indira Gandhi to punish King Mahendra for allowing greater presence of the Chinese. But this strategy could not succeed due to the declaration of Emergency in India in 1975 and Gandhi's defeat in the election of 1977. Although the 1975 context is over, bureaucrats and intelligence personnel seem to be romanticised by the idea and may have been pursuing Indian political leaders to adopt a policy of keeping Madhes under its control, if not annexing it to India.

But in the context of presumed heavy engagement of China in Nepal due to vulnerability of her soft belly, Tibet, it may be wiser on the part of political stakeholders in India not to engage in confrontation with China in Nepal and ensure that it remains emotionally and politically united and economically prosperous, taking into account the intrinsic or inalienable linkages that exist between its three ecological regions—Himalayan, mountainous and Tarai/Madhes. If Nepal turned into a rogue state, it would create more problems for the neighbouring countries, as well as the international community.

In the light of the above, it can be said that a number of social, economic and political issues do exist in the Tarai/Madhes. However, the genuine problems of the real Madhesis are far from being addressed by any of the so called champions of the Madhesi cause. The social fabric, hitherto found harmonious and peaceful, faces the risk of breaking down under intensifying political conflicts between the plain and hill leaders.

There is a perennial problem of citizenship certificate distribution, which remains unresolved. The genuine residents of Nepal are being deprived of citizenship, but those who are temporary migrants get it easily. This discrepancy is attributed to the role of illegal money, the deciding factor in the issue. A majority of the people in Tarai/Madhes are as nationalistic as the people from the mountains and hills. The people of Tarai/Madhes have shown great courage in safeguarding their motherland from encroachment by outside forces on many occasions. Hence, their love for the motherland is unquestionable.

In Conclusion

Nepal suffered large-scale damage to human lives and material property due to the ten-year Maoist armed movement. But it ended neither with a clear victory nor defeat in the battlefield. The Maoists joined tacitly the second peaceful people's movement (launched by the political parties spearheaded by G.P. Koirala in 2006) against the rule of King Gyanendra. When the movement succeeded in emasculating kingship, the signatories of the 12-point New Delhi agreement appeared at the political centre stage and wielded state power. It was the time when all high-level decisions were virtually made by two leading personalities—Koirala and Dahal.

Looking back at the Maoist conflagration after twenty years of its inception, it must be admitted that they have been able to bring about some fundamental changes in the structuring of the state, like the abolition of the 240-year-old monarchy, adoption of federalization of the state and ethnic awakening and getting a new constitution, prepared and adopted by the people of Nepal although many of its features are contested. As a result, changes are, however, yet to take root in the Nepalese society, which is showing utter uneasiness in the new phenomena in the political spectrum.

In the meantime, however, they should also be held responsible for creating prolonged instability for ten years since they joined the mainstream politics, with no sign of it ending soon. They must be credited, on the one hand, for social and cultural awakening and, on the other hand, they must accept discredit for mismanaging the ethnic- and identity-based tensions threatening to tear the country apart and growing mal-governance and corruption in the country, which have disillusioned the people. The biggest challenge to the new order of Nepal is to accommodate the regional aspirations, especially those spearheaded by the Tarai/Madhes-based parties, which they have raised once again even after the formation of governments both at the provincial and federal levels as well as having participated in the election in all the three levels of government including 753 local government bodies.

In addition, people from different regions, castes or religions have to be brought to the mainstream, politically and socially, as all Nepalese people have to live together, whichever ecological area they belong to. Nepal cannot compromise on its national sovereignty and territorial integrity in the name of satisfying the demands of one group or other. Furthermore, the neighbouring countries and international community must honour its territorial integrity and national sovereignty rather than supporting sectarian elements.

∽

***Aditya Man Shrestha** is a senior journalist of Nepal.*

***Chiranjibi Bhandari** is Assistant Professor at the Department of Conflict, Peace and Development Studies, Tribhuvan University.*

***Rajib Timalsina** is Assistant Professor at the Department of Conflict, Peace and Development Studies, Tribhuvan University.*

Bibliography

Government and Allied Publications

Government of Nepal/Ministry of Home Affairs/United Nations Development Programme (GoN/MoHA/UNDP). Armed Violence Reduction and Strengthening Community Security (AVRSCS). Annual Progress Report 2014.

Government of Nepal/National Planning Commission/United Nations

Development Programme (GoN/NPC/UNDP). Nepal Human Development Report 2014: Beyond Geography: Unlocking Human Potential.

Ministry of Peace and Reconstruction/Nepal Peace Trust Fund (NPTF). 2010. Program Document. Kathmandu.

Other Publications

Adhikari, S.P. 1982. *Integrated Rural Development in Nepal.* Kathmandu: Sahayogi Press.

Beyerle, S. 2014. *Curtailing Corruption: People Power for Accountability & Justice.* London: Lynne Rienner Publishers.

Bhandari, C. 'Reintegrating Maoist Army Combatants into Nepali Society'. *Economic and Political Weekly*, 2015, Vol. 9, No. 50.

Dhakal, A. 2009. 'The People's Liberation Army'. In: Sapkota, B. (Ed.) *The Nepali Security Sectors: An Almanac.* Kathmandu: Geneva Centre for Democratic Control of Armed Forces and the Centre for European Studies.

Dhungel, D.N. 2004. 'Achieving Peace and Order in Nepal in the Context of Maoist Insurgency'. Conference paper submitted to Public Service Commission, Government of Samoa and Eastern Regional Organization of Public Administration (EROPA) at Apia, Samoa.

Grävingholt, J., et al. 2013. *Struggling for Stability: International Support for Peace and Democracy in Nepal.* Bonn: German Development Institute.

Gurung, H. 1997. 'State and Society in Nepal.' In: Gellner, D.N., Pfaff-Czarnecka, J. and Whelpton, J. (Eds.). *Nationalism and Ethnicity in Nepal.* Amsterdam: Harwood Academic Publishers.

Jha, P. 2014, *Battles of the New Republic: A Contemporary History of Nepal.* New Delhi: Aleph Book Company.

Jha, H.B. 2013. 'Role of Economic Activities and Funding in Peacebuilding in Nepal'. Seminar paper presented in a national seminar on Non-linearity of Peace Process in Nepal. Kathmandu: Centre for Economic and Technical Studies (CETS) and Friedrich-Ebert-Stiftung (FES).

Jha, P. 2012. 'A Nepali Perspective on International Involvement in Nepal'. In: Einsiedel, von S., Malone, D.M. and Pradhan, S. (Eds.) *Nepal in Transition: From People's War to Fragile Peace.* New Delhi: Center on International Cooperation, Cambridge University Press.

Jha Ahiraj, Rajesh. 'Madhes: Problem or Opportunity'. Unpublished article in Nepali Language.

Joshi, B.L. and Rose, L.E. 1966. *Democratic Innovations in Nepal.* Berkeley: University of California Press.

Keshar Bahadur, K.C. 1976. *Nepal After the Revolution of 1950.* Kathmandu: Sharada Prakashan Griha.

Khanal, G. 2017. *Bhoo-rajneeti (Geo-politics).* Kathmandu: Phoenix Books.

Koponen, J. 2010. 'The Security-Development Nexus: State Fragility and State Building.' In: Alava, H., (Ed.). *Exploring the Security-Development Nexus.* Helsinki: Ministry for Foreign Affairs of Finland.

Mishra, B. 2009. *Nepalese Peace Process.* Kathmandu: FinePrint.

Mishra, C. 2007. 'Locating the "causes" of the Maoist Struggle.' In: Mishra, C. (Ed.). *Essays on the Sociology of Nepal.* Kathmandu: FinePrint.

Muni, S.D. 2012. 'Bringing the Maoists down from the Hills: India's Role.' In: Einsiedel, von S., Malone, D.M. and Pradhan, S. (Eds.) *Nepal in Transition: From People's War to Fragile Peace.* New Delhi: Center on International Cooperation, Cambridge University Press.

Paudyal, M. 'At India's door.' My Republica, 8 September 2015, http://admin.myrepublica.com/opinion/story/27789/at-india-s-door.html

Paudyal, M. 'It's secession, stupid.' My Republica, 20 February 2017.

Shah, S. 2010. 'From Evil State to Civil Society.' In: Dixit, K. and Ramachandaran, S., (Eds.). *State of Nepal (8th Printing).* Kathmandu: Himal Books.

Shah, V.K. and Adhikari, S. 2010. *Maile Dekheko Durbar.* Kathmandu: Yeti Publications.

Sharma, P. 2014. *Some Aspects of Nepal's Social Demography: Census Update.* Kathmandu: Social Science Baha/Himal Books.

Shrestha, A.M. 2014/15. *Resurrection.* Kathmandu: Shami Sam Prakashn Griha.

Shrestha, C.B. 2004. *Nepal: Coping with Maoist Conflict.* Kathmandu: Chetana Lokshum.

Slavu, C. 2012. 'The 2008 Constitution Assembly Election: Social Inclusion for Peace.' Einsiedel, von S., Malone, D.M. and Pradhan, S. (Eds.). *Nepal in Transition: From People's War to Fragile Peace.* New Delhi: Cambridge University Press.

Thapa, D. 2010. 'The Maobadi of Nepal.' In: Dixit, K. and S. Ramachandaran (Eds.). *State of Nepal.* Kathmandu: Himal Books.

Timalsina, R. 'The Promise and Perils of Aid: The Role of the Nepal Peace Trust Fund (NPTF) Framework in Facilitating Post-Conflict Development in Nepal.' *Asian Journal of PEACEBUILDING, 2016,* Vol. 4, No. 1.

Upadhya, S. 2010. 'A Dozen Years of Democracy: The Games that Parties Play.' In: Dixit, K. and S. Ramachandaran (Eds.). *State of Nepal.* Kathmandu: Himal Books.

Yadav, R.K. 2014. *Mission R&AW.* New Delhi: Manas Publications.

Newspapers and Websites

Kantipur, 30 November 2016
Nagarik daily, 3 December 2016
My Republica, 5 December 2016
The Himalayan Times, 30 November 2016 and 21 August 2017
http://federalsocialist.org/?cat=139
http://kathmandupost.ekantipur.com/news/2017-04-05/3-parties-merge-to-form-nepal-loktantrik-forum.html
http://kathmandupost.ekantipur.com/news/2017-04-20/five-madhes-based-parties-unite-to-form-rastriya-janata-party.html
http://english.onlinekhabar.com/2017/10/03/407359.html
https://en.wikipedia.org/wiki/Nepalese_local_elections,_2017

Annexure 1: Text of 40-point demands of the Maoists submitted to the Prime Minister Sher Bahadur Deuba

4 February 1996

Demands:

Concerning nationality

All discriminatory treaties, including the 1950 Nepal-India Treaty, should be abrogated.

The so-called Integrated Mahakali Treaty concluded on 29 January 1996 should be repealed immediately, as it is designed to conceal the disastrous Tanakpur Treaty and allows Indian imperialist monopoly over Nepal's water resources.

The open border between Nepal and India should be regulated, controlled and systematized. All vehicles with Indian licence plates should be banned from Nepal.

The Gurkha/Gorkha Recruitment Centres should be closed. Nepali citizens should be provided dignified employment in the country.

Nepali workers should be given priority in different sectors. A 'work permit' system should be strictly implemented if foreign workers are required in the country.

The domination of foreign capital in Nepali industries, business and finance should be stopped.

An appropriate customs policy should be devised and implemented so that economic development helps the nation become self-reliant.

The invasion of imperialist and colonial culture should be banned. Vulgar Hindi films, videos and magazines should be immediately outlawed.

The invasion of colonial and imperial elements in the name of NGOs and INGOs should be stopped.

Concerning people's democracy

A new Constitution should be drafted by representatives elected for the establishment of a people's democratic system.

All special privileges of the king and the royal family should be abolished.

The army, the police and the bureaucracy should be completely under people's control.

All repressive acts, including the Security Act, should be repealed.

Everyone arrested extra-judicially for political reasons or revenge in Rukum, Rolpa, Jajarkot, Gorkha, Kavre, Sindhupalchowk, Sindhuli, Dhanusa, Ramecchhap, and so on, should be immediately released. All false cases should be immediately withdrawn.

The operation of armed police, repression and State-sponsored terror should be immediately stopped.

The whereabouts of citizens who disappeared in police custody at different times, namely Dilip Chaudhary, Bhuwan Thapa Magar, Prabhakar Subedi and others, should be investigated and those responsible, brought to justice. The families of victims should be duly compensated.

All those killed during the People's Movement should be declared martyrs. The families of the martyrs and those injured and deformed should be duly compensated, and the murderers brought to justice.

Nepal should be declared a secular nation.

Patriarchal exploitation and discrimination against women should be stopped. Daughters should be allowed access to paternal property.

All racial exploitation and suppression should be stopped. Where ethnic communities are in the majority, they should be allowed to form their own autonomous governments.

Discrimination against downtrodden and backward people should be stopped. The system of untouchability should be eliminated.

All languages and dialects should be given equal opportunities to prosper. The right to education in the mother tongue up to higher level should be guaranteed.

The right to expression and freedom of press and publication should be guaranteed. The government mass media should be completely autonomous.

Academic and professional freedom of scholars, writers, artists and cultural workers should be guaranteed.

Regional discrimination between the hills and the tarai should be eliminated. Backward areas should be given regional autonomy. Rural and urban areas should be treated at par.

Local bodies should be empowered and appropriately equipped.

Concerning livelihood

Land should belong to 'tenants'. Land under the control of the feudal system should be confiscated and distributed to the landless and the homeless.

The property of middlemen and comprador capitalists should be confiscated and nationalized. Capital lying unproductive should be invested to promote industrialization.

Employment should be guaranteed for all. Until such time as employment can be arranged, an unemployment allowance should be provided.

A minimum wage for workers in industries, agriculture and so on should be fixed and strictly implemented.

The homeless should be rehabilitated. No one should be relocated until alternative infrastructure is guaranteed.

Poor farmers should be exempt from loan repayments. Loans taken by small farmers from the Agricultural Development Bank should be written off. Appropriate provisions should be made to provide loans form small farmers.

Fertilizer and seed should be easily available and at a cheap rate. Farmers should be provided with appropriate prices and markets for their produce.

People in flood- and drought–affected areas should be provided with appropriate relief materials.

Free and scientific health services and education should be available to all. The commercialization of education should be stopped.

Inflation should be checked. Wages should be increased proportionate to inflation. Essential goods should be cheaply and easily available to everyone.

Drinking water, roads and electricity should be provided to all villagers.

Domestic and cottage industries should be protected and promoted.

Corruption, smuggling, black marketing, bribery, and the practices of middlemen and so on should be eliminated.

Orphans, the disabled, the elderly and children should be duly honoured and protected.

We would like to request the present coalition government to immediately initiate steps to fulfil these demands which are inextricably linked with the Nepali nation and the life of the people. If there are no positive indications towards this from the government by 17 February 1996, we would like to inform you that we will be forced to adopt the path of armed struggle against the existing state power.

Thank you.

Dr Baburam Bhattarai
Chairman Central Committee,
United People's Front, Nepal

Source: Nepalma Janayuddha (People's Ware in Nepal), Nepal Rastriya Buddhijibi Sanganthan (Nepal National Intellectual Organization), Kathmandu, 2001.

Annexure 2: Human cost during the armed conflict

S. N.	Category	Number
1	Deceased persons	17,886
2	Disappeared persons	1,530
3	Displaced persons	79,571
4	Abducted persons	3,142
5	Disabled persons	8,935
6	Widows	9,000
7	Individuals property damaged	17,484
8	Martyrs of people's movement	26
9	Those injured during the people's movement	4,014
10	Orphans	620

Source: Ministry of Peace and Reconstruction, information received from Post Conflict Rehabilitation and Reconstruction unit, 2016.

Annexure 2.1: Destruction of physical infrastructure

S. N.	Category	Number
1	Schools	2,149
2	Village Development Committee Offices	2,072
3	Government offices at district headquarters	986
4	Government offices at local level	1,047
5	District development committees and municipalities	130
6	Suspension bridge	101
7	Others	2,032

Source: Nepal Institute for Policy Studies' paper 2013, in Nepal's Peace Process: A brief overview

Annexure 3: Timeline of major activities of Maoist conflict and peace building

S. N.	Date	Activities
1	May 1994	CPN-M boycott general election
2	4 February 1996	40-point demands forwarded to government related to 'nationalism, democracy and livelihood'
3	13 February 1996	The Nepal Communist Party (Maoist) began their insurgency
4	August 1997	Government declared Maoists' activities as terrorist activities
5	1 June 2001	Royal massacre (King Birendra and members of his family were shot dead)
6	30 August 2001	First peace talk between government and the Maoists started in Kathmandu
7	23 November 2001	First round of peace talks failed, and Maoists launched attacks on army and police posts
8	4 October 2002	The King dismissed the prime minister and assumed executive power
9	30 January 2003	Second peace talk between government and the Maoists started
10	1 January 2005	King Gyanendra dismissed the government and assumed direct rule
11	22 November 2005	12-point agreement between Maoist and Seven Political Parties
12	5 April 2006	The people's movement started with the SPA general strike and Maoist blockades
13	24 April 2006	King Gyanendra surrendered power and agreed to reinstate the parliament after street protests
14	18 May 2006	Proclamation of the HoR; monarchy paralyzed; power given to Prime Minister with few legal changes; the official name, 'His Majesty's government', changed into 'Nepal Government'
15	26 May 2006	Maoists and SPA signed a ceasefire code of conduct
16	16 June 2006	Formation of the interim constitution drafting committee

17	9 August 2006	Maoists and SPA sent parallel letters to the UN Secretary-General requesting monitoring of arms and elections
18	21 November 2006	SPA and Maoists sign the Comprehensive Peace Agreement ending the war
19	28 November 2006	Agreement on Monitoring of the Management of Arms and Armies signed by the Maoists and SPA
20	16 December 2006	Maoists and SPA agree on the interim constitution
21	15 January 2007	An interim constitution was adopted by Nepal's HoR, which dissolved itself to make way for the interim parliament. CPN-M representation to parliament; seventy-three members nominated for the Parliament
22	23 January 2007	The Security Council passed Resolution 1740 establishing the UN Mission in Nepal for an initial period of 12 months (UNMIN)
23	1 April 2007	An interim government, power sharing government, established, consisting of eight political parties, including the Maoists
24	Spring 2007	Madhesi uprising in Tarai
25	Mid-February 2008	Madhesi groups call a sixteen-day strike in the Tarai region
26	28 February 2008	The government signs an accord with the United Madhes Democratic Front (UMDF) umbrella group giving greater representation to minorities in state and local authorities and agreed to autonomous regions for the Madhesi under a future Federal Democratic Structure
27	10 April 2008	CA elections held; Maoists emerge as the single largest party
28	28 May 2008	The CA convened for the first time and proclaimed Nepal a republic
29	August 2008	Maoist leader Pushpa Kamal Dahal aka Prachanda forms coalition government, with NC in opposition

30	21 October 2008	Agreement made by all parties to form a special committee for the integration and rehabilitation of the Maoist combatants
31	4 May 2009	Prime Minister Prachanda resigns following a row with President Yadav over the integration of former rebel fighters into the military
32	16 December 2009	Government and Maoist party agree to release verified minor and late recruit combatants
33	7 January 2010	3,000 former Maoist combatants begin to be discharged
34	15 January 2011	United Mission in Nepal ceases its operation
35	1 November 2011	Parties sign 7-point agreement. Agree to integrate 6,500 combatants in NA-led directorate
36	28 May 2012	The CA is dissolved after failing to produce a draft constitution.
37	18 June 2012	Mohan Vaidhya led CPN-M announced a separate political party
38	19 November 2013	Second CA election held with NC emerging victorious, pushing the former ruling Maoists into third place and leaving no party with a majority.
39	20 September 2015	Parliament passes a landmark constitution, which defines Nepal as a secular country, despite calls to delay voting after more than forty people are killed in protests
40	3 August 2016	Parliament elects former communist rebel leader and Maoist party leader Pushpa Kamal Dahal 'Prachanda' as Prime Minister for the second time
41	3 October 2017	Declaration of the two parties, CPN-UML and CPN-MC, to form an alliance and going to the general elections held in November and December 2017 with one Manifesto and merge two parties into one

Source: Compiled from various sources

Annexure 4: Timeline of Tarai/Madhes movement since 2007

S. N.	Date	Activities
1	16 January 2007	Madhes uprising started, led by Upendra Yadav from Madhesi Janadhikar Forum (MJF)
2	19 January 2007	Maoists clash with Madhesi activists in Lahan, killing student Ramesh Kumar Mahato
3	20 January 2007	Curfew imposed
4	20 January to 7 February 2007	Movement picks up against the government, with huge public support and mass defiance of curfews, clashes between police and protestors; almost 40 killed.
5	30 August 2007	22-point agreement between government and MJF
6	28 February 2008	8-point agreement between government and 'Samyukta Loktantrik Madhesi Morcha', including MJF, TMLP, Sadbhavana Party (agreed on Nepal to be Federal democratic republic and there will be an autonomous Madhes state)
7	3 June 2007	The first phase of the formal talks between the government and the MJF ended with agreement reached on one half of the 26-point demands put forth by the Forum
8	10 April 2008	First CA election; CPN-M, NC, CPN-UML and MJF become the 1st, 2nd, 3rd and 4th party, respectively
9	28 May 2008	First CA meeting declares Nepal to be Federal Democratic Republic by 560-4 votes
10	31 March 2011	Meeting of Madhesis takes place in Kathmandu after twenty-two years; C.K. Raut appeals for a stronger coalition to take the Madhes Movement to the global level
11	21 May 2011	Alliance for Independent Madhes (AIM) announces manifesto and plans

12	8 June 2015	16-point agreement between four major parties (NC, CPN-UML, CPN-M, Madhesi Janadhikar Forum-Democratic)
13	9 June 2015	16-point agreement between four major political parties (Congress, UML, Maoist and Forum-Democratic). They also agree on eight-state model; but boundaries not finalized. Maoist led 30-party alliance split
14	8 August 2015	Four major political parties (Congress, UML, Maoist and Forum-Democratic) agreed on a new six-states model. All new six states to have boundary with India. Four states (except Lumbini & Madhes) to have boundary with China as well
15	21 August 2015	After several protests in two weeks, Congress, UML and Maoist now agree on a new seven-states model. The three parties have combined 451 (75 per cent) seats in CA. The fourth party from earlier agreement (Forum-Democratic) opposes the agreement
16	16 September 2015	Nepal's Constitution 2072 B.S. endorsed by the CA meeting by 2/3 majority
17	20 September 2015	President Ram Baran Yadav promulgates the Constitution of Nepal in the last meeting of CA
18	23 September 2015	Start blockade in Nepal as an effect of struggle in Madhes
19	11 February 2016	UDMF decides to induct three fringe Tarai/ Madhes-based parties—NMSP, NSP and MJF-R—into the front
20	12 February 2016	The joint meeting of the task forces of the three major parties and agitating UDMF decide to form a political mechanism to address the concerns of the front regarding the provincial demarcation

21	5 January 2017	NC, CPN-MC and UDMF at a tripartite meeting held at the Prime Minister's residence in Kathmandu decide to table the constitution amendment bill at the parliament meeting scheduled for 8 January
22	8 January 2017	Government tables the Constitution Amendment Bill amid protests from opposition party lawmakers

Source: Compiled from different public documents

Annexure 4.1: Agreements with various armed groups of Tarai/Madhes

S. N.	Date	Activities
1	11 December 2008	Four-point agreement between government dialogue team and Madhesi Virus killers team
2	26 December 2008	Five-point agreement between government dialogue team and Samyukta Janatantrik Tarai Mukti Morcha
3	24 December 2008	Agreement between government dialogue team and Tarai Samyukta Jankranti Party
4	10 January 2009	Agreement between government dialogue team and Janatantrik Terai Mukti Morcha (Rajan Group)
5	21 February 2009	Agreement between government dialogue team and Liberation Tiger of Tarai Elam (LTTE)
6	20 March 2009	Agreement between government dialogue team and Madhesh Mukti Tigers team
7	7 May 2010	Agreement between government dialogue team and Akhil Tarai Mukti Morcha (establishment) team
8	8 August 2011	Agreement between government dialogue team and Akhil Tarai Mukti Morcha (establishment) team

9	13 August 2011	Agreement between government dialogue team and Samyukta Janatantrik Tarai Mukti Morcha (Pawan group)
10	2 December 2011	Agreement between government dialogue team and Samyukta Jantantrik Tarai Mukti Morcha (Pawan group)
11	19 August 2011	Agreement between government dialogue team and Smayukta Jantantrik Tarai Mukti Morcha (Aajad)
12	4 November 2011	3-point agreement with government dialogue team and Samyukta Jantantrik Tarai Mukti Morcha (establishment)
13	24 November 2011	Agreement between government dialogue team and Samyukta Janatantrik Tarai Mukti Morcha (Kautilya Group)
14	12 January 2012	Agreement between government dialogue team and Samayukta Janatantrik Tarai Mukti Morcha (Aajad)
15	21 January 2012	Agreement between government dialogue team and Akhil Tarai Mukti Morcha (Jayakrishna Goit Group)
16	6 March 2012	Agreement between government dialogue team and Janatantrik Tarai Mukti Morcha (Jayakrishna Goit Group) team
17	6 March 2012	Agreement between government dialogue team and Janatantrik Tarai Madhes Mukti Party (Bhagat Singh)
18	14 March 2012	Agreement between government dialogue team and Janatantrik Madhes Tarai Mukti Morcha (Jhabar Sah, Pratap)
19	18 April 2012	Agreement between government dialogue team and Janatantrik Madhes Tarai Mukti Morcha

Source: http://www.peace.gov.np/content.php?id=167

Annexure 4.2: Tarai/Madhes-related political parties which participated in the CA election of 2013 and the number of seats secured

Names	Number of seats secured
Sanghiya Samajbadi Forum, Nepal	15
Madhesi Jana Adhikar Forum, Nepal (Loktantrik)	14
Tarai-Madhes Loktantrik Party	11
Sadbhavana Party	06
Rastriya Madhes Samajwadi Party	03
Tarai/Madhes Sadbhavan Party	03
Tharuhat Tarai Party Nepal	02*
Madhesi Janadhikar Forum (Ganatantrik)	01
Sanghiya Sadbhavana Party	01
Madhes Samata Party, Nepal	01
Sanghiya Loktantrik Rastriya Manch (Tharuhat)	01*
Nepal Sadbhavana Party	01
Bahujan Shakti Party	01
Madhes Tarai Fourm	
Madhesi Janaadhikar Forum, Madhes	
Rashtriya Madhes Bahujan Samajwadi Party	
Nepal Sadbhavana Party, Gajendrawadi	
Nepal Sadbhavana Party, United	
Janatantrik Tarai/Madhes Mukti Tigers	
Rastriya Madhes Ekta Party, Nepal	
Nepal Madhesi Janata Dal	
Total:	**50**

***Note:** Counted in the total because Tharus do not consider themselves as Madhesis.

Source: Legislature/Parliament Nepal [http://parliament.gov.np/np/publications.html] and Election Commission Nepal [www.election.gov.np].

Annexure 4.3: Tarai/Madhes-related political parties which participated in the CA election of 2008 and the number of seats secured

Names	**Number of seats secured**
Madhesi Jana Adhikar Forum	54
Tarai Madhes Loktantrik Party	21
Sadbhavana Party	09
Nepal Sadbhavana Party (Anandi Devi)	03
Total:	**87**

Source: Election Commission of Nepal

Results of elections held on 26 November and 7 December 2017 for Federal House of Representatives

Party	**Votes secured**	**Percentage**	**Out of 165**	**PR 110**
CPN-UML	3173494	33.25	80	41
NC	3128389	32.78	23	40
CPN-MC	1303721	13.66	36	17
RJP	472254	4.95	11	6
FSFN	470201	4.93	10	6
Bibekshil Sajha Party	212364	2.22		
RPP	196782	2.06		
Rastriya Prajatantra Party (Democratic)	88377	0.93		
NSPN	81837	0.86		
Rastriya Janamorcha	62133	0.65		
Others	355227	3.72	5	
Total	9544779	100	165	110

Source: Election commission of Nepal

Results of elections held on 26 November and 7 December 2017 for provincial legislatures

Party	**FPTP**	**PR**
CPN-UML	167	75
NC	41	72
CNP–CPN-MC	74	35
RJP	16	12
FSFN	24	13
Naya Shakti Party, Nepal	2	1
Rastriya Janamorcha	2	2
NMKP	1	1
Independents	3	
Bibekshil Sajha		3
RPP		3
Rastriya Prajatantra Party (Democratic)		1
Nepal Sanghiya Samajbadi		1
Sanghiya Lokatantrik Rastriya Manch		1
Total	330	220

Source: Election commission, 2017

Note: From the above figures, it is evident that left alliance of CPN-UML and CPN-MC has secured large number of seats in the National legislature and provincial legislatures. Also the seats secured by the Tarai/Madhes parties were mainly from Tarai/Madhes constituencies

Annexure 5.1: Tarai/Madhes-related political parties which participated in the general elections held in 2017 and the number of seats secured in the HoR

Party	**Vote secured**	**Percentage**	**Out of 165**	**Out of 110 under PR**
RJP	472,254	4.95	11	6
FSFN	470,201	4.93	10	6

Source: Election Commission, Nepal

Note: Mostly, the seats were secured from the Tarai/Madhes constituencies falling under Province No. 2 and only these two parties representing Tarai/Madhes had participated in the elections

Annexure 5.2: Tarai/Madhes-related political parties which participated in general elections held in 2017 and the number of seats secured in Seven Provincial Legislatures under FTTP and proportional representation

Party	FPTP out 330	Out of 220
RJP	16	12
FSFN	24	13

Source: Election Commission of Nepal

Note: Mostly these parties in Tarai/Madhes constituencies falling under Province No. 2. Only these two parties representing Tarai/Madhes had participated and secured these seats in the elections.

Annexure 5.2.B: Tarai/Madhes-related political parties which participated in the local elections held in 2017 and the number of seats secured

Party	Mayor	Deputy Mayor	Ward Chairperson	Ward Member
FSFN	34	32	262	1,111
RJP	25	30	195	862
Nepal Loktantrik Forum	9	8	88	356
Total	68	70	545	2,329

Source: Elections 2017 and https://en.wikipedia.org/wiki/Nepalese_local_elections,_2017

Note: The total number of positions at the 753 local government units are 35,041 (753 mayors, 753 deputy mayors, 6,742 ward chairpersons and 26,790 ward members), out of this number the three parties representing Madheshi parties secured 2,329 positions, meaning 6.64 per cent of the positions. Mostly, they secured the positions at the Tarai/Madhes districts falling under the Province number 2.

Endnotes

1 On 22 November 2005, a 12-point agreement was signed between the seven main political parties and the CPN-M in New Delhi which agreed to collectively reduce the power of the monarchy and restore parliamentary democracy. This instigated a popular uprising orchestrated by the SPA and the CPN-M. The protest lasted for nineteen days and led to an acceptable environment for the signing of a Comprehensive Peace Accord (CPA) between the government and the CPN-M in November 2006. The agreement was instrumental in ending the ten year armed conflict in Nepal initiated by the CPN-M.

2 The main features of the amendment were: (i) proposal to form another Tarai province with six districts—Nawalparasi (Bardaghat Susta west), Rupandehi, Kapilvastu, Banke, Dang and Bardiya. This would be called as Province 5; (ii) putting hill districts of the existing Province 5 into Province 4. Province 4 will, thus, have Gorkha, Lamjung, Tanahun, Kaski, Manang, Mustang, Parbat, Syangja, Myagdi, Baglung, Palpa, Gulmi, Arghakhanchi, Nawalparasi (Bardaghat Susta east), Ropla, Pyuthan and Rukum (eastern part); (iii) forming a commission to address concerns about five districts Jhapa, Morang, Sunsari, Kailali and Kanchanpur; (iv) Forming a commission through an executive order to address all concerns about boundaries. The commission to have the mandate to prepare its report after studying all concerns about boundaries, the reports of erstwhile State Restructuring Commission and the agreements signed in the past with stakeholders including Janajatis; (v) the Upper House, will have three representations from all provinces—differently-abled, Dalit and minority representatives—and thirty-five members on the basis of population. Among them, fourteen will be female representatives; (vi) to list all the mother tongues of Nepal in the schedule of the constitution on the recommendation of the Language Commission. Also all languages recommended to be official languages by the Language Commission will be listed in the constitution's schedule; and (vii) foreign women married to Nepali men can obtain naturalized citizenship after initiating the process to renounce their citizenship; however the bill does not say anything about the rights of the naturalised citizens and citizens by birth (*The Himalayan Times*, November 30, 2016)

3 The revised bill sought to have: (i) an electoral college comprised of the members of the provincial legislatures for the election of a 56-member upper house of parliament of which twenty-one members (at least one women,

one dalit and one disabled or marginalised person from each of the seven provinces and remaining thirty-five members to be elected on the basis of the population ratio of the said provinces; (ii) provide naturalized citizenship to a foreign woman married to a Nepali citizen provided she had initiated the process to relinquish the citizenship of the country at the time of her marriage on the basis of the law passed by the federal parliament; (iii) form a federal commission to review the number and boundary of provinces and make suggestion for changes as per the terms of reference and working procedure decided by the government; (iv) provide federal parliament power of approving the bill submitted by the government in relation to changing the number and boundary of the provinces on the basis of the recommendation of the federal commission; and (v) include all mother languages in the annex of the constitution on the basis of the recommendation of a Language Commission and also include a list of approved languages by the GoN on the recommendation of the Language Commission as official working languages in the annex of the constitution (Legislative–parliament secretariat and Ekantipur, 30 April 2017).

4 Rastriya Janta Party Nepal (RJPN) was founded on 20 April 2017 through a merger of these Tarai based parties: Tarai-Madhesh Loktantrik Party (TMLP), Sadbhavana Party (SP), Rastriya Madhes Samajwadi Party (RMSP), Tarai Madhesh Sadbhawana Party (TMSP), Madheshi Jana Adhikar Forum (Republican) and Nepal Sadbhawana Party with a system collegiate leadership. (http://kathmandupost.ekantipur.com/news/2017-04-20/five-madhes-based-parties-unite-to-form-rastriya-janata-party.html)

9

CORRUPTION: THE BANE OF NEPALI GOVERNANCE

Dwarika Nath Dhungel
Dipak Gyawali
Mahendra Raj Sapkota

One of the Divya Upadesh given to his successors by King Prithvi Narayan Shah, the founder of modern Nepal, specified corruption as the biggest enemy of the state as follows:

> *Niyanisaf bigarnya bhanyako ghus dinya ra ghus khanya. En dui ko ta dhan jib gariliyako pani paap chhaina. Ee rajaka mahasatur hun.*
>
> (Justice is crippled with bribe giving and bribe taking. If the life and property of these two are taken, no sin is incurred. They are the greatest enemies of the King.)

The historical roots of this moral foundation of the state go back about a century and a half before King Ram Shah of Gorkha, whose righteous rule was characterized by the popular saying, *'Nyaya napaye Gorkha janu'* (If you want justice, go to Gorkha). It is widely acknowledged that today's Nepal has fallen far below from those sublime heights and is mired in unprecedented corruption that is as widespread as it is blatant. Almost every morning when a random scanning of newspapers or surfing of Nepali news websites are done, one can find a plethora of big and small corruption stories. Thus the Nepali state's current reputation is indeed a far cry from the standards set by King Ram Shah or Prithvi Narayan Shah. This chapter is an attempt to not only describe the pathology of corruption in Nepal but also theoretically examine the basis and drivers of this complex socio-political phenomenon and suggest remedies.

Corruption: Some Annotations

Contrary to people's aspiration that the restoration of democracy in 1990 will result in a free political and administrative atmosphere and severe measures to combat corruption will be taken, the degree of corruption and misuse of national wealth took an all-time upward leap. Not only have the limited resources of the country been misused, even ordinary citizens face the burden of corruption in their day-to-day life, as bribery has become an essential component of any transaction. How bad the situation is can be assessed by the fact that even the courts of justice are also alleged for not being free from corruption.

Corruption in Nepal has become a pernicious problem. Political corruption has gone beyond the pursuit for personal gain by the political parties, politicians and their henchmen. Political bigwigs have gone to the extreme extent of providing protection to their family members, friends and party workers who are among the beneficiaries of commission mongering, influence peddling and cashing in on the proximity to the powers.

At the political level, corruption is adopted as a modus operandi for gaining power, keeping hold and to generate additional resources for an enduring grasp on power. Principles play no role in political contest. As such, political parties, particularly the larger ones, aspire to attract cadres and supporters by promising lucrative rewards at the public expense. This has led to dishonesty as the bottom line, no matter whether it is in public employment, in dispensing of services, in provision of public resources and in implementation of development policies and programmes.

The elected representatives of different political parties have been governing Nepal since the restoration of a democracy in 1990.

Nevertheless, the representative character of the successive governments has eroded because of the high pecuniary value attached to elections along with the influence of illicit elements. Even a comparatively sincere politician finds him/herself politically immobilized to do a bit in the cause of national interest.

Individuals seek plum and lucrative positions, and then use their position to serve their own greedy interests. From the executives of big enterprises to even a village schoolteacher, appointments are more by kickbacks than by normal and established criteria. The same is true of promotions, placements and transfers. This has demoralized, politicized and even criminalized the bureaucracy, disabling it from performing its normal expected functions. A systematic, stable, self-regulating and specialized administration is a hindrance to politicians who need public servants to carry out their command. Almost all levels of government suffer from this malaise. The confidence and spirit of sincere civil servants has ebbed so low to instigate positive decisions and actions.

It is undisputable that corruption—not just financial, which is or can be the end results, but also behavioural and moral as more insidious—has eaten into the sinews of the Nepali state. The country has not improved in the latest Corruption Perception Index of TI. In 2012, Nepal's position was 139th with a score of 27 points; the position was almost same at 122nd with a score of 31 points after six years in 2017. In 2017, among South Asian nations, Nepal was just ahead of Afghanistan (177th with 15 points) and Bangladesh (143rd with 28 points).

Types of Corruption

There are various forms of corruption, starting from those that are faced every day by common citizens which are much talked about, and working up to white collar and policy crimes that are obvious but difficult to pin down. Indeed, the higher one goes, the more arcane and intricate becomes the modus operandi of the perpetrators, so much so that charges against them are often thrown out by the courts on equally esoteric legalistic grounds and very few indictments actually take place. It then feeds the growing public perception that only the small fry get caught while the big fish slip away, or as a Nepali saying has it, '*Saana lai ain, thula lai chain*' (force of law on the ordinary people, comfort for the influential ones).

Basic service delivery

Every Nepali citizen is entitled to receive a citizenship certificate without which no formal business can be conducted, whether it is opening a bank account, getting water and electricity connections, availing of public resources such as government grants and subsidies or buying property. This certificate is issued by the District Administration Office (DAO) on the recommendation of local government units[1]. These units are expected to be accountable and have a sense of service towards the citizens.

However, such is not the case. Public officials still consider themselves as masters, not servants, with a feudalistic attitude, procrastinate simple tasks for days, and wait for rent-seeking opportunities before they deliver the services they are obliged to.

Two studies were conducted by TI-Nepal, in twenty-one districts covering agencies responsible for delivery of services. They present a very gloomy picture of the state of governance. Table 1 depicts that service recipients had to pay extra money to receive services from the land revenue office (34.1 per cent), land survey office (27.3 per cent) and land reform office (29.0 per cent) in the case of the nine districts covered by the first study. In the case of the twelve districts, 51 per cent of the recipients had paid extra money to the land reform and revenue office and 47 per cent to the land survey office (Table 2).

Table 1: Extra money paid for completion of work on time

SN	Offices	Yes	No	Total	% paid
1	Land Revenue office	157	303	460	34.1
2	Land Survey office	50	133	183	27.3
3	Land Reform office	9	22	31	29.0
4	District Administration office	30	334	364	8.2
5	District Development committee	14	55	69	20.3
6	Municipality office	21	495	516	4.1
7	Village Development Committee office	28	292	320	8.8
8	District Education office	2	31	33	6.1
9	District Agriculture Development office	3	44	47	6.4
10	District forest office	2	10	12	16.7
11	Transport Management office	19	54	73	26.0
12	Water Supply Corporation	7	95	102	6.9
13	Revenue and Tax office	11	104	115	9.6
14	Judiciary	4	26	30	13.3

Source: A Survey on Public Service Delivery, TI Nepal, 2015

Table 2: Corruption experienced by household in different service sectors

Sectors	Number of service taken incidences from each service sector	Percentage
Land reform and revenue	1058	51
Land survey	742	47
Transport	928	42
Forest	207	37
Customs/Tax	604	33
Municipality	1501	30
Agriculture	429	28

Police	440	27
District Administration office	1178	26
Health	1323	25
Electricity	1536	24
Water	1091	23
Communication	955	15

Source: Satisfaction Survey on Public Service Delivery, TI Nepal, 2016

It was revealed that land reform/revenue and survey offices were the most corrupt. Next to them was the transport management office. Strangely, most of the citizens seem fatalistic and do not complain because they doubt that any action would be taken even if complaints were filed.

Bureaucracy

With the increase in import, export, capital budget amount (budget allocated to activities other than the administrative and management expenses), procurement volume, donor support to the country and more and more involvement of brokers/commission agents in the government's decision-making process, there is hardly any sector or government agency and personnel which is not involved in corrupt behaviour.

In really chronically and structurally corrupt systems, not only will the entire edifice be 'in on-the-take' (as, for instance, public works departments, which are heavily into construction work where skimming starts at the lowest level of overseers and the percentages filter up all the way to the level of the chief), but very rarely will the matter come to the knowledge of the public or the media. It is only when a disgruntled employee acts as a whistle-blower that the scandal breaks. This is primarily because much of this type of corruption occurs not by breaking the rules or law but by operating within its maze and thickets that are intelligible or penetrable only to the initiated within the structure. This is also the reason courts and commissions for corruption control fail to indict major perpetrators since they only see if rules have been broken and only the really stupid ones indulge in corrupt acts by breaking the rules. Thus, corruption exists across the bureaucracy. As a result, the Nepali public officials/civil service/bureaucracy is considered to be one of the most corrupt institutions by 85 per cent of the people in the country (Table 3).

Political corruption

The syndicate culture in Nepali politics[2] started in the 1990s and continues to thrive. The situation greatly aggravated after the adoption of a mixed electoral system of territorial and proportional representation in the national legislature, first under the interim constitution of 2007 and now under the Constitution of Nepal 2015. The persons elected under the proportional representation are nominees of political parties as per their share of popular votes and decided by the respective political parties on the basis of the list submitted by them to the Election Commission (EC) at the time of filing nomination to the general elections. The mixed electoral system has created a situation where a political party gaining a majority could be rare. It means the country may, time and again, face the situation of a coalition government and with it the sordid drama of corruption will continue. The result is that the country, by January 2017 had seen more than two dozen prime ministers (some multiple times) since 1990, ten of them within the last decade. In essence, such coalition governments cannot be considered more than a syndicate of political parties (or mathaadhish-tantra, the rule by oligarchs). The interests of most of the ministers of such governments will naturally be to misuse power and amass wealth to the maximum extent possible for personal benefit as well as to finance the next election.

Within the party itself, sources of funding remain confined to a select few, including the top leaders and their coterie, often key family members. Also, because of the costs involved in the elections, those who can afford to spend are taking greater interest in getting party tickets, even if they have little experience or acumen for mass politics or the national executive office. When that happens, bargaining takes place between the influential leaders of the respective political parties and the prospective candidates, with the highest bidder getting the party ticket to stand for elections. The going market rate, as generally whispered, is millions of rupees. Such candidates who have spent millions to get elected hope to recoup their investments by influencing the decision-making process, getting contracts awarded to the preferred firms and contractors, getting preferred persons/officials to lucrative positions or acquiring a berth in the cabinet, especially in what are called 'lucrative ministries' with lots of procurement or construction contracts.[3]

A proportional representation system, as opposed to a first-past-the-post, was devised to ensure that all votes cast were represented in the parliament and marginalized sections of society were represented in the national policymaking process. In theory, these arguments may be correct, but in real life, the expectations were belied by the political parties. Proportional representation is one of the most misused systems in the current political culture. What was surprising about the proportional representation nomination to the CAs and parliaments was that it included spouses of party leaders and big business houses—'crown prince of trading houses'. As a result, contractors, bank promoters (those in the management of commercial/development banks), private school owners, executives of NGOs, including international NGOs, and promoters of hydropower projects, secured birth in the legislature having purchased their way in. When someone buys a parliamentary seat, s/he would definitely like to get back with compound interest what was invested, which is possible only through blatant misuse of the state apparatus.

One structural imperative for the blatant corruption in the political parties is that, over the years, general elections have become an expensive affair, costing millions of rupees for the party and the candidates that is way above what is prescribed by election regulations. Consequently, there is a nexus between the business or trading houses and the political parties, making the activities of the political parties, especially fund mobilization and funding sources, more and more dubious and non-transparent. Due to all this, the political parties were found to be the most corrupt (Table 3).

The members of the parliament have been involved in drafting laws as per their interests. Particularly, members who are also owners of private schools and chairpersons of private commercial banks are highly involved in influencing the process of law-making during drafting the bills of their interest. Their most controversial involvement was seen during the drafting of the bill on Education Act and Bank and Financial Institution Act (BAFIA).[4]

Dismal judiciary

The rot has hit the judiciary too, and political interference has entered this sector with a vengeance. Currently, the Judicial Council (JC), which recommends the appointment of judges other than the Chief Justice of the Supreme Court, is composed of the Chief Justice as chair, law minister, seniormost judge of the supreme court, and two members appointed by the President on the recommendation of the Nepal Bar Council and the Prime Minister. Except for the Chief Justice and the seniormost judge of the Supreme Court, the other three members are basically political in nature. If the Bar Council happens to be in control of the supporters of the party in government, its nominee would naturally be the supporter of the government. Similarly, the prime minister may recommend a candidate from amongst his/her supporters. In such a case, the judges, other than those coming from regular judicial service, are picked from among party loyalists. In case the nominee of the Bar Council is not the supporter of the government or when there is a coalition government, members of the JC decide to pick up candidates from among coalition partners.

Nepal established the Special Court in 2009 to hear corruption cases filed by the CIAA. But the court came under fire after it acquitted a string of high-profile political leaders, government officials and police officers. Also, some of the cases did not lead to any punishment and the public reacted with outrage. As such the credibility of the Special

Court is being challenged time and again on the basis of its decisions on known corruption cases, in which top guns were involved. Also, some decisions of the Supreme Court and other courts have also not been free from criticism.

The consequence of all these shenanigans has led to a decline in the credibility of judges in the society, with the perception of corruption in the judiciary quite rampant. From the large number of corruption cases pending before the Supreme Court, one could doubt the credibility of the highest court of justice. And the number is rising—in 2012–13 it was 480, which went up to 545 in 2013–14 and further to 661 in 2014–15. The former Chief Justice, Sushila Karki, in a public forum, had stated that a few legal professionals had made illegal earnings under the garb of the lawyer's black coat by working together with brokers engaged in land dealings (*Annapurna Post,* 12 August 2016). It is worth mentioning here that the 2016 country reports on Human Rights Practices released by the US State Department has put a serious question on the independence of the Nepali courts, as it claims, 'The law provides for an independent judiciary, but courts remained vulnerable to political pressure, bribery and intimidation.'[5] The issue of corruption in judiciary has been empirically proved and cited in the Shree Hari Aryal Committee Report of 2064 BS (2008). The Supreme Court Bar Association had constituted this committee to recommend measures on increasing the trust of the people in the judiciary.

NGOs and donors

NGOs, national as well as international, have become part of Nepali life since the 1980s. They are engaged in various sectors, especially in the socio-economic as well as disaster relief activities. However, the NGOs in Nepal run a parallel government. They are supposed to be registered with the Social Welfare Council (SWC)—a national body that is to regulate, supervise and monitor their activities. In reality, the NGOs just ignore it and decide their own agenda in cohort with their international donors. The SWC, despite its claims of monitoring the activities of the NGOs, is in a state of hopelessness vis-à-vis the NGOs, mainly because they are politically patronized, while politicization of the SWC in the appointment of its office-bearers is the other side of the coin. On the whole, neither SWC nor the Ministry of Women, Children and Social Welfare (MoWCSW)—responsible for NGO-related matters—is in a position to tell which NGOs are working in which sector and in which part of the country.

A recent example is the mismanagement of funds collected for the relief work after the massive earthquake in 2015. A news report by Akhanda Bhandari and Chandra Sekhar Adhikari, entitled '*Kahan Janchha Yeti Dherai Paisa?*' (Where did so much money go?), provides graphic details of the NGOs' operation based on the latest annual report of the Auditor General (*Kantipur*, 20 August 2016). As per these contributors, billions of rupees were raised by international NGOs, of which only a small portion reached the affected people[6]. So, the question that arises is: Where has the money gone? In this context, the Auditor General has recommended to the government that there is a need for monitoring the NGOs' work.

In infrastructure works, the massive corruption that goes on with the public, the consumer and the taxpayer being defrauded colossal sums of money happens within the ambit of the law. Hildyard (2016) shows how privatization of infrastructure building has resulted in the phenomenon of, what he calls, 'licensed larceny'. It is a grand theft that is wholly legal in terms of contracts, MoUs and the like, even if wholly immoral and illegitimate when money is being siphoned off from the world's poorest 99 per cent to the richest 1 per cent both in the Global North and the Global South.

Taking off from this line of argument, Gyawali (2016) shows how the German-aided Middle Marsyangdi project was a 'perfectly legal and wholly illegitimate' case. The 70 MW Middle Marsyangdi was to be built with some 82 per cent of the required finance as grant, while Nepal government and Nepal Electricity Authority (NEA) were to come up with 18 per cent of the remaining amount, with the legal caveat that any cost increase would be borne by the Nepali side. It was completed at a cost about five times higher than the going market rate with fifty months of time overrun. This meant that, in reality, Nepal ended up paying some 70 per cent of the total increased project cost, which essentially meant that it was not German aid to Nepal but its reverse: Nepali government and consumers paying massively to German businesses, a phenomenon that is legally impeccable but morally dubious!

Policy corruption

In the name of policy decisions, the Council of Ministers (Cabinet)—the highest policymaking body in the country, whose decisions cannot be challenged in any court[7] or against whom nobody can file petition to the corruption control agency—has been taking all kinds of decisions, which on any ground cannot be considered as policy decisions. Some of the cabinet decisions include financial assistance worth billions of rupees (NPR 3.63 billion during the past ten years from 2006/07 to 2015/16) to different persons, and amendment to the required minimum qualification for appointment to the post of advisers to the prime minister so as to make the qualifications suitable to the person intended to be appointed.

Overall Corruption Scenario

An old Russian saying has it that a fish always rots and smells from the head, not the tail, meaning, corruption starts at the top and if only the ones at the top were clean, it would become so much more difficult for those at the lower echelons to engage in rent-seeking. During the Rana rule, until 1951, while the Rana families enriched themselves enormously, it was not through corruption per se but through 'savings from taxation' that was accepted as a given right of higher officials. The Ranas were pretty strict with rule breakers, including their own kith and kin who could be banished for such crimes.

While specific data to clinch the debate does not exist, there is widespread perception that the parliamentary democracy that replaced the Rana rule in the late 1950s was more corrupt than what preceded it; that the late Panchayat was more corrupt than the early Panchayat or Rana rule; that the restored multiparty democracy of the 1990s is perceived as a shade more venial than the Panchayat it replaced; and that the Republican Nepal has 'hundreds of mini-corrupt kings replacing one king of the past'. Thus without minimizing its importance, it can be said that with democracy—and more and more democratization—corruption has also become a more mass-scale phenomenon and is prevalent in all sectors (Table 3).

Table 3: Corruption by sector

S. No.	Sector	Score	Percentage of respondents
1.	Political Parties	4.6	90
2.	Public Officials/Civil Servants/ Bureaucracy	4.4	85
3.	Police	4.3	80
4.	Parliament/Legislature	4.2	79
5.	Judiciary	4.1	77
6.	Business/Private Sector	3.5	54
7.	NGOs	3.2	46
8.	Education System	3.2	45
9.	Military	3.2	43
10.	Medical and Health	3.0	37
11.	Media	2.8	33
12.	Religious Bodies	2.9	33

Source: Global Corruption Barometer, TI, 2013

Note: Score scale 1–5, where 1 means not at all corrupt, 5 means extremely corrupt

Reasons for Corruption

A number of questions arise: Why has corruption increased? Is it because the country does not have a state policy against corruption or is it not a signatory to the international convention against corruption? Or is it because there is no legal framework and institution for corruption control? Or is it due to the absence of oversight bodies or the parliament has not created its own oversight body?

Answers to these questions would be 'No' because there exist several measures to combat corruption in the country, including constitutional pronouncements on corruption control,[8] a strong legal system or existence of laws[9] against corruption, a constitutional body (CIAA) to investigate the cases of corruption on the basis of anti-corruption laws and a special court where the anti-corruption cases are being filed by the CIAA and other agencies. In addition, there are other constitutional bodies such as an independent Office of the Auditor General, PSC, JC, Judicial Service Commission and EC. Besides, there were parliamentary oversight committees such as the Public Accounts Committee (PAC), State Affairs Committee (SAC) and Good Governance and Monitoring Committee (GGMC). Within the government are the National Vigilance Centre (NVC) and different departments such as the Department of Revenue Investigation (DRI), Department of Money Laundering Investigation (DMLI), Public Procurement Monitoring Office (PPM), National Information Commission, Financial Information Unit (FIU) at the Nepal Rastra Bank (NRB) and seventy-five district administration offices. Furthermore, at the NGO level, there exist a number of public watchdog institutions, the most important one of which is TI-Nepal and the media, which is recognized as a strong mechanism to expose corruption and build support on the efforts to combat corruption. Yet, corruption is rampant in Nepal. Some of the major reasons are as follows:

Auctioning of public office

Public offices ostensibly belong to the whole nation, and the officials should be appointed on the basis of merit. But most of the important public positions including constitutional positions, ambassadors, secretaries, director generals and chief of the public institutions are decided on the basis of political leaning, especially the party or parties in power, although there is a façade of parliamentary hearing for judging the suitability of candidates in case of constitutional positions and ambassadors. As a consequence, there is a general feeling in the country that the public officials are the representatives of political parties rather than national officials.

Actually, as per an investigative journalist, it is the civil service trade unions affiliated to the party concerned, that negotiate with the prospective candidates and decide who is to be recommended by the party for placement, promotion and granting other benefits.

Decreased risk level/impunity

During the Panchayat period (1961–90), which was directly under the active leadership of kings, the country witnessed and faced a number of corruption scandals (Thapa, 2002 and Dhakal, 2005). But the risk level, unlike at present, used to be high, as public officials used to be afraid of being caught and loss of image in society. Over the period, the risk level has gone down and the word 'fear' does not seem to exist any longer. And the feelings of '*I can do whatever I like*' and '*Who is to control me*?' seem to have replaced the term 'fear' in the minds of the public officials. Whenever actions are initiated against public officials, the party concerned politicizes the matter and considers as an example of political vendetta by the anti-corruption agency.

The most important anti-corruption generic law in the country is the Prevention of Corruption Act (PCA) 2002. The PCA, 2002, defines corruption and categorizes corruption, punishments, fine and imprisonment for corrupt activities and investigation/inquiry procedures and filing of cases at the Special Court established under the Special Court Act 2002. The CIAA Act 1991 mainly deals with the investigation process and filing of cases in the Special Court on the basis of the PCA provisions. The CIAA Act also defines the term '*Anuchit Karya*' (improper conduct) of persons holding public offices and actions that could be initiated by the CIAA for such improper conduct. However, this provision has been deleted from the constitution. Looking at the provisions of these Acts, one can hardly find deficiency in the laws to deal with corruption, as the definition of corruption is comprehensive and corrupt activities have been categorised into as many as twenty-one types (Chapter 2 Section 3 of The Prevention of Corruption Act 2002) from the standpoint of punishment. Punishment ranges from a fine of minimum NPR 5,000 to maximum of NPR 5,00,000 and/or imprisonment ranging from one month to ten years depending upon the nature of offence.

Nepal is a signatory of the United Nations Convention against Corruption (UNCAC), and the country has also ratified the convention in February 2011. In order to fulfil the UNCAC obligations, the government adopted the Second National Anti-corruption Strategy in 2012. As part of its obligation, the government has to review and update its anti-corruption laws and bring them in line with the convention. Although the Prevention of Corruption Act 2002 is the most important and wide-scoped anti-corruption generic law in the country, it does not cover officials of the private sector, NGOs, military and judiciary. Also, employees of international organizations are not covered by the Act. Due to the absence of bilateral agreements with several countries, those who have fled the country after committing corruption-related crimes could not be penalized. Because of this reason, the NVC, in its 14th annual report, has drawn the attention of the government and suggested it to act upon fulfilling the UNCAC obligations of reviewing the existing corruption-related laws to encompass the organizations not covered so far, including the NGO, private sector, etc.

Image problem of corruption controlling agencies

As a constitutional body, CIAA is mandated to investigate cases of corruption and file cases at the Special Court as per the provisions of the CIAA Act. This is the most important anti-corruption body in the country. The Constitutional Council (CC), composed of the Prime Minister, Leader of the Opposition Party, Chief Justice of the Supreme Court, Speaker and Deputy Speaker of the Legislature-Parliament, recommend the President to appoint the Chief Commissioner and other Commissioners of CIAA. This Council was supposed to ensure fairness and impartiality in recommending candidates. For this purpose, the Council Secretariat, i.e. Office of the Prime Minister and Council of Ministers (OPMCM) was also supposed to maintain a roster of persons, eligible to be appointed to the constitutional bodies. While recommending candidates, the Council was supposed to consider, among other criteria, the candidate's social prestige and his/her high moral character (Article 283 [6] [5]), public opinion about him/her and his/her service record. At face value, everything looks perfect and flawless.

But, since the appointment of a litigious person Lokman Singh Karki as Chief Commissioner of the CIAA, the anti-corruption body has become more controversial. Karki was recommended on 5 May 2013 and the then President appointed him as Chief Commissioner on 8 May 2013. His name was selected by a unanimous decision of the leaders of the major political parties. Karki's appointment became controversial because he was held guilty of suppressing the Peoples' Movement in April 2006 when he was Chief Secretary. He was also accused of amassing property through illegal means during his tenure as Director General of the Department of Customs. A large section of civil society and Kathmandu intelligentsia had seriously objected to his appointment, citing his pro-royal, anti-democratic, and opportunistic antecedents. Surprisingly, the honchos of the major political parties who run the country's political syndicate supported him with unanimity.[10] Soon after Karki's appointment, a case was filed in the Supreme Court on 16 May 2016 against the decision. After deferring the hearing on this petition several times, the court gave the verdict that Karki did not meet the qualifications required to hold the position of the Chief of the CIAA. Since Karki's appointment was by the President of the country on the CC's unanimous recommendation, the court judgement puts an ethical question mark on the entire top echelon of Nepal's governance (Ghimire, 2017). The Karki episode has gravely tarnished the public image of CIAA. It seems that a long time will take to build up a positive public image of CIAA.

Not only Karki, but the appointment of other commissioners in the CIAA is also not free from controversies as they are appointed mainly on a partisan basis. As such, questions have been raised many times about the integrity and impartiality of the CIAA and its activities have been criticized as politically motivated actions. The CIAA has also been charged for not taking any action against the 'big fish' but being concentrated only on tiny corruption cases.

From the viewpoint of functional areas, the other important body within the government organization is the NVC established under the provision of the PCA 2002. This agency has been established within the government with a secretary-level officer as its administrative head and under the direct control and supervision of the Prime Minister in order to effectively control corruption-related activities and promote people's awareness against corruption. But this Centre has not been as effective as it should have been due to the frequent transfers of its administrative heads. It also suffers from a number of problems such as lack of clear-cut and specific laws to facilitate corruption control and preventive functions, duplication among the corruption controlling agencies about the functional areas and lack of resources and trained personnel, particularly technical persons to perform technical audits (NVC: 14th Annual Report).

Commenting on the effectiveness of some of the anti-corruption bodies—DRI, DMLI, FIU, PPMO—Koirala, et al. (2015), in their study, have stated that 'the executive functions of...Department of Revenue Investigation (DRI), Department of Money Laundering Investigation (DMLI) and Public Procurement Monitoring Office (PPMO) is overlapping. With the supervising ministries of DRI and DMLI being the MoF, these agencies are not as effective as they should have been'. Similarly, parliamentary oversight committees such as the PAC, and the JC have also not been found to be effective at all.

Political instability

Since 1990, Nepal has seen as many as twenty-seven prime ministers. And, since the first coalition headed by the NC in September 1995, the country has been ruled by one coalition or another. Almost all coalition governments have been jumbo in size, and ministers from the coalition partners have been found to be running the ministries and departments as their personal fiefdom and as a milking cow to extract resources by any means for personal and family benefit and to the benefit of their political parties. Interestingly, whenever a new government assumes office, the new prime minister does not forget to mention that the government is committed to controlling corruption, but in reality the Prime Minister and his party just turn a blind eye to this burning issue.

After the general elections in 2017, a new coalition government of the Left Alliance, i.e. CPN-UML and CPN-MC, was formed in February-March 2018, and has also expressed its commitment to curb corruption. This government is expected to be stable and take stern actions against corruption.

Non-state funding of political parties and costly elections

So far the main sources of income of the political parties are levy from their members and donations, particularly from the big industrialists and business houses. Being the main players in the national politics and running and managing the state affairs, political parties are supposed to be transparent from all perspectives, including their financial resources and expenditures. But their sources of income remain undisclosed (Mainali, 2015) and their expenses are dubious.

The EC decides how much a political party and candidate can spend during the election. But because the elections have become a very costly affair, the parties and candidates make huge expenses than what is prescribed by the EC. After the election, both the candidates and political parties have to submit their expenses to the EC. The financial reports they submit to the EC, as per the election laws, are unconvincing.

> None of the election expense details submitted to the EC is real. Is NPR 1 million enough to run the election campaign? When I contested from Gorkha for the first time, it cost me NPR 600,000. When I contested the elections for a second time, I found that the

> real electoral expenses are many times higher [than the limit set by the commission]. They were well beyond my affordability. Even after support from friends, I was hard-pressed. Looking at the campaign expenses of candidates, I found that NPR 1 million is largely insufficient. But we are lying to everyone.
>
> —Former Prime Minister Baburam Bhattarai in the BBC Nepali service interview aired on 28 October 2015 (quoted in Mainali, 2015).

Wealth: Symbol of social prestige

Personal standing in Nepali society is largely dependent on how much wealth a person has, no matter s/he is in the political or bureaucratic field or in any other field and whether s/he has earned by legitimate means. Any person, especially from public life, failing to make money is considered to be unsuccessful and not capable of harnessing the opportunity through position. Within the family or clan also, such persons are considered idealistic and dogmatic. Because of the prevalence of such criteria for measuring success or standing in society, the moment one joins a public position, there is severe family and community pressure to gain maximum benefits from the position, whether by hook or by crook.

Explaining Corruption from a Theoretical Perspective

In addition to the reasons discussed above, why corruption has remained a serious problem in the country could also be analysed from the conceptual point of view as corruption is an elusive and complex phenomenon requiring more insights from the social sciences. The best of scholars have had great difficulty getting to theoretical grips with it. However, management sociologist Mars (1983), having spent a great deal of ethnographic time among waiters, dockyard workers, moonlighters and a host of others in the informal as well as black and illegal occupations, concludes that rule bending is not new, it is ancient, it is ubiquitous; and it has to be understood only through the total rewards system that are governed by covert institutions of occupational life. They grow 'in reaction to the ever-growing controls that derive from government' and find acceptance if the government in question is perceived as unfair and, worse, heavily rent-seeking. They are engaged in by individuals as well as collectives, and often they are also tolerated by those at the very top of the hierarchy as a necessary evil that compensates for low pay.

Klitgaard, et al. (2000), writing on behalf of the World Bank Institute and the Institute for Contemporary Studies, define it as a misuse of office—a position of public trust—for personal gain. It can be found in the public, private and non-profit sectors; it can be an individual 'freelance' act or that of a cabal within an organization; or, most damaging, it can be systemic when the entire edifice is structurally corrupt as with match-fixing in lucrative spectator sports. The authors list seven excuses that justify this type of behaviour—it is everywhere; has always existed; the concept is vague and culturally determined; it would require impossibly wholesale change in societal attitude and values; it is not that harmful as it greases the wheels of the economy; that nothing can be done when the ones at the top are corrupt; and it is superfluous to worry about it as market growth and democracy will overcome it anyway. They, however, add that, 'Systematic corruption generates economic costs by distorting incentives, political costs by undermining institutions, and social costs by redistributing wealth and power towards the undeserving.'

Theobald (1990), looking at political corruption of the public sphere rather than individual moral decay, writes: '...corruption, like many other forms of behaviour when placed under the scrutiny of the social science lens, proves to be an elusive and complex phenomenon: in fact the more one examines it the more difficult it becomes to separate corruption from other forms of social exchange.'

Starting with Max Weber's ideal type of rational bureaucracy, he goes on to discuss the conditions for its existence in both developed and developing countries. While it was fashionable in Western circles to paint corruption as a Third World phenomenon, the writer shows that it is as prevalent in developed countries as in underdeveloped ones. With examples ranging from Reagan administration's subverting environmental laws for a beer baron who was his big supporter and its sleazy defence contract deals (including the Iran Contra affair) to the Freemasonry corruption of the British police force, he shows how patronage dispensing patrimonialism is also pervasive in countries of the Industrialized North.

He argues with data that, in the underdeveloped countries of the Global South, corruption cannot be explained on the basis of poverty alone. Indeed Tanzania is much poorer than Mexico but is generally accepted as a much more honest country than the latter. The reason corruption seems more obvious in underdeveloped countries than in developed ones is not because the latter and their bureaucracy are more 'rational' in the Weberian sense but because of the fact that, in the former, underdevelopment 'considerably restricts local opportunities for economic advancement' with less access to lucrative employments, to access to capital and such.

Also, the presence of a strong market provides ample opportunities for advancement as well as favour dispensing in developed countries than in underdeveloped ones where the government (and jobs as well as procurement processes within it) is often the only game in town. That is also the reason that comes to prominence as scandal in developing countries is about collusion or favouritism of politicians and decision-makers with particular market cronies, whereas in underdeveloped countries it is direct corruption in the public sector.

Susan Rose Ackerman, in her work on corruption and government, especially her discussion of corruption and politics, talks of corruption from the perspective of Kleptocratic system (corruption at the top) and other states where 'bribery is the province of large number of low level officials' (1999). Also, she thinks that it has to be understood from the perspective of the 'bribery market'. In this regard, she is of the opinion that the corruption situation should be dealt with from the point of view of whether in a state there exists a small number of major private actors or is the payment of bribes decentralised across a large number of people and firms?[11]

Advocates of Cultural Theory (i.e. the neo-Durkheimian theory of plural rationalities or new institutionalism) argue that more in-depth examination of corruption would often reveal what is a corrupt cabal of politician-bureaucrat-consultant/contractor nexus that collaborates to undermine the system and benefit themselves. It has also been called, in the case of US defence contract scandals or that of Bihar's irrigation mafia, an 'iron triangle' of politician-bureaucrat-contractor clique. It is 'dharma gone wrong', as argued by Gyawali and Thompson (2016), where each of the three active social solidarities—market individualism, bureaucratic hierarchism and activist egalitarianism—undermines its own way of organizing by debasing the very principles on which it is founded. Vishwanathan and Sethi (1998), chronicling fifty years of corruption in India—from touts in front of courts, to politicians—describe the tight nexus between the tout, the clerk and the policeman, which controls the functioning of corruption in modern India. Indeed, they go on to argue that this triad exists from the village all the way up to the highest echelons of government in Delhi where 'briefcase (full of cash) politics' is what holds sway. They cynically conclude that a bribe is a badge of citizenship in India as that is the only point at which a citizen comes into contact with the state.

Propositions for Improving the Situation

Countries like Nepal would continue to suffer from corruption due to the very nature of the society and polity. However, efforts to curb corruption must be continued. Therefore, the following measures must be considered to improve the situation:

1. Impartial and strict pursuance of law is a must in terms of investigation, filing of case and penalizing of culprits. Moreover, the fines and punishments stipulated in the PCA are not so severe and, therefore, they need to be made harsher. There are even demands for awarding life imprisonment to those who have been convicted of serious types of corruption cases and confiscation of property earned through corrupt means.

2. The officials of CIAA (Chief Commissioner and other Commissioners) should not be appointed on partisan basis and totally transparent selection process should by adopted to appoint them. The parliamentary hearing to endorse their appointment should not merely be a formality but more rigorous. The provision of requiring two-thirds majority of the parliamentary hearing committee for rejection should be lowered to a simple majority.

In case of the NVC, there is a need of clear delineation of its functional areas, powers and responsibilities, along with its power to take legal action for defiance of its decisions and directions through the amendment of the PCA. In order to avoid duplication in the functional areas, there should be clear-cut distinction between the CIAA and the NVC with precise institutional relationship between them. In addition, NVC should be strengthened with capable human resources and provided adequate budget for independently undertaking the technical audit function. Frequent transfers of NVC heads, which has, so far, remained a serious issue, should be stopped and one should be posted at least for full term.

Both the DRI and DMLI have not been effective mainly due to being under the MoF. Because, one department taking actions against colleagues working under or affiliated to the same parent ministry is not easy, if not impossible. Also there was a need to have the institutional relationships between Centre and the RID, DMLI and FIU, clearly established. In this regard, the NVC, in its 14th report had suggested that all three agencies, viz. NVC, RID and DMLI, should be integrated into one agency and be placed under the direct supervision and control of the Prime Minister. In order to address this issue and implement the recommendation of the NVC, Prime Minister Oli has brought the RID and DMLI under his direct administrative supervision and control. In other words, all three institutions—NVC, RID and NVC—are, now, under the umbrella of the OPMCM. However, if the concentration of excessive power at the hand of the Prime Minister is not misused by those who are in his/her inner circle, and those who can influence the

Prime Minister, mainly political characters, there is a possibility of improvement in the governance situation of the country and decreasing the level of corruption from the public sector.

In addition, an independent financial intelligence unit (FIU) is needed instead of the present FIU under the NRB with the power to take actions against illegal cross-border money transactions, because the existing FIU lacks power to take action against such transactions.

3. Funding of political parties from the state could be a measure to address the problem of the issue of a nexus between the political parties and business community—one of the main reasons of the growing corruption in the country.
4. Anti-corruption civil societies (such as TIN) should support the media to undertake investigative journalism on corruption cases, bring out facts and figures to public notice for building pressure against corrupt activities and put pressure on the government and other public agencies for following accountable and transparent behaviour in discharging their functions and responsibilities. Nevertheless, the media should be careful and see that their political bias does not reflect in their writings.
5. The growing corruption is because of the moral degradation of people holding public positions, such as contractors, dons and dampatis (people with money). As such, those persons who show strong moral value in professional life should be duly recognized. In addition, children and students should be taught lessons in morality and ethics. For this, ethical and moral values should be included in school curricula to help students build strong moral personality during professional life.
6. Growing use of discretionary power of the Council of Ministers should be curbed as this has been one of the major causes of corruption. For this, there is need for clear definitions as well as contents of policy decisions.
7. Although it is not under the control of a particular political party, they may collectively consider re-thinking the present mixed election system (first-past-the-post and proportional) with a view

to lessening of corruption.

8. A thorough review of the composition of the JC and appointment procedure to the judiciary, especially the judges, is urgent to improve the credibility of the judiciary.

In Conclusion

The country may have strong legal and institutional frameworks to deal with corruption, but the image of the country has been going from bad to worse from all indications. So long as the mindset of those who are responsible for running the affairs of the country does not change, they will not behave in an accountable manner and implement the provisions of the law in letter and spirit; no matter how strong the anti-corruption agencies or severe punishment provisions are made in the law, the corruption situation is not going to improve. In other words, as long as public officials and the private sector are guided by self-interests and are not accountable and transparent in their functioning, Nepal's corruption image will not improve.

So, public officials and other leaders must show their leadership in words and deeds in relation to maintaining and upholding moral values and performing their functions in an accountable and transparent manner along with the change in their mindset. Furthermore, civil societies could build opinion against corruption and corrupt persons and motivate society to socially boycott corrupt persons, right from the primary-level, education courses (Administrative Reforms Commission Report, 1991) where the importance of ethical values and morality may be given.

With the coming of a government, i.e. headed by K.P. Sharma Oli (as of April 2018) having majority in the HoR after the elections of 2017, political stability with an accountable and transparent government seems to be a possibility now. With such a mandate, the Oli government could take concrete measures to control corruption and improve the image of the country. But, so long as the mindset of the political leadership and other concerned remains the same, corruption control would remain a mere wishful thinking.

ᔕ

***Dwarika Nath Dhungel** is currently a senior researcher of Social Sciences. He is Former Executive Director, Institute for Integrated Development Studies (IIDS), Kathmandu, and Former Secretary, Government of Nepal.*

***Dipak Gyawali** is Chair, Nepal Water Conservation Foundation and academician at Nepal Academy of Science and Technology (NAST). He has also served as Minister of Water Resources, Government of Nepal,*

***Mahendra Raj Sapkota** is a freelance social science researcher.*

Bibliography

Government and Allied Publications

Constitution and Laws

Constitution of Nepal 2015
Commission for the Investigation of Abuse of Authority Act 1991
Corruption Prevention Act 2002
Good Governance (Management and Operation) Act 2008
National Vigilance Centre (Working Procedure) Regulations 2008–09
National Vigilance Centre Working Procedure 2003–04

Other documents

Public Accounts Committee: 18th Report of the Public Accounts Committee 2016.

Commission for the Investigation of Abuse of Authority (CIAA). 25th Annual Report (summary version), February 2016.

Office of Auditor General (OAG). Office of Auditor General Report, 2010/11.

Government of Nepal, Ministry of Finance (GoN/MoF). Economic Survey, 2015/16.

Department of Printing and Publication. Administrative Reforms, Commission Report: 1991.

National Vigilance Centre Kathmandu. 14th Annual Report, July 2016.

Other Publications

Arora, R.K. *Comparative Public Administration.* New Delhi: Associated Publishing House, nd.

Cheema, G.S. 2005, *Building Democratic Institutions: Governance Reforms in Developing Countries.* Bloomfield: Kumarian Press Inc.

Dhakal, B. 2005. *Empire of Corruption.*

Dhakal, B, 2006. *AdalatmaBhrastachar (Corruption in Courts).*

Dhungel, D.N. 2007. *Inside out: Political Parties of Nepal.* Kathmandu: Institute for Integrated Development Studies and International IDEA.

Dhungel, D.K. and Rajbhandary, A.B. 2004. *Introducing Good Governance in the Public Administration of Nepal.* Kathmandu: Centre for Studies on Democracy and Good Governance.

Dhungel, D.N., 'Value-based System for Public Sector Governance in Nepal.' *Administration and Management Review, A Journal of the Nepal Administrative Staff College,* August 2003, Vol. 15, No. 2.

Lalitpur Sub-Municipality, *Dibya Upadesh of Shree Panch Bada Maharadhiraj Prithvi Narayan Shah* (Divine Dictums), nd.

Gyawali, D. and Thompson, M. 'Restoring Development Dharma with Toad's Eye Science?' *IDS Bulletin: States, Market and Society: New Relationships for a New Development Era,* November 2016, Vol. 47, No. 2A.

Gyawali, D. 2004. 'Governance, Corruption and Foreign Aid.' In: Sharma, S. et al. (Eds.). *Aid Under Stress: Water, Forests and Finnish Support in Nepal.* Lalitpur, Nepal: Himal Books, with Institute of Development Studies, University of Helsinki and Interdisciplinary Analysts, Kathmandu.

Hildyard, N. 2016. *Licensed Larceny: Infrastructure, financial extraction and the Global South.* U.K.: Manchester University Press.

Klitgaard, R., Maclean-Abaroa, R. and Parris, H.L. 2000. *Corrupt Cities: a practical guide to cure and prevention.* Oakland: ICS Press and Washington, DC: World Bank Institute.

Koirala, B.P., Khadka, K. and Timsina, Y. 2015. *Anti-Corruption Interventions in Nepal: Policy, Practices and Possible Collective Interventions.* Kathmandu: Royal Norwegian Embassy.

Mars, G. 1983. *Cheats at Work: An anthropology of workplace crime,* London: Unwin Paperbacks.

Rose-Ackerman, S. 1999. *Corruption and Government: Causes, Consequences, and Reform.* Berkeley: Cambridge University Press.

Shrestha, R.S. 2017. 'Large Hydro: Failure of Financial Engineering.' In: Gyawali, et al. (Eds.). 2017. *Aid, Technology and Development: The lessons from Nepal.* U.K.: EARTHSCAN/Routledge.

Subedi, M.S. 'Corruption in Nepal: An Anthropological Inquiry'. *Dhaulagiri Journal of Sociology and Anthropology, 2005,* Vol. 1.

Supreme Court Bar Association. 2008. 'Nayapalikaprati Jana AsthaAvibridhi: AdhyanPratibedan 2064 (Study Report: Raising People's Faith in Judiciary: 2008)'.

Thapa, H.B. and Bhandari, B. 2008. *Rajnitik Daupech Bhitra Karmacharitantra(Bureaucracy under the Politics of Political Parties).* Kathmandu: Media and Governance Study and Consultancy Centre.

Thapa, H.B. 2002. *Anatomy of Corruption.* Kathmandu: Sangita Thapa.

Theobald, R. 1990. *Corruption, Development and Underdevelopment.* Durham, North Carolina: Duke University Press.

Transparency International Global. *Corruption Barometer 2013.*

Transparency International Global. *Report on Corruption 2015.*

Transparency International–Nepal. 2012. 'Gap Analysis of UN Convention against Corruption and Its implementation in Nepal'.

Transparency International–Nepal. 2015. A Survey of Public Service Delivery.

Transparency International–Nepal. 2016. Satisfaction Survey on Public Service Delivery 2015.

Visvanathan, S. and Sethi, H. 1998. *Foul Play: Chronicles of Corruption 1947-97.* New Delhi: Banyan Books.

Articles, Newspapers and Websites

Articles

Basnet, G. 'Nepal: The Demise of the Judiciary', http://www.eurasiareview.com/29052014-nepal-the-demise-of-the-judiciary-oped/

Bhandari, A. and Adhikari, C.K. *Kaha Jaanchha Yati Dherai Paisa?* (Where does so much Money go?)'. *Kantipur,* 20 August 2016.

Bhattarai, P. 'Revitalising Local Governments Political Commitment is needed'. *The Rising Nepal,* 28 March 2015, http://therisingnepal.org.np/news/2494

Dahal, B. 'Judicial match-fixing', http://nepalitimes.com/regular-columns/Legalese/ judicial-match-fixing

Dixit, K. 'Kritichorni Upakulpati (Vice Chancellor is a Plagiarist)', http://setopati.com/ bichar/58195/

Gautam, B. 'Government disappoint Nepalese by recommending Karki for CIAA chief', 7 May 2013, http://www.theasian.asia/archives/71458

Ghimire, Y. 'Uccha Naitik Charitrako Prashna (Question of high moral character)', 13 January 2017, http://www.annapurnapost.com/news/62484

Gyawali, D. 'Grand Larceny: Reverse Robin Hood behind the Privatization of Infrastructure, *Spotlight*, 2016, http://www.spotlightnepal.com/News/Article/GRAND-LARCENY-Reverse-Robin-Hood-Privatization-Inf

Mainali, M. 'Income of the Political Parties', http://southasiacheck.org/in-public-interest/income-of-the-political-parties/#sthash.JmV3KUbu.dpuf

Marasini, M. 'Daijolepahelpurmantriharu (Ministers Encrusted in Dowry Gold', 2017, http://kantipur.ekantipur.com/news/2017-01-09/20170109074844.html

Pandit, S. 'Bhagbandama 24 Sachhiv Badhuwa (Promotion to the post of 24 Secretaries under Political Quota)', *Naya Patrika*, 25 July 2009.

Newspapers

Kantipur, 20 August 2016

Nagarik, 19 November 2016 and 14 October 2017

Naya Patrika, 25 July 2009

Nepal Today, 18 June 2013

Spotlight, 24 August 2012

Spotlight, 30 August 2013

The Himalayan Times, 12 December 2015

The Himalayan Times, 27 January 2016

The Rising Nepal, 28 March 2015

Websites

http://admin.myrepublica.com/society/story/26851/names-of-vcs-recommended-for-four-universities.html

http://english.onlinekhabar.com/2017/01/13/393752.

http://peoplesreview.com.np/2017/01/18/

http://pubad-ias-blogspot.com/2011/09 riggesian-models-and their-critique.html

http://ranabhola.blogspot.com/2013/06/final-day-for-voter-registationkathmand.html

http://southasia.com.au/2017/03/05/americas-2016-human-rights-report-claims-nepali-courts-are-vulnerable-to-bribery/

http://therisingnepal org.np/

http://www.camelotintl.com/village/society.html

http://www.ekantipur.com/the-kathmandu-post/2012/03/01/

http://www.ekantipur.com/the-kathmandu-post/2012/03/01/top-story/jc-shortlists-complaints-against-12-judges/232142.html

http://www.hamrosandesh.com/2016/08/56711.html

http://www.hamrosandesh.com/2016/08/56711.html
http://www.karobardaily.com (September, 12, 2012)
http://www.karobardaily.com, September, 12, 2012
http://www.nonstopkhabar.com/detail_page.php?id=6215
http://www.nrb.org.np/fiu/
http://www.thehimalayantimes, 17 June 2013.
www.annapurnapost.com, 12 August 2016.
www.annapurnapost.com, 12 August 2016.
www.can.gov.np/np/legislature/phsc.html
www.ekantipur.com, February, 28, 2015
www.track.unodc.org/.../Nepal/Authorities/Anti-Corruption%20 Authorities%20-%20...

Endnotes

1. There are seventy-seven districts in the country. Regarding the tier and number of local government bodies, there is a two tier system, district level and sub district level bodies. Each of the district has a district coordination committee. At the sub district level, there is rural local government (Gaun Palika) and at the urban areas, urban local government (Nagar Palika). There are altogether 766 local government units in the country.
2. 'Syndicate' is a popular term in Nepali, e.g. a bus 'syndicate', aggregate supply 'syndicate', etc. It refers to cartelling and also goes by a more local Nepali name *'bhagbanda'* or apportioning and sharing of spoils. Syndicate is mostly applied to economic cartelling whereas *bhagbanda* is mostly used in the context of political parties and their representatives sharing the spoils of office.
3. During the government headed by Puspa Kamal Dahal 'Prachanda' (4 August 2016 to 7 June 2017) Prabhu Shah, the member of the Legislature-Parliament from the UCPN-MC was offered the portfolio of Minister of Law and Justice, he declined the offer because Shah wanted to be the minister of a lucrative Ministry of Federal Affairs and Local Development (MoFLDA). In his decline statement, Mr Shah said, 'it is better to be the Chairman of a [parliamentary] committee than to be the Minister of Law. What to do by being the Minister of Law? Distribute law books to the public?' (*Onlinekhabar*, 14 July 2016).
4. The private school lobby is strong, and it wields clout in terms of both resources and political advocacy. Similar to the polarity and political

fragmentation in different walks of life, private schools are organised and have created their organizations or unions more or less in accordance with their political affiliations. As most of the private schools have been networked around these unions, an orchestrated voice has been articulated to oppose the government move to regulate them better. There is a strong presence of the private school lobby in the national legislature since school operators themselves have a berth in the national law-making institution. They tend to stand united and seek to scuttle attempts to regulate them in public interest. Whether it is the issue of regulating the process of raising fees by setting minimum yardsticks or standardising the curriculum and textbooks or opening new schools, discernible resistance has been mounted by the private school lobby. As a result, none of the government attempts have succeeded fully because the lobby has been able to exert influence as they have access to the corridors of power.

In case of BAFIA, regarding the tenure of the bank board directors, the original Act of 2006 (2063), provided: 'the tenure of office of a director of a bank or financial institution shall be as provided in its articles of association, but not exceeding four years' and 'a person retired from the office of director on expiry of his or her tenure of office shall be eligible for reappointment to the office of director.' Thus, there was no term restriction of directors. But, the amendment bill proposed that the term of the directors of private commercial banks should not be for more than two terms. This change was intended to avoid the situation of operating a financial institution run by the public deposit as private property of the directors. But the Legislature-Parliament members-cum-chairpersons of private commercial banks were adamant to change this provision and retain the earlier provision.

5. http://southasia.com.au/2017/03/05/americas-2016-human-rights-report-claims-nepali-courts-are-vulnerable-to-bribery/
6. Akhanda Bhandari and Chandra Sekhar Adhikari cite the Auditor General's Report of 2016, according to which, 111 NGOs and 121 international NGOs seemed to have provided cash and kind contributions to the tune of NRS 5 billion and 730 million to the earthquake-affected people. In addition, sixty-nine NGOs had secured permission for spending NRS 1 billion and 160 million for eighty-five projects and fifteen international NGOs have secured the permission of spending NRS 12 billion and 716 million rupees for sixteen programmes. One international NGO, Lutheran World Federation, before getting permission for the

collection of the fund, had already collected $15.5 million.

7. As per Article 82 of the Constitution of Nepal, 2015, 'the business of the Government of Nepal shall be allocated and transacted in accordance with the rules approved by the Government of Nepal. (2) No question may be raised in any court as to whether or not the rules under clause (1) have been observed'.
8. Part 4, Article 51 of the Constitution of Nepal 2072 (Policies of the State) provides Policies relating to political and governance system of State (sub-Article 51b). Among others, one of the four provisions under this sub-Article is to guarantee good governance by ensuring the equal and easy access of the people to the services and facilities delivered by the State, while making public administration fair, competent, impartial, transparent, free from corruption, accountable and participatory.
9. The most important anti-corruption generic law in the country is the Prevention of Corruption Act (PCA) 2002. Besides, there are several other laws aimed at controlling corruption, some of which are: Commission for the Investigation of Abuse of Authority Act 1991 (CIAA Act 1991), Audit Act 1991, Special Court Act 2002, Revenue Leakage (Investigation and Control) Act 1996, Money Laundering Prevention Act 2008, Prevention of Organized Crime Act 2013, Extradition Act 1988, Foreign Exchange (Regulation) Act 1962, Nepal Treaty Act 1990, Public Procurement Act 2007, Right to Information Act 2007, and Mutual Legal Assistance Act 2015.
10. Karki was recommended by the then Constitutional Council (CC) headed by the then Chairperson of the Council of Ministers/incumbent Chief Justice of the SC on 5 May 2013 and the then President appointed him as Chief Commissioner on 8 May 2013. His name was selected by a unanimous decision of the leaders of the major political parties. Karki's appointment became controversial because he had been held guilty of suppressing the people's movement in April 2006 as the Chief Secretary of the government. He was also accused of amassing property through illegal means during his tenure as Director General of the Department of Customs. A large section of civil society and Kathmandu intelligentsia had seriously objected to his appointment, citing his anti-democratic, and opportunistic antecedents. Surprisingly, the honchos of the major political parties who governed the country's political syndicate supported him with unanimity.
11. In her discussion on corruption and politics, Ackerman (1999) writes that 'democracy is simply too general a term to capture the range of

government forms that come under that rubric. Furthermore, a government structure that works well in one country may be dysfunctional in another context. Widespread, entrenched corruption is one form of dysfunction'... Kleptocracy, bilateral monopolistic situation, mafia dominated state and in a state of competitive bribery situation, could also be used to understand Nepal's growing corruption problem. Nepal suffers from the problem of corruption at the top—Kleptocrats, the influence of the commission agents—especially somebody having the monopoly supplying situation in negotiating and bargaining with the different levels of the decision-makers for the cost of a particular supply or the project at the cost of the country or people with a promise to share the profits with all of them. Over the period, mafia of different sorts is getting influential in the political parties and through them, influencing the decision-making process and extorting resources.

INDEX